THE I TATTI
RENAISSANCE LIBRARY

James Hankins, General Editor

CICERONIAN CONTROVERSIES

ITRL 26

CICERONIAN CONTROVERSIES

EDITED BY

JOANN DELLANEVA

ENGLISH TRANSLATION BY

BRIAN DUVICK

THE I TATTI RENAISSANCE LIBRARY

HARVARD UNIVERSITY PRESS

CAMBRIDGE, MASSACHUSETTS

LONDON, ENGLAND

2007

Series design by Dean Bornstein

Library of Congress Cataloging-in-Publication Data

Ciceronian controversies / edited by JoAnn DellaNeva ;
English translation by Brian Duvick.
p. cm. — (The I Tatti Renaissance library ; ITRL 26)
Includes bibliographical references and index.
Letters in Latin with English translations.
ISBN-13: 978-0-674-02520-2 (alk. paper)
ISBN-10: 0-674-02520-2 (alk. paper)
1. Cicero, Marcus Tullius — Criticism and interpretation — History.
2. Humanists — Italy — Correspondence.   3. Latin letters, Medieval and
modern — Translations into English.   4. Imitation in literature.
I. DellaNeva, JoAnn.
PA6346.C53 2007
875'.01 — dc22   2006100633

Contents

꒰꒱

· CONTENTS ·

Introduction

When the Roman humanist Paolo Cortesi (1465–1510) painstakingly collected and sent to his mentor, the famous scholar-poet Angelo Poliziano (1454–1494), a set of letters written by other scholars in what he thought was an admirable Ciceronian style, he could not have imagined that his innocent, collegial gesture would provoke what was to become known as the Ciceronian Quarrel, the single most important literary debate of the Renaissance.[1] But that is precisely what happened, for, upon receiving this gift, Poliziano dashed off a short and rather ungracious letter of acknowledgment that chastised his former pupil and friend for his undue and unseemly attachment to the Ciceronian style. In turn, Cortesi defended his position in a longer letter that was to go unanswered by the eminent humanist. This exchange of letters, which is undated but probably occurred in the mid-1480s, constitutes the first of many polemical writings concerning the proper mode of literary imitation in the Renaissance. To subsequent players in the debates, Cortesi seemed to be the prototypical staunch Ciceronian who advocated the use of a single model of stylistic excellence for the modern Latinist attempting to achieve a correct classical style. His adversary, Poliziano, on the other hand, became the hero of the Eclectics, who found stylistic excellence in a variety of models and ridiculed the foolish self-imposed limitations of the Ciceronians.

The battle of the Ciceronians and the Eclectics was to be replayed again and again throughout the Renaissance, particularly in Italy. Indeed, within a generation, a second set of letters was exchanged between the philosopher Gianfrancesco Pico della Mirandola (c. 1469–1533), nephew of the more famous Giovanni Pico, and Pietro Bembo (1470–1547), the most famous Ciceronian of the age, later a papal secretary and cardinal. These letters reprised many of the arguments first made in the Poliziano-Cortesi debate. In fact, the Pico-Bembo exchange (1512–13) explicitly refers to the earlier Poliziano-Cortesi debate in two of its three letters and clearly presents itself as a continuation of that quarrel. Roughly twenty years later, a third set of polemical epistles was exchanged between Giambattista Giraldi Cinzio (1504–1573), who later became a famous writer of tragedies and novels in Italian and a source for Shakespeare, and his teacher Celio Calcagnini (1479–1541), a professor of rhetoric at the University of Ferrara. These were written in 1532 though not published in complete form until 1537. This exchange also explicitly presented itself as the direct descendant of both the Poliziano-Cortesi and the Pico-Bembo correspondence.

The first two of these three debates attracted considerable attention at the time from other Renaissance humanists. Both quarrels, for example, were commented upon by the celebrated Dutch humanist Desiderius Erasmus (c. 1466–1536) in his *Ciceronianus* of 1528. In this remarkable and witty dialogue, Erasmus ridiculed the strict Ciceronians and championed the cause of the Eclectics. But Erasmus hardly had the last word on this issue. On the contrary, an extensive series of rejoinders encompassing dozens of texts over the next several years assured that the Ciceronian quarrel was to remain a hotly debated issue throughout the sixteenth century.[2]

While the first two exchanges, Erasmus' *Ciceronianus* and the many replies to Erasmus have been studied by literary historians, the third set of polemical letters — that between Cinzio and Calcagnini — has been largely ignored and indeed recently dismissed as being "academic."[3] Because these letters were disseminated nine years after the publication of the *Ciceronianus*, they obviously could not have been commented upon by Erasmus and thus did not figure in the series of polemical writings generated in response to that dialogue. It is perhaps for this reason that the

Cinzio-Calcagnini letters were relatively neglected by Renaissance humanists and later scholarship.

Yet these letters certainly did have their impact on literary history, albeit in a round-about fashion. For eventually they were to form a bridge between the decidedly Renaissance issue of Ciceronian imitation and the classicizing treatises on educational matters that proliferated especially among Jesuit theorists in the seventeenth century. From there, they form the forgotten basis of theories of originality that were to preoccupy writers of the Romantic movement and beyond. The first to comment upon this exchange was Lilio Gregorio Giraldi (1479–1552), who was asked by his kinsman Giraldi Cinzio to bring these letters to the attention of their mutual acquaintance Gianfrancesco Pico. In response, Lilio recounted Pico's views on the debate, the latter being apparently considered an expert on matters of imitation. Indeed, Lilio's epistle—though even less well known than the original Cinzio-Calcagnini letters themselves—is a crucial document in the history of Ciceronianism, for it names all six of the participants in these Italian polemical exchanges. In so doing, it offers a remarkable compromise solution that would be critical in the ultimate resolution of the debate in the early part of the seventeenth century.

Although this letter appears to have been disregarded for a period of almost fifty years after its initial publication in 1537, it was the subject of renewed interest towards the turn of the seventeenth century. In 1593, the Jesuit diplomat and educational theorist Antonio Possevino (c. 1533–1611) published in Rome his first edition of the *Bibliotheca selecta*, an encyclopedic work that brought together excerpts from a vast array of published texts and was intended as a curricular guide for Jesuit colleges across Catholic Europe. In the section entitled the *Cicero*, which deals with the issue of imitation, he provides a transcription of Pico's second letter to Bembo and an extensive paraphrase of Lilio's letter to Giraldi

Cinzio, outlining his compromise solution to the quarrel. Ten years later, in 1603, Possevino published a new edition of his *Bibliotheca selecta*, this time including an extensive transcription of another text that was influential in the Ciceronian quarrel: the *Epistolica Institutio* of the Flemish humanist Justus Lipsius (1547–1606), which outlines a compromise solution remarkably similar to the one suggested by Lilio Giraldi. Possevino comments upon this similarity between Lipsius and his presumed, but unacknowledged, source, delicately implying Lipsius' indebtedness to Lilio and thus reclaiming for Italy the ultimate resolution of the Ciceronian quarrel.

Thanks to the Jesuits' great interest in education, the issue of Ciceronianism — or at least the question of how to develop an excellent style in Latin — survived well into the seventeenth century, though by now the question of imitation was largely reformulated in other terms. Later Jesuit rhetoricians nevertheless had recourse to Possevino's work and, thus, by extension, to the whole of the Ciceronian quarrel as it had played out among Italian humanists in the Renaissance. Thus the Ciceronian texts presented here can be seen as fundamental to larger issues of educational theory and practice and, ultimately, to the development of the concept of innovative imitation, or what was in the Romantic period to become known as the prized literary virtue of "originality."

The three polemical exchanges and their subsequent commentaries span a period of over 125 years and clearly form a discrete unit in the history of literary imitation. Moreover, the textual affiliations among the three quarrels — their common themes, images, and explicit references to each other — are paralleled by the close biographical ties (familial, geographical or intellectual), that bind their various players.[4] Just as it is Pico who eventually became the most important source for the Jesuit understanding of imitation and originality, so too is it Pico who is the pivotal figure linking all six participants. Gianfrancesco Pico was the nephew, biographer and editor of the famous Renaissance philosopher Giovanni Pico della Mirandola (1463–1494). Only six years younger than his uncle, he had passed much of his youth in the company of the elder Pico's friends, including Pico's closest friend, Poliziano. The younger Pico was thus well acquainted with the members of Lorenzo de' Medici's circle in Florence, including the Platonic philosopher and translator of Plato, Marsilio Ficino (1433–1499). Both Poliziano and Ficino, along with the elder Pico, were influential in Gianfrancesco's intellectual development, and despite the younger Pico's explicit embrace of skepticism and fideism in his own philosophical writings, his understanding of Ideal Form, which was to become crucial to his imitation theory, bears the impress of Florentine Platonism. Not surprisingly, then, when the younger Pico took up the issue of imitation with Bembo, he reprised the role played by his compatriot and master, Poliziano.

It is Pico, too, who shifts the site of the imitation debates from Florence to Rome. Pico had been embroiled in considerable familial strife, as a result of which he was stripped of his claim to the lordship of Mirandola. This was being held under the control of his mother and brothers who, reportedly, had attempted to have him killed. In 1512 Pico journeyed to Rome to seek the Pope's help in his quest to be restored to his lost title. It was at this time that he met Bembo and began the correspondence on the subject of imitation. Bembo for his part was familiar with intellectual circles in Florence and had hosted at his father's home in Venice, a scant three years before Poliziano's untimely death in 1494, both the elder Pico and Poliziano. Nevertheless, Bembo's education and cast of mind put him in closer alliance with the humanists in Rome, especially those affiliated with the Church. These included Pope Leo X (Giovanni de' Medici, 1475–1521), the first Medici Pope and a literary patron, as well as Jacopo Sadoleto (1477–1547), who in 1513 was to be appointed Apostolic Secretary, together with

Bembo. In this role Sadoleto and Bembo were responsible for composing the official correspondence of the Holy See, so that the issue of style and imitation became a professional one as well as a matter of personal taste. Although there is no evidence that Bembo had ever met or corresponded with Paolo Cortesi, who had died at the age of forty-five, just two years before the Pico-Bembo quarrel began, Bembo apparently knew his work and quotes freely from the older scholar, who in his time had also served as Apostolic Secretary. It is likely, though, that the younger Pico was acquainted with Cortesi, for the latter had been a student of Poliziano's and had corresponded with the elder Pico.

Later, Pico again shifted the site of the quarrel, this time to the Duchy of Ferrara, a prosperous and innovative intellectual center revolving around the Este court and the local university. In Ferrara, Pico was befriended by both Calcagnini and Lilio Giraldi (who, like Bembo, had just escaped the horrors of the sack of Rome), and the three carried on an extensive correspondence with each other, some of which is preserved in editions of their works.[5] Calcagnini, a scientist as well as literary critic and rhetorician, had also corresponded with Erasmus and occupied the chair in rhetoric and literature at the University of Ferrara; Giraldi Cinzio had numbered among his former pupils and was to succeed him in his academic post when Calcagnini died at the age of sixty-two in 1541.[6] Given Lilio Giraldi's kinship with Giraldi Cinzio as well as his friendship with both Calcagnini and Pico, it is fitting that he should have been asked by Giraldi to comment upon the imitation debates that had occupied three generations of Italian humanists.

It was left then to Possevino, who had been born around the time when the Cinzio-Calcagnini debate took place, to resurrect interest in these quarrels roughly sixty years after the initial publication of the last installment of letters and to preserve Lilio Giraldi's compromise solution in his encyclopedic work. Possevino had demonstrated an interest in literary matters as a very young man and seems to have been especially interested in the vernacular theory of Giraldi Cinzio, an acquaintance whom he may first have met when the two men were both connected with the University of Ferrara in the mid- to late 1550s. It was at this time that Possevino wrote a treatise in defense of Giraldi Cinzio's theory of dramaturgy, rejecting the charges of plagiarism brought by Cinzio's former student, Giovan Battista Pigna, against his mentor.[7] Presumably, Possevino maintained his interest in Cinzio's literary theory and remembered the exchanges that had transpired within the Ferrarese circle — which included Cinzio, Lilio, Calcagnini, and Pico — when he set out to write his encyclopedic work, conceived in the 1570s though not published until 1593. He was thus in a position to provide transcriptions or paraphrases from the letters of Pico and Lilio in his own work.

While the texts of the Ciceronian controversy are closely interrelated, they cannot be divorced from prior discussions of imitation that took place in the Renaissance and indeed in classical antiquity itself. Because the Renaissance treatment of this issue was so heavily influenced by classical works on the subject, some familiarity with earlier texts is essential (and additional sources and parallel passages will be pointed out in the notes to the English translations in this volume). It is surely no coincidence that early Renaissance interest in the subject of imitation took on a new life precisely at the moment when many classical texts on the subject — including Cicero's *Orator* and *De oratore* and Quintilian's *Institutio oratoria* — had just been rediscovered in their complete form. Other influential classical works included the anonymous *Rhetorica ad Herennium* (which in the Renaissance was widely believed to be by Cicero), the eighty-fourth epistle of the younger Seneca and the writings of the Roman satirist Horace. On the other hand, Greek imitative theory — including the *Poetics* of Aristotle, the works of Dionysius of Halicarnassus, Hermogenes of Tarsus and the writer known as "Longinus" — were either unknown or ignored until the late Renaissance. Their gradual emergence as important sources for Renaissance imitative theory is in part chronicled by the series of polemical exchanges in this volume.

But by far the most influential classical sources pertinent to these three quarrels remain the works of Cicero, Quintilian, Seneca and Horace, all of whom treated the crucial issue of whether or not one should choose a single excellent model or a variety of excellences in different authors in order to achieve the best Latin style. For the most part, these classical theorists were proponents of eclecticism and often gave strong warnings against excessive imitation of any single model. Cicero, for instance, recounted the story of Zeuxis in his early work *De inventione*. Unable to find a single woman incorporating all the beauties of Helen, whom he had been commissioned to paint, Zeuxis compensated by combining the best features of five beautiful maidens. Later, in the *De oratore*, Cicero warns the aspiring writer not to succumb to a servile imitation of faults and to be aware of the suitability of particular models in the development of one's own, individual style. Finally, in the *Orator*, Cicero elaborates upon the notion of an "ideal of perfect eloquence" that was to serve as the ultimate model for writers. Each of these texts was echoed repeatedly in the Renaissance and served to fuel a seemingly endless debate about the proper selection of literary models.

It has been suggested that it is Quintilian who must be recognized as the first proponent of Ciceronianism, for he clearly saw in that orator the foremost model of eloquence. Yet Quintilian could not be considered a Ciceronian as that term was later to be understood among the Italian humanists, for nowhere does he propose that Cicero be an *exclusive* model of eloquence. Moreover Quintilian, like Cicero before him, warned of the dangers inherent in imitation. Indeed, it is his insistence that new writers not hesitate to rely on their own inner talent, their *ingenium*, that remains, perhaps, his foremost contribution to Renaissance debates on literary imitation.

One feature characteristic of many classical works on imitation — and in particular Quintilian's *Institutio oratoria* — is their highly metaphorical quality, that is, the abundance of figures and images they use to describe both proper and improper imitative techniques. Most prominent among these metaphors was the digestive image, where external materials, like food digested so as to become consubstantial with the person consuming it, are transformed into the very substance of the new writer. While Quintilian seems to be the favored source for many Renaissance metaphors of imitative theory, few of these images actually originated with him and can often be found in the earlier writings of Seneca and Horace, who shared Quintilian's penchant for arguing by analogy. Seneca, for example, likened the proper resemblance between model and imitation to that between father and son, as distinct from that between sitter and painted portrait. Seneca and Horace also popularized what was to become the virtual emblem of "innovative imitation" using multiple models: the image of the bee that flits about from flower to flower in order to transform that nectar into a honey of its own making. In all these analogies, similarity, not sameness, is clearly the preferred quality.

Just as Quintilian can be seen as the first classical Ciceronian, there is a sense in which Francesco Petrarca (1304–1374), known to the English speaking world as Petrarch, can be seen as the first Renaissance Ciceronian. He, too, admired Cicero beyond all other writers of Latin prose and famously engaged in an imaginary correspondence with the Roman orator. But Petrarch, like Quintilian before him, was hardly adverse to the practice of eclectic imitation and indeed expounded its virtues in a series of letters in which he treats the topic of imitation. His influence can easily be seen in the quarrels of later humanists. This influence is most marked in the images Petrarch uses to describe both proper and improper imitative techniques, images that derive from the classical triumvirate of sources: Seneca, Horace, and Quintilian. These include the ridiculous crow clothed in borrowed plumage (Horace), the father-son analogy (Seneca), the bee that draws nectar from various flowers (Seneca and Horace), and the digestive process which turns food into one's own body (Quintilian). Just as these images were borrowed from classical sources, so too will Petrarch's arguments be re-appropriated by the Eclectics in the later quarrels.

After Petrarch, a host of other early humanists — including Gasparino Barzizza (1360–1430), Leon Battista Alberti (1404–72), Pier Paolo Vergerio the Elder (1370–1444), George of Trebizond (1395-c. 1489), and Guarino da Verona (1374–1460) — treated the subject of imitation. While both Barzizza and his pupil Alberti continued the Petrarchan tradition of eclectic imitation and the importance of adding something of one's own to the written text, Vergerio, Guarino, and George all proposed a different understanding of imitative technique, one that emphasized resemblance rather than innovation and stylistic integrity rather than variety. Though these theorists disagreed with the prevailing theories of the time, their treatises were not polemical in nature, in that they did not specifically denounce the ideas of a particular opponent. But other theorists, such as Coluccio Salutati (1331–1406) and Leonardo Bruni (1370–1444), as well as Lorenzo Valla (1406–1457) and Poggio Bracciolini (1380–1459), did engage in polemical exchanges on the matter of imitation. Salutati, who was a contemporary of Petrarch, shared in that great humanist's predilection for eclecticism and, like him, stressed the importance of adding something new and modern — an element of originality — in composing the imitative text. His former protégé Bruni, on the other hand, sought to develop a style of Latin that would be characterized by its resemblance to the Ciceronian model. The great Roman humanist Lorenzo Valla proposed that a wide variety of authors could serve as models for eloquence, while his antagonist, Poggio, affirmed the preeminence of Cicero and maintained a high degree of reverence for the model text, which, he maintained, did not require the addition of something new to achieve eloquence. Thus the lines between the Ciceronians (such as Vergerio, George of Trebizond, Bruni, Poggio, and Guarino) and the Eclectics (such as Barzizza, Alberti, Salutati, and Valla) were already being drawn in the first generations of the humanist movement. Poliziano's letter to Cortesi, which (with the help of the printing press) launched the Ciceronian Quarrel onto the wider European stage, must be viewed in this context.

Poliziano makes it clear from the outset that he sees nothing but danger in Cortesi's implied approval of imitating Cicero to the exclusion of all other authors. Drawing on Seneca, Quintilian and Horace, Poliziano denounces the imitation of superficial features that could easily degenerate into caricature and proposes a different sort of imitation that allows for self-expression and the development of one's own natural ability or *ingenium*. This is to be accomplished through the broad reading of many texts whose individual excellences can be assimilated and forged into a single new style. Poliziano's emphasis on self-expression, however, was understood by his opponent Cortesi to amount to disapproval of imitation as such. Thus Cortesi devotes the better part of his letter to a justification of the very idea of literary imitation. Cortesi also questions how individually pleasing elements from various authors could possibly be integrated into a single harmonious whole. Hence the Poliziano-Cortesi debate focuses on the relationship between external influences and internal creative resources. While Poliziano expressed faith in the writer's ability to assimilate multiple outside influences which become the stuff of self-expression, Cortesi was adamant that internal creative resources could not be depended upon to produce eloquence without the guidance of a single great model such as Cicero. Appearances aside, however,

Cortesi's response to Poliziano is not so radically opposed to the thesis of his mentor as he would have us believe. Cortesi, like Poliziano, worries about excessive similitude, as is revealed by his use of the father-son analogy. The use of this image likewise points to the influence of Petrarch's letters behind Cortesi's epistle and indeed behind Poliziano's as well. Petrarch would remain a quiet presence on both the Eclectic and Ciceronian sides throughout the Quarrel.

Poliziano's letter to Cortesi was not the only work in which the humanist proclaimed an affinity for eclecticism. Indeed, one could argue that his entire literary production is a testament to his preference for eclectic imitation. Poliziano's poetry—both in Latin and in the vernacular Italian—is notable for its use of a wide array of sources, often obscure ones, and its non-classical tendencies, most especially the trademark use of diminutives that pepper his style. His Italian vernacular poetry demonstrated a similar predilection for the rare and witty, a characteristic he shared with the early *Petrarchisti*, who likewise exaggerated some of the rhetorical mannerisms of their master Petrarch.

Among Poliziano's other theoretical writings on the subject, his *Oration on Quintilian and Statius* is of particular interest and would become especially pertinent in the Pico-Bembo debate.[8] In that inaugural speech, delivered when he first assumed his professorial chair in 1480, Poliziano affirmed that a wide variety of authors—including minor or second-rate figures—might prove valuable sources for the aspiring writer, particularly in the earliest stages of his career. It is here that Poliziano develops an apprenticeship model of imitative practice, whereby younger writers are advised to use inferior models first. This is because they are incapable of achieving the eloquence of great models such as Cicero—who are indeed virtually inimitable—at this early stage of their careers. Eventually, however, these apprentice writers can turn with confidence to greater models, that is, to texts that are more difficult to imitate. This distinction among imitative practices suitable for different age groups will become a crucial element in the ultimate resolution of the Ciceronian quarrel by the end of the sixteenth century, though later theorists will invert Poliziano's proposed sequence of models.

Other works, written after his exchange with Cortesi, reaffirm Poliziano's eclecticism and would again prove influential when the debate was revisited by Pico and Bembo. Among these is a letter addressed in 1493 to the humanist chancellor of Florence, Bartolomeo Scala (1430–1497). Here Poliziano suggests that excellent writers such as Demosthenes and Cicero often differ greatly from each other, and that this fact proves a variety of stylistic excellences are possible. He also criticizes here those who in their zeal for creating an authentic Ciceronian discourse eschew the use of words that they believe have not been used by Cicero. The problem, declares Poliziano, is that later discoveries sometimes reveal that Cicero did indeed use a particular word in a text that had hitherto been lost; conversely, words deemed to be authentically Ciceronian are sometimes found to be inauthentic because they occur in manuscripts later proved to be corrupt or even fraudulent. This issue of authenticity will also be raised in the Pico-Bembo debates and will be revisited by Erasmus.

Paolo Cortesi's later literary works are equally pertinent to the Ciceronian quarrel and its resolution. His first major work, the *Dialogus de hominibus doctis*, finished soon after his debate with Poliziano, contains a number of passages that repeat almost verbatim whole sections of his letter to Poliziano. In one such passage Cortesi even borrows from Poliziano's letter to him, employing the ape image which the elder humanist had used to warn against improper imitation. In a later text, the *De cardinalatu* (1510), Cortesi explicitly refers to his quarrel with Poliziano and continues to criticize the latter's flamboyant, eclectic style. Nevertheless, it has been suggested that Cortesi's own style towards the end of his career, as demonstrated by the *De cardinalatu*, was far from strictly Ciceronian and even approached the eclectic quality he had criticized in Poliziano's style. Still, despite evidence that Cortesi may have modified his strict Ciceronian position, later debaters saw him as a model of rigid Ciceronianism, alternately praised and ridiculed.

The second generation of Ciceronian debates began in 1512, when Pico sent his friend Bembo an essay he had composed, entitled *De imitatione*, which Pico had been inspired to write following recent conversations on the subject between the two men. In this letter Pico describes his preferred method of imitation. Recalling Horace, he denounces slavish imitators and proclaims that the best writers are not satisfied merely to imitate past greatness but seek to surpass it. Emulation, unlike mere imitation, allows new writers to cultivate their individual genius, though it is in its turn dependent upon the imitation of multiple models. Pico's major contribution to the Ciceronian quarrel lies in the notion of the Idea or Form of beauty and eloquence as a principle of discernment in the selection of appropriate models. Pico suggests that this Idea might be innate, but he also acknowledges that it can be developed empirically by analyzing a variety of good sources. This abstract Idea or Form, synthesized from a multiplicity of real objects but distinct from any single instantiation of it, had been discussed by Pico in an earlier tract, *De imaginatione* (1501), which seems to have informed some of the thinking developed in the *De imitatione*. Once this Idea of beauty is formed, it becomes the standard by which an aspiring writer can judge the particular worth of any individual source; it thus acts as a safeguard against the apish imitation of faults that strict Ciceronians might fall into accidentally, simply because these features happen to occur in a text thought to be authentically Ciceronian. But perhaps the most significant aspect of Pico's letter is his use of the novel term *genius*, as opposed to the more common term *ingenium*, to describe individual natural talent, a concept that will eventually take on modern connotations of creative ability and self-reliant inspiration.[9] In this way, Pico firmly places himself in the shadow of Poliziano, who in his letters to Cortesi and Scala likewise championed eclecticism, individual talent and self-expression, and who likewise warned against faults that could arise from over-zealous reproduction of a single, possibly inauthentic, Ciceronian text. Pico's first letter also explicitly mentions for the first time two recently rediscovered classical sources: the Greek works of Dionysius of Halicarnassus and Hermogenes of Tarsus, both of which helped Pico articulate his position on the artful blending of a variety of styles into a single, harmonious discourse.

Pico's affinity for Poliziano was no doubt obvious to Bembo, who began his response, dated 1 January 1513, with a reference to the Poliziano-Cortesi debate. Indeed, it is quite possible to read Bembo's letter as a response primarily aimed at Poliziano rather than at Pico himself, for he challenges many ideas expressed by Poliziano but not repeated by Pico, even though he does not always explicitly name the elder humanist. While Bembo couches his argument in exceedingly polite phrases, being sure to compliment Pico for his astounding wisdom and philosophical expertise, the polemical nature of this exchange is still obvious and extends beyond Pico himself to all those associated with the Florentine humanists. For Bembo it is axiomatic that there is a single best model in Latin prose, Cicero, and he declares that he is naturally attracted to that best model alone. Bembo goes on to take issue with Pico's notion of the Idea of eloquence, challenging the assertion that such an Idea could possibly be innate (he chooses not to deal with Pico's alternative explanation of an empirically derived Ideal). Moreover, he attacks Pico's eclecticism, claiming, like Cortesi before him, that the imitation of multiple models can lead only to an inharmonious juxtaposition of styles. He then relates some of his own past failures, including an apprenticeship process wherein he attempted to imitate only mediocre models at first, in the hope of eventually arriving at a level of excellence which would allow for the imitation of the best models. This plan, which sounds suspiciously like the one outlined by Poliziano in his *Oration on Quintilian and Statius*, was unsuccessful, for he merely acquired the bad habits inherent in bad writing, which proved difficult to unlearn. Eventually, Bembo saw the light and turned to the best models for imitation. But in speaking of "best models" in the plural, it is clear that Bembo was not so exclusively Ciceronian as he is sometimes portrayed. Indeed, he makes a gesture in the direction of eclecticism at the end of his letter when he draws a distinction between borrowing material (which can be taken from a variety of sources) and imitating style (which should be taken from a single source). He suggests that Pico did not make this distinction himself and that this error may be the cause of their disagreement.

But Pico does not take up this distinction in his second letter to Bembo. Instead, he reiterates many of the arguments presented in the initial treatise and develops his concept of the Idea or Form of eloquence, located in the mind's eye, which is to be used as a guide in the selection of models. He further emphasizes the notion of individual skill and creative resources in the development of stylistic excellence, notions which were precursors of the concept of originality as it was to be developed among later theorists. Moreover, he explicitly and repeatedly cites Cicero himself on the question of imitation in the hope of persuading Bembo of the inadequacy of his theory.

Finally, Pico ends his epistle with a reference to two earlier humanists, namely, his uncle, Giovanni Pico della Mirandola and Ermolao Barbaro (c. 1453–1493), who exchanged letters on stylistic matters in 1485. The issue there concerned the relative importance of *verba* and *res*, of words and matter, or of rhetorical power and philosophical precision.[10] While the elder Pico had upheld the primacy of *res* over *verba*, or of theological and philosophical truth over stylistic eloquence, Barbaro appeared to privilege style over substance. In his letter to Bembo, the younger Pico reaffirms his uncle's stance, insisting on the importance of wisdom rather than superficial eloquence. This opposition, of course, did not originate with Pico and Barbaro, but can trace its development to the works of Plato and, later, to Cicero, who lament the dichotomy of eloquence and wisdom. But the elder Pico does more than state that rhetorical eloquence is unnecessary in the pursuit of philosophical truth; he implies that such ornamentation may even be detrimental to the philosopher who wishes to pursue truth, a task which Pico sees as inconsistent with that of the rhetorician. Indeed, by the Renaissance, the fields of eloquence and philosophy were so far apart that no writer who aspired to stylistic excellence would be entirely flattered to be called a philosopher, for that would imply a neglect of stylistic beauty in favor of unadorned wisdom. So Bembo's seeming compliment on Pico's philosophical expertise is a barbed one; in the Renaissance context it was tantamount to a criticism of Pico's Latin style. At any rate, the explicit reference to the Pico-Barbaro letters signals their underlying importance in the Pico-Bembo exchange. The younger Pico quotes repeatedly from his uncle's letter, while Barbaro seems here and in other letters to anticipate some of the views that will be espoused by his fellow Venetian Bembo, particularly the distinction between borrowing material from many sources and the need to form one's style from a single model.

The linking of the two Picos with the Florentine cultural scene, taken together with the alliance of the two Venetian humanists, Bembo and Barbaro, serves to highlight the geographical context of the Ciceronian quarrel. Bembo, like the prototypical Ciceronian George of Trebizond, was a citizen of Venice whose clerical responsibilities brought him to Rome. In some sense, then, Venice should be considered the first home of Ciceronianism, thanks to its association with George, Barbaro, and, finally, Bembo. But it is

Rome that is most closely associated with the triumph of Ciceronianism, and it is not surprising, therefore, that Bembo felt a great affinity with Cortesi, who likewise lived in Rome and was employed by the Curia. For these Roman humanists, whose job it was to write important ecclesiastical documents in a correct and eloquent Latin, the issue of Ciceronianism was of vital practical concern and not just a theoretical intellectual debate. They saw themselves as the direct descendants of the great Roman writers of antiquity in a way that the humanists of Florence (and later of Ferrara) simply could not appreciate. For them, Ciceronianism had a political and religious import; their exclusive imitation of Cicero was a way of re-establishing Rome and the Church as the true and unique inheritors of the aesthetic values of antiquity. It is in part thanks to this patriotic and religious zeal that rigid Ciceronianism would eventually come to be derided as the "Italian sect."

Similarly, Pico's reference to his uncle also serves as a reminder that his familial connections made him part of the same Florentine intellectual community to which the elder Pico, Poliziano, and their compatriot Marsilio Ficino all belonged. Bembo was fully aware of this common intellectual heritage and alludes to it in passing at the end of his letter, where he refers to the younger Pico's ongoing philosophical project, the *De amore divino*. This work treats the subject of love, a topic he had already touched upon in his earlier work, the *De venere et cupidine expellendis carmen*. In both texts Pico developed in a particular direction the Florentine Platonic tradition popularized by Marsilio Ficino in his commentary on Plato's *Symposium*, the *De amore* (1469). In so doing, however, he showed himself to be once again at odds with Bembo, who had treated Platonic love in his vernacular tract, the *Asolani*, in a strikingly different manner.[11] Both Bembo's allusion to Pico's ongoing work and Pico's own reference to his uncle's Florentine intellectual circle thus underscore the degree to which the issue of imitation was only one among many topics that Bembo and Pico disagreed on profoundly. These references also indicate the extent to which Bembo was taking on in his polemical writings not just the younger Pico but all the renowned Florentine men of letters of the preceding generation, including Poliziano and the elder Pico.

Bembo's conflict with Pico and, by extension, with Poliziano and other Florentines, is also a crucial component of his vernacular treatise on literary matters, the *Prose*, first published in 1525 but probably begun in its initial form at the same time that he was engaged in his polemics with Pico. His interest in vernacular literature is, in fact, one of the ways Bembo distinguishes himself from other strict Ciceronians, who tended to eschew all but the production of perfect Latin prose. Bembo himself realized that his writing in Italian might have been detrimental to the development of his Latin style, for he alludes to this predicament in his letter to Pico. Yet in many ways the theoretical concerns of Bembo's writings in Italian mirror those of his Latin works. For the *Prose*, like the *De imitatione*, proposes the imitation of a single model of excellence and warns against the dangers of mixing a variety of sources. Likewise, the *Prose* also contains a number of passages which can be read as thinly veiled criticisms of Poliziano and his flamboyant Italian style, reminiscent of other *Petrarchisti* such as Antonio Tebaldeo (1463–1537). On the other hand, Bembo's poetry — which he extensively revised in an effort to purge his verse from corrupt influences of the *Petrarchisti* and perhaps of Poliziano himself — proclaims the pre-eminence of a single poetic model, namely Petrarch. It is in part thanks to this consistent stance concerning the necessity of imitating a single model that led to Bembo's reputation as a strict, if not eccentric, Ciceronian, who was rumored to have collected classical relics. These he supposedly venerated in a manner that led some to identify him as the ridiculous imitator Nosoponus, caricatured by Erasmus in the *Cicero-nianus*, whose excesses were said to characterize the "Italian sect" in its worst form.

Nearly twenty years after the Pico-Bembo exchange took place, Giraldi Cinzio launched a new episode of the Ciceronian quarrel. Writing to Calcagnini, his former teacher, Cinzio immediately reveals his alliance with Cortesi and Bembo against the likes of Poliziano and Pico. Like Cortesi and Bembo before him, Cinzio asserts the necessity of imitation and chastises Poliziano for his apparent anti-imitative stance. He denies the sufficiency of relying on one's own talent or *ingenium*, a position which he claims was wrongly espoused by Poliziano and, more recently, by Erasmus. Hence Cinzio appears to repeat Cortesi's misrepresentation of Poliziano's stance. Or at least he seems unable, like Cortesi before him, to imagine a kind of imitation that would also allow for the development of one's own personal style or self-expression. Again like Cortesi, Cinzio calls into question the ability of an imitator to attain a single harmonious style when he has recourse to multiple models. Yet Cinzio is by no means a strict advocate of the exclusive imitation of Cicero. Instead, he admits that young writers can certainly benefit from wide reading, though he recommends that this eclectic reading take place only after the young writer's style has been sufficiently formed in the Ciceronian manner. Thus Cinzio advocates the opposite of the failed apprenticeship experiment described by Bembo in his letter to Pico and the successful one proposed by Poliziano in his *Oration on Quintilian and Statius*. According to Cinzio, instead of attempting to imitate mediocre models first, then turning to the best models later, novice writers should read only the best writers first, then widen their repertoire once their style is formed. It is precisely this notion of successive stages of imitation that was to become the essential component of the compromise solution established by Lilio Giraldi and later Lipsius and Possevino. Despite this nod to eclecticism, however,

Cinzio is far closer in spirit to his Ciceronian predecessors, particularly in his understanding of imitation as a quest for similitude and not differentiation.

Calcagnini's cordial response is composed of two parts. The first is merely a cover letter that introduces the formal treatise to follow. From the start, it is clear that Calcagnini does not view Cinzio as an adversary whom he wishes to engage in heated polemics. Instead, he praises profusely both the wisdom and eloquence of his correspondent. But this apparent flattery perhaps once again carries a deeper significance: besides placing this exchange of letters within a tradition that can be traced back to the Pico-Barbaro exchange, it seems also to imply that wisdom and eloquence—which Pico had seen as diametrically opposed—can in fact be reconciled. This spirit of reconciliation is indeed a determining characteristic of Calcagnini's response; it ultimately generates a solution to the polemics on imitation theory as it was debated among Italian humanists.

Calcagnini agrees with Cinzio that imitation is necessary, particularly for Neo-Latin writers who are not composing in a language known since infancy. He asserts that the serious writer of Latin should avoid writing in the vernacular, which tends to interfere with the development of a truly eloquent style. Here Calcagnini seems to be alluding to Bembo, who also lamented the contamination of his Latin style that came from composing Italian prose and poetry. But Calcagnini also offers some criticism that would apply to Bembo's adversary, Pico, for he condemns those philosophers of the previous generation who were more concerned with obscure studies than with eloquence. He goes on to criticize writers who rely only on their own inner resources—their *ingenium*—in the process of writing, and who do not recognize the need to imitate the best writers of antiquity. In this way, Calcagnini, like his eclectic predecessors Petrarch, Poliziano and Pico, gives attention both to *ingenium* and imitation. But while those earlier Eclectics considered the two as allies, and held multiple-model imitation to be the technique that liberates genius, Calcagnini sets them in opposition, in a manner reminiscent of the Ciceronian Cortesi.

Later, however, Calcagnini will introduce a new element into the imitative debate: the notion of inspiration. For him inspiration is an ally of imitation, a force that emanates from without, a genuine *influence* from others, rather than the mark of self-sufficient genius that the Romantics will later make it out to be. Here Calcagnini clearly aligns himself with the Eclectics in his openness to a wide variety of possible sources; indeed, Calcagnini suggests, in a manner reminiscent of Poliziano, that even second-rate authors may display occasional flashes of brilliance. He also recalls the Eclectics in his aversion to excessive similitude. Finally, Calcagnini develops Cinzio's notion of the appropriate stages of imitative practice and suggests that the mature writer should in fact forgo imitation in favor of genuine emulation, which he understands to be a combative, antagonistic struggle with the precursor. To illustrate his point, Calcagnini recounts the story of Eros and Anteros, claiming that it was only when engaged in a struggle with his brother and rival that Eros could fully mature.

Although this treatise did not evoke a direct response from Cinzio, it did become the subject of a third letter, this one written by Cinzio's kinsman, Lilio Gregorio Giraldi. Here, Lilio also focuses on the issue of the proper stages of imitative practice discussed by Giraldi and later developed by Calcagnini. To Lilio, it is clear that the solution to the Ciceronian dilemma is one that combines the best features of the theories offered by the Ciceronians, such as Bembo, along with other advice culled from the Eclectics. Specifically, Lilio suggests that the apprentice writer follow Bembo's advice of exclusive imitation of the best model in the earliest stages of his career. This apprenticeship period should be followed by a more advanced stage, characterized by a more liberal approach to imitative practice. In this stage the young writer would be free to choose from a wide variety of possible sources, as the Eclectics suggested. Moreover, Lilio warns against the commission of a stylistic sin which he refers to as *inepta imitatione*, a Latin equivalent of the Greek term κακοζηλία that was used by Quintilian to describe an "extravagant affectation" or excessiveness that must be avoided. Although this letter is brief, it is of critical importance in the history of Ciceronianism, for it was to be paraphrased and quoted at length by both Lipsius and Possevino.

Years after his youthful exchange with Calcagnini, Giraldi Cinzio composed a host of prefaces, letters, and formal treatises that dealt with the matter of imitation. In these writings, Cinzio seems to have abandoned his adherence to single-model imitation, even reprising the Zeuxis story to make his point, and, moreover, adamantly voices the modern writer's need to modify ancient literary discourse to conform with the realities of the contemporary world. This appeal to the notion of historical decorum, a hallmark of the anti-Ciceronian position espoused by Erasmus, demonstrates that, in the wake of his exchange with Calcagnini, Cinzio came to have greater affinity with the Eclectics than with the Ciceronians. Ultimately, like Calcagnini, he suggests that aspiring writers should eventually be free to forgo imitation entirely and forge their own style. Again like Calcagnini, he invokes the notion of inspiration which he sees as emanating from an outside source, but nonetheless reminds his reader that much labor is necessary to achieve eloquence. This combination of inspiration and labor — or, as Cinzio puts it in a marginal comment to his treatise, of work and grace — will reappear in the theories developed by the Jesuit Possevino in identical terms.[12]

After the Cinzio-Calcagnini exchange, there appears to be a lull in the polemical discussion of imitative theory, at least among Italians, so that there were no further epistolary debates on the matter. This is not to say, however, that the issue of Ciceronianism was completely resolved; other theorists, particularly outside Italy, took part in the Ciceronian quarrel, responding directly to the *Ciceronianus* of Erasmus, but in formal treatises rather than through an exchange of letters. Some of these treatises—including those of Scaliger and Dolet—comment explicitly on the debates between Poliziano, Cortesi, Pico and Bembo. Other treatises, which dealt with the issue of imitation while not directly confronting the *Ciceronianus*, likewise referred to some of the players in the Italian exchange of letters.[13] Significantly, however, none of these subsequent texts allude to the whole of the Cinzio-Calcagnini-Lilio exchange, which was to prove so influential later in the century, and only one (the preface to Johannes Sturm's *De imitatione*) mentions even one part of this correspondence (namely Calcagnini's formal treatise addressed to Giraldi Cinzio).

The next and final chapter of the Ciceronian quarrel begins with the publication of Possevino's *Bibliotheca selecta* in 1593. The purpose of this encyclopedic text was to provide excerpts of important literary and philosophical works that might aid in the education of young people in a way not pernicious to their spiritual welfare. It is evident from Possevino's first edition of this encyclopedic text that the issue of developing an eloquent style in Latin was of great importance to this Jesuit educator. In a treatise entitled the *Cicero*, Possevino discusses the Ciceronian quarrel and its major players. This section, which constituted an appendix to the Roman edition of the *Bibliotheca selecta* of 1593, printed with its own title page and separate pagination, was also published independently in the same year at Lyon, Cologne and Padua. In the *Cicero*, Possevino chooses to include in its entirety the third letter of the Pico-Bembo debate, that is, Pico's little-known and rarely published second letter to Bembo. Possevino's decision to include this text not only testifies to his eclectic sympathies but also to his desire to ensure that Pico's contribution to the quarrel would not be forgotten. It is also a testament to the religious orthodoxy which underpins Pico's imitative theory. While Pico's letter was the only document from the quarrel that Possevino transcribes in its entirety, another important letter — the epistle of Lilio Giraldi, which comments upon all the quarrels — is quoted extensively in the following chapter. Yet Possevino does not provide any comments of his own on this debate, which is perhaps why he revisits the subject ten years later in his second edition of the *Bibliotheca*, published in 1603.

This time, Possevino begins his treatment of the issue by referring to those who have, in his opinion, best studied the issue, including Pico, Lilio and Lipsius, and goes on to give an extensive paraphrase of Lipsius' chapters dealing with imitation taken from the *Epistolica Institutio* of 1591. Though it is written by a non-Italian who is conscious of his status as a foreigner in the debate, the *Epistolica Institutio* is definitely a product of the Italian Ciceronian quarrels. It consists of a set of lecture notes composed by Lipsius while he was professor of rhetoric at the University of Leiden in 1587. Here Lipsius is specifically interested in the art of letter writing, a subject which had already been treated by previous participants in the Ciceronian quarrel, including Erasmus, and traces of the latter's theories can be found throughout the text.[14] Lipsius is quick to condemn "certain recent Italians" who propose that Cicero alone was suitable reading material for the aspiring writer. Yet the Ciceronians are not completely ridiculed by Lipsius and, indeed, their point of view is vital to the first stage of imitative practice that he describes. The youthful imitator is urged to adopt the practice of the "sect of the Italians," or, more literally, to follow the "Italian heresy," that is, the exclusive, almost sacramental imitation of Cicero alone. This would allow them to hone their style on a single authoritative master, assuring that they will achieve the kind of harmony that Bembo and Cortesi were certain could not be attained through eclectic imitation. Next, for a period of two years, the adolescent writer is advised to widen the scope of his readings to include those classical authors whose style is most like Cicero's himself. Finally, the mature writer is free to take ornamentation from a vast array of authors from all periods of literature. In addition to this notion of the gradual expansion of the canon of acceptable authors for imitation, Lipsius suggests that the manner of imitation employed by the novice writer should likewise change as he grows and matures. The youngest writers should adhere most strictly to the Ciceronian style; the adolescent author is urged to be more moderate; while mature writers are expected to develop a style uniquely their own, the product of their individual genius. It is here that Lipsius warns writers to avoid "bad emulation," the same expression borrowed from Quintilian which had appeared in the letter of Lilio Giraldi.

It is significant that Possevino in his paraphrase—which otherwise borders on an exact transcription of chapters eleven through thirteen of the *Institutio*—takes pains to eliminate all negative references to the Italian literary quarrels, including the allusion to those recent fastidious Italians who read no one but Cicero as well as the designation of strict Ciceronianism as the "sect of the Italians." Possevino apparently sought to rehabilitate the Italian Ciceronians despite his own predilection for the Eclectics. What is more, Possevino takes pains to ensure that the role played by the Italians in the ultimate resolution of the Ciceronian quarrel would not go unnoticed, for, as he will go on to suggest, Lipsius' new program of imitative practice is virtually identical to Lilio's solution to the dilemma. Though Lipsius himself did not give credit for these ideas to Lilio or to any of the seven principal correspondents on the matter, Possevino apparently noticed the similarity, thanks in large part to Lipsius' use of the key Greek term κακοζηλία, used by Lilio in his letter to Giraldi, and thus gives due recognition to the neglected Lilio and his intellectual predecessors. This is accomplished in the chapters he devotes to a general discussion of imitation, where he explicitly refers to the Pico-

Bembo debate and analyzes the hitherto overlooked letter of Lilio Giraldi. Here Possevino shows how Lilio reconciled the Ciceronian and eclectic approaches to imitation by showing how both theories could be put into practice sequentially. Moreover, he also points out how Lilio warned against "inept imitation" or "bad emulation," the same phrase that had appeared in Lipsius' tract. While Possevino never explicitly accuses Lipsius of having stolen his plan from Lilio, the implication is certainly there to be discovered by the attentive reader.

But in case the reader misses these subtle correspondences, Possevino (or his editor) makes the connection between Lipsius and Lilio absolutely certain, thanks to the marginal annotations that accompany the tract. The first of these notations is located in chapter seventeen, where Lipsius is quoted as admonishing the mature imitator to resist "bad emulation." The notation reads: "Haec eadem Gregorius Giraldus ad Cinthium Giraldum." In the beginning of the next chapter, Possevino summarizes Lilio's letter, mentioning his use of that same Greek term. The marginal annotation here reads simply: "Idem Lipsius," thus assuring that the reader is again aware of the connection between Lipsius and Lilio. In this way, Possevino succeeds in reclaiming for Italy what he perceived to be the best solution to the Ciceronian quarrel that had preoccupied his countrymen for well over a century.

Possevino's interest in literary matters is apparent from another treatise that was published as a section of the *Bibliotheca selecta* of 1593 and later published separately under the title *Cultura ingeniorum*. This text—which was apparently deemed important or popular enough to be translated almost immediately into Italian and published in 1598 under the title *Coltura degl'ingegni*—provides another forum for Possevino to display his alliance with the Eclectics.[15] It is particularly reminiscent of Pico in its assertion of the primacy of *res* over *verba*. More importantly, it proclaims the importance of natural talent in the creative process and conceives of this genius as working in conjunction with art or technique. It is thus reminiscent of the comment made by Cinzio regarding the alliance of labor and inspiration which, he claims, is analogous to the relationship in the theology of salvation between works and divine grace. Indeed, Possevino makes precisely the same analogy, implying that genius or talent, like grace, constitutes a potential artistic excellence that requires the artist's full cooperation with God's gift in order to come to fruition. Thus, Possevino's understanding of genius is consistent with the position he and other Jesuit thinkers (such as the theologian, Luis de Molina, 1535–1600) held with regard to the issue of divine grace and its relationship to the free actions of men.[16] It is this understanding that underpins their unique resolution of the thorny issues that haunted Jesuit theologians: namely, how to counteract the Protestant insistence on the predominance of grace over works and to reconcile a strong notion of creaturely freedom with the image of a God who providentially cares for his creation. Possevino's theological commitments lead him to develop a notion that might be called "teachable genius": a divinely-infused power of eloquence that nevertheless needs to be cultivated and requires genuine labor. By insisting on the necessity of labor, Possevino acknowledges the pertinence of the Ciceronians' reliance on laborious imitative technique, which is akin to relying on free will or works alone to achieve salvation. But by balancing this emphasis on labor with a recognition of the need for innate talent or genius, analogous to divine grace, Possevino also shows respect for the eclectic position which emphasized the use of one's own inner resources to the neglect of laborious technique.

The Ciceronian quarrel, as it played out in Italy between the 1480s and the 1600s, can thus be seen as belonging to the wider cultural debates of the time. It certainly is related to the famous *Questione della lingua* (the debate over whether one should write in Latin or

Italian, and what kind of Italian should be used);[17] it played a major role in the development of Jesuit pedagogical theory that culminated in the development of the *Ratio studiorum;*[18] and consequently it is inevitably bound up with the religious turmoil that characterized much of the later Renaissance. After Possevino reconciled the two warring camps, his novel solution to the problem — or rather the solution suggested by Lilio — was promulgated throughout the seventeenth century, especially among French Jesuits and most notably in the *De eloquentiae sacrae et humanae parallela* (1619) of Nicholas Caussin (1583–1644). From his reuse of many of their favorite analogies such as the Zeuxis image, the father/son dichotomy, and the digestive metaphor, it is clear that Caussin sympathizes with the Eclectics. Yet it is also clear that Caussin thought of himself as a Ciceronian, but in the manner of Petrarch and other early humanists: one who regarded Cicero as a prime model, but certainly not one to be followed to the exclusion of all other authors. Ciceronianism, it seems, had taken three centuries to come full circle.

I have incurred a number of debts in the course of finishing this book, and it is my pleasure to acknowledge them now: David Bachrach, Maureen Boulton, Theodore Cachey, Rachel Doggett, John P. Donnelly, S. J., Br. Michael Grace, Mary Louise Gude, C. S. C., Walter Nickorgski, David O'Connor, Daniel Sheerin, and Alison Sproston all helped provide answers to many questions. I must also acknowledge countless library staff, especially at the Newberry Library, the Folger Shakespeare Library, the Library of Congress, the British Library, the Bibliothèque Nationale in Paris, the Library Company of Philadelphia, and the libraries of the University of Pennsylvania, Princeton University, the University of Chicago, the University of Michigan, and Loyola University. My largest debt, of course, is to the efficient and helpful staff of the Hesburgh Library at the University of Notre Dame. I am also extremely grateful for the financial benefits I received from Notre Dame's Institute for Scholarship in the Liberal Arts, in the form of research and materials grants as well as to the College of Arts and Letters for giving me the release time to work on this project. I should also like to thank Jill Bodensteiner, Kay Henderson, Phyllis Shelton-Ball, and Gregory Sterling for their roles in the completion of this work and especially want to acknowledge the help I received from my collaborator, Brian Duvick, in establishing the Latin text of this edition. I also wish to recognize the expert attention James Hankins bestowed on this volume, making it a far better book. Finally, my deepest gratitude is for my husband, Thomas Flint, and for my daughter, Christine Flint, who have both added much joy to my life.

J. D.

I would like to acknowledge the following for their assistance in the completion of this project: Hervé Pasqua of the Institut Universitaire de St.-Melaine, Georges Fresneau, and Robert Welshon of the University of Colorado. I especially want to thank Richard Duvick, my family for their patience and support, and JoAnn DellaNeva for her sound judgment, constancy and friendship over the years.

B. D.

This book is dedicated to the memory of our sisters, Helen DellaNeva Hollingsworth and Kimberly Marie Duvick.

NOTES

1. For more on the Ciceronian quarrel, see the works by Sabbadini, Scott, Fumaroli, and McLaughlin cited in the Bibliography.

2. These responses include the *Oratio pro M. Tullio Cicerone contra Desiderium Erasmum* and the *Oratio secunda*, published, respectively, in 1531 and 1535 by Julius Caesar Scaliger (1484–1558), an Italian living in France, and the *De imitatione Ciceroniana, adversus Desiderium Erasmum Roterodamum, pro Christophoro Longolio* (1535) by Etienne Dolet (1509–1546), a Frenchman who had spent considerable time in Italy (see Scaliger and Dolet under ABBREVIATIONS; the Dolet edition has an extensive bibliography of primary sources, compiled by E. V. Telle, on 439–460). An analysis and English paraphrase of the Scaliger and Dolet texts can be found in Scott 1: 42–62 and 63–97, respectively. For more on these debates, the reader is referred to Scott, Sabbadini, and especially to Pigman, "Imitation and the Renaissance Sense of the Past." Other responses of some interest include (1) Giulio Camillo's *Trattato della imitatione* (c. 1530), found in Weinberg, 1: 161–185, in which Camillo felt Erasmus must have written the *Ciceronianus* in jest; (2) the *Dialogus* of the anti-Ciceronian Nicholas Bérauld (1534); (3) the *Cicero relegatus et Cicero revocatus* (1534) of Ortensio Landi, which mocked both sides of the debate; (4) the *Succisivarum lectionum libri III* (1539) of Francesco Florido (1511–1548), which defended Erasmus against Dolet; (5) the *De imitatione Ciceroniana adversus Floridum* (1540), Dolet's response to Florido; and (6) the *Adversus Doleti calumnias* (1541), Florido's second response to Dolet.

3. McLaughlin, *Literary Imitation*, 3.

4. An excellent source for information on these filiations is Girolamo Tiraboschi's *Storia della letteratura italiana* (Milan, 1822–26), especially volumes 6 and 7.

5. See Book VIII of Calcagnini's *Epistolae* (in Calcagnini, 104–105, 106–107, 111–112) for some of Calcagnini's letters to Pico and Book VII (ibid. 95) and Book XVI (ibid. 211) for his letters to Lilio Giraldi. See also Pico's *Opera omnia* (1573), 2: 1281 and 1358 for the Pico-Calcagnini letters and 2: 1364 for the letter to Lilio Giraldi. Lilio's letters to Pico were also published in Pico's *De amore divino* (1516).

6. See Calcagnini's letters, Book XII (Calcagnini, 166–167), and the *Opus Epistolarum Desiderii Erasmi Roterodami*, eds. P. S. Allen and H. W. Garrod (Oxford, 1906–58), 10: 303–304, no. 2869, for Calcagnini's correspondence with Erasmus, dated 17 September 1533, in which he expresses general agreement with Erasmus about the ability of modern authors to equal the achievement of Cicero.

7. This work, entitled *Due discorsi. L'una in difesa di messer Giovanni Battista suo fratello dove si discorre intorno all'honore et al duello, l'altro in difesa del signor Giovanni Battista Giraldi dove si trattano alcune cose per iscriver tragedie* (Rome, 1556), is cited in several bibliographical references, but is exceedingly rare. I am indebted to John P. Donnelly, S. J., for providing me with a photocopy of it.

8. The Latin text of the *Oratio super Fabio Quintiliano et Statii Sylvis*, along with an Italian translation, can be found in Garin, 870–885.

9. For more on Pico's understanding of "genius" see Jean Lecointe, *L'Idéal et la Différence*, 46, 219–225, and 375–468.

10. See Pico-Barbaro for an English translation. The correspondence has been reedited with Italian translation and commentary in *Filosofia o eloquenza? Ermolao Barbaro, Giovanni Pico della Mirandola*, ed. Francesco Bausi (Naples, 1998).

11. Bembo's theory of Platonic love would later be expounded by the character of Pietro Bembo at the end of Book IV of Baldassar Castiglione's *Courtier*.

12. "There is need for study in order to compose well, and for *exercitatio*, aided by divine grace" (Cinzio 1968, 166, translation modified). "Vi è bisogno di studio a ben comporre, e di esercitazione, la quale aiutata dalla divina grazia" (Cinzio 1864, 1: 35).

13. These include the *De elocutionis imitatione ac apparatu* (1537) of the German Jacobus Omphalius (1500–1567); *In M. T. Ciceronis Tusculanarum Quaestionum commentarii* (1538) of Joachim Camerarius (1500–1574); *De imitatione libri tres* (1545) of Bartolomeo Ricci (1490–1569); the *Ciceronianus* (1557) of Peter Ramus (1515–1572); the *Scholemaster* (published posthumously in 1570) by Roger Ascham (1515–1568); the preface to the *De*

imitatione oratoria (published in 1574, though probably written earlier) of Johannes Sturm (1507–1589); the *Ciceronianus* (1577) of Gabriel Harvey (1550–1630); and the preface to a collection of letters in the Ciceronian style edited by Henri Estienne (Bunel et al.)

14. See the *De conscribendis epistolis* (1522) of Erasmus.

15. The first edition of the *Cultura ingeniorum* constitutes the introduction to *Bibliotheca Selecta* (Rome: Bibliotheca Apostolica Vaticana, 1593) and is found on pp. 11–147; likewise it serves as the first book of the 1603 edition of the *Bibliotheca selecta*, where it occupies pp. 1–49, and in the reprint of 1607, where it can be found on pp. 1–44. The text was published individually in 1604 as the *Cultura ingeniorum* (Venice: Ciottus, 1604). For the Italian translation, see the *Coltura degl'ingegni*, ed. Mariano Lauretti (Venice: Greco, 1598).

16. Marc Fumaroli likewise mentions in passing in a footnote that "il y a, à notre sens, un rapport profond entre la Querelle du Cicéronianisme, entendue au sens large, et la Querelle de la Grâce. L'importance que les Jésuistes accordent dans leurs enseignement rhétorique, à la nature et à l'art, correspond à leur théologie de la liberté. Et la valeur qu'ils accordent aux vraisemblances oratoires correspond à leur théologie de la 'science moyenne'. . . " See *L'âge de l'éloquence*, 182, n. 282.

17. See Vitale, *La questione della lingua*, and Grayson, *A Renaissance Controversy: Latin or Italian?*

18. See Brizzi, *La "Ratio Studiorum."*

CICERONIAN
CONTROVERSIES

1   Angelus Politianus Paulo Cortesio suo salutem dicit

Remitto epistolas diligentia tua collectas, in quibus legendis (ut libere dicam) pudet bonas horas male collocasse. Nam praeter omnino paucas, minime dignae sunt quae vel a docto aliquo lectae, vel a te collectae dicantur. Quas probem, quas rursus improbem, non explico. Nolo sibi quisquam vel placeat in his auctore me vel displiceat. Est in quo tamen a te dissentiam de stilo nonnihil. Non enim probare soles (ut accepi) nisi qui liniamenta Ciceronis effingat. Mihi vero longe honestior tauri facies aut item leonis quam simiae videtur, quae tamen homini similior est. Nec ii, qui principatum tenuisse creduntur eloquentiae, similes inter se, quod Seneca prodidit. Ridentur a Quintiliano qui se germanos Ciceronis putabant esse, quod his verbis periodum clauderent: esse videatur. Inclamat Horatius imitatores ac nihil aliud quam imitatores. Mihi certe quicunque tantum componunt ex imitatione, similes esse vel psitaco vel picae videntur, proferentibus quae nec intellegunt. Carent enim quae scribunt isti viribus et vita; carent actu, carent affectu, carent indole; iacent, dormiunt, stertunt. Nihil ibi verum, nihil solidum, nihil efficax. Non exprimis, inquit aliquis, Ciceronem. Quid tum? Non enim sum Cicero. Me tamen (ut opinor) exprimo.

2   Sunt quidam praeterea, mi Paule, qui stilum quasi panem frustillatim mendicant, nec ex die solum vivunt, sed et in diem; tum nisi liber ille praesto sit ex quo quid excerpant, colligere tria verba non possunt. Sed haec ipsa quoque vel indocta iunctura vel barbaria inhonesta contaminant. Horum semper igitur oratio tremula,

Angelo Poliziano to Paolo Cortesi

Angelo Poliziano sends greetings to Paolo Cortesi.   1

I am returning the letters that you collected with such diligence. If I may speak freely, I am ashamed to have so badly spent
so many good hours reading them. Except for a very few, they are
unworthy of having been read by a learned man or of having been
collected by you. I will not say which I approve of and which not.
I do not wish that anyone be either pleased or displeased with
himself with regard to them on my account. Still, there is a point
regarding style that I disagree with you on. For you generally do
not approve of anyone, as I understand it, unless he copies the features of Cicero.[1] To me the face of a bull or a lion seems far more
honorable than that of an ape,[2] which nonetheless is more like a
man than they are. The men who are believed to have held the
pinnacle of eloquence are not similar to one another, as Seneca has
demonstrated.[3] Quintilian laughs at those who considered themselves brothers of Cicero because they closed a period with the
phrase, "it would *seem* so." [4] Horace rebukes imitators who are
nothing but imitators.[5] In my view, anyone who composes by imitation alone is like a parrot or a magpie,[6] seeming to voice what he
does not understand. For what men of this type write lacks force
and life; it lacks drive, emotion, talent; it falls flat, dozes, snores.[7]
Nothing there is true, nothing solid, nothing effective. "You do not
write like Cicero," someone says. So what? I am not Cicero. Yet I
do express myself, I think.[8]

There are also men, Paolo, who go begging for their style piece 2
by piece, as though it were bread.[9] And they live this way not only
day-to-day but everyday. Then, unless they have their book at
hand from which to draw excerpts, they cannot put three words

vacillans, infirma, videlicet male curata, male pasta, quos ferre profecto non possum. Iudicare quoque de doctis impudenter audentes, hoc est de illis quorum stilum recondita eruditio, multiplex lectio, longissimus usus diu quasi fermentavit.

3   Sed ut ad te redeam, Paule, quem penitus amo, cui multum debeo, cuius ingenio plurimum tribuo, quaeso, ne superstitione ista te alliges, ut nihil delectet quod tuum plane sit, et ut oculos a Cicerone numquam deicias. Sed cum Ciceronem, cum bonos alios multum diuque legeris, contriveris, edidiceris, concoxeris et rerum multarum cognitione pectus impleveris, ac iam componere aliquid ipse parabis, tum demum velim (quod dicitur) sine cortice nates, atque ipse tibi sis aliquando in consilio, sollicitudinemque illam morosam nimis et anxiam deponas effingendi tantummodo Ciceronem tuasque denique vires universas pericliteris. Nam qui tantum ridicula ista quae vocatis liniamenta contemplantur attoniti, nec illa ipsa (mihi crede) satis repraesentant, et impetum quodammodo retardant ingenii sui, currentique velut obstant, et (ut utar Plautino verbo) remoram faciunt. Sed ut bene currere non potest qui pedem ponere studet in alienis tantum vestigiis, ita nec bene scribere qui tamquam de praescripto non audet egredi. Postremo scias infelicis esse ingenii, nihil a se promere, semper imitari.

    Vale.

together; but these too they spoil with either an unlearned conjunction or undignified barbarism.[10] As a result, the speech of
these men, whom I really cannot bear, is always tremulous, hesi-
tant, infirm, clearly ill-prepared and ill-cultivated.[11] And they have
the impudence to dare judge even the learned, that is, men whose
style has long fermented, if you will, with recondite learning,
broad reading and extensive practice.

But to return to you, Paolo, whom I cherish deeply, to whom I   3
am much indebted, whose natural ability I value highly, I ask that
you not so shackle yourself with this superstition that you be
pleased with nothing of your own and never shift your eyes from
Cicero.[12] But after you have read Cicero and other good writers
widely and at length, after you have consumed, thoroughly learned
and digested them,[13] and have filled your heart with the knowledge of many matters,[14] and you prepare to compose something
yourself, then at last I would wish you to swim (as they say) without a preserver,[15] take your own counsel sometimes, put away that
excessively fastidious and anxious preoccupation that you have
with copying Cicero alone, and finally put the totality of your
wide-ranging powers to the test.[16] Those who are so very stunned
by their contemplation of those ridiculous things that you call
"features," believe me, do not even reproduce them satisfactorily;
in a sense they retard the momentum of their own natural talent,
struggle against the current, and if I might use a Plautine word,
"side-track" themselves.[17] But as you cannot run well if you strain
to put your feet only in other people's tracks,[18] neither can you
write well unless you dare depart from what has been prescribed,
as it were. Finally, I hope you know that it is in the nature of a
barren talent to produce nothing of its own but rather always to
imitate.[19]

Farewell.

1   Paulus Cortesius Angelo Politiano suo salutem dicit

Nihil umquam mihi tam praeter opinionem meam accidit quam redditus a te liber epistolarum nostrarum. Putabam enim illum tibi in tantis occupationibus excidisse. Nunc autem lectis tuis literis video illum non modo a te gustatum, sed etiam plane devoratum, cum et scripseris puduisse te in eo legendo bonas horas male collocasse, et eas ipsas minime tibi dignas videri, quae vel ab aliquo docto lectae vel a me collectae fuisse dicantur, praeter nescio quas hominum perpaucorum. Ego autem totum istud tibi remitto, nec plane iudicium meum interponam, cum nefas sit quodammodo a te dissentire. Et ego is sim, qui de altero iudicium facere (ut ait Marcus Tullius) nec velim si possim,[1] nec possim[2] si velim. Sed veniam ad illud in quo te dicis a me quam maxime dissentire.

2   Scribis enim te accepisse me neminem probare, nisi qui liniamenta Ciceronis consectari videantur. Ego vero quantum repetere memoria possum, nec istud recordor umquam dixisse, nec dictum volo. Quae enim stultitia esset, ut cum tam varia sint hominum ingenia, tam multiplices naturae, tam diversae inter se voluntates, eas velle unius ingenii angustiis astringi et tamquam praefiniri? Sed quoniam me in hanc disputationem vocas, non erit fortasse alienum tempus purgandi iudicii nostri et tuendi mei, cum plane cognoscam verba tua esse suasoris, non lacessentis. Et primum de iudicio libenter fatebor, cum viderem eloquentiae studia tamdiu deserta iacuisse et sublatum usum forensem et quasi nativam

Paolo Cortesi to Angelo Poliziano

Paolo Cortesi sends greetings to Angelo Poliziano.   1

   Nothing so contrary to expectations has ever happened to me
as when you returned my book of letters. For I thought that, in
the midst of all your business, you had forgotten it. Now, however,
after reading your letter, I see that you have not only sampled it
but completely consumed it, since you write that you are ashamed
to have so badly spent your good hours in reading it, and that the
letters themselves seemed to you unworthy of the claim of having
been read by a learned man or of having been collected by me, except for those (I do not know which) of a very few men. For my
part, I grant everything you say, and will not present my judgments frankly, since it is almost irreligious to disagree with you. I
too am the sort of person, as Cicero says, who would not wish to
judge another, even if I could, nor could I, even if I wanted to. But
let me address that passage where you say that you disagree with
me most of all.

   You write that you have understood me to approve of none but   2
those who seem to follow and imitate the features of Cicero.
Really, as far as I can recall, I have never said such a thing, nor do
I wish I had. When the talents of men are so varied, their natures
so manifold, their wills so different from one another, what stu-
pidity it would be to wish them bound and restricted by the con-
straints of a single talent.[1] But since you call me into this controversy, perhaps this is an opportune moment to justify my opinion
and defend myself, since I recognize clearly that yours are words of
persuasion, not provocation. First, about my opinion I shall willingly confess that, when I saw the pursuit of eloquence lying so
long deserted,[2] public speaking so neglected and our people lack-

quandam vocem deesse hominibus nostris, me saepe palam affir-
masse nihil his temporibus ornate varieque dici posse, nisi ab iis
qui aliquem sibi praeponerent ad imitandum. Cum et peregrini ex-
pertes sermonis alienas regiones male possint sine duce peragrare,
et anniculi infantes non nisi in curriculo aut nutrice praeeunte
inambulent. Cum autem multi in omni eloquentiae genere floruе-
rint, memini me unum Marcum Tullium ex doctorum acie ab-
duxisse, in quem omnium ingeniosorum hominum studia con-
ferenda putarem. Non quod ignorarem multos dicendi gloria
praestitisse qui et acuere industriam et multis oratoriis virtutibus
alere ingenia possent, sed et quia videbam hunc unum omnium
saeculorum consensu principem esse iudicatum, et quia a puero
didiceram in omni numero semper optimum esse eligendum. Cor-
rupti stomachi et intemperantis aegri esse putabam deteriorem ci-
bum seligere, salutarem et optimum aspernari. Ausim nunc etiam
affirmare idem quod saepe: neminem post Marcum Tullium in
scribendo laudem consecutum, praeter unum aut alterum, qui non
sit ab eo eductus et tamquam lactis nutrimento educatus. Sed erat
tum quaedam certa imitandi ratio, qua‹e› et fastidio similitudinis
occurrebatur et nitidum illud genus hilaritate quadam aspersa
condiebat[ur]. Nunc autem illa ab hominibus nostris aut neglecta
est aut ignorata. Similem volo, mi Politiane, non ut simiam hominis, sed ut filium parentis. Illa enim ridicula imitatrix tantum de-
formitates et vitia corporis depravata similitudine effingit. Hic autem vultum, incessum, statum, motum, formam, vocem denique et
figuram corporis representat, et tamen habet in hac similitudine
aliquid suum, aliquid naturale, aliquid diversum, ita ut cum comparentur dissimiles inter se esse videantur.

ing a kind of native voice, I often and openly asserted that nothing
in these times could be said with elegance and variety[3] except by
those who set out a model for themselves to imitate,[4] just as trav-
elers ignorant of the local language have difficulty traversing foreign lands without a guide,[5] and toddlers cannot get about except
in a stroller or led by a nurse.[6] Although many have flourished in
every genre of eloquent speech, I recall that I chose Cicero alone
from the ranks of learned men, and thought that every talented
person should concentrate his studies on him. It was not that I
was ignorant of the many men who had excelled in the glory of
fine speech, who were able both to sharpen one's diligence and to
nurture one's talents with their many rhetorical virtues, but because I saw that the general consensus of all the ages had judged
him the sole champion, and also had learned as a boy that one
should always choose the best of any group. I considered it the
sign of a ruined digestion and a sickness born of intemperance to
choose inferior food but spurn the healthy and best.[7] Even now I
would dare assert what I often said before: apart from one or two
exceptions, no one after Cicero has earned praise for his writing
who was not raised by him and nourished, if you will, on his
milk.[8] But there was at that time a definite method of imitation
that ran counter to the distaste for similarity and used to season
this attractive genre of writing with a certain cheerfulness. Now,
however, our people have either neglected or are simply ignorant
of that method. I wish to be similar to Cicero, my Poliziano, not
as an ape to a man but as a son to a father.[9] For the ape, that ridiculous imitator, mimics only the deformities and faults of the body
in a sort of depraved likeness.[10] The son, however, reproduces the
appearance, walk, posture, motion, form, voice and finally the
shape of his father's body, but still has something of his own in
this likeness,[11] something natural, something different. So when
compared, they still seem dissimilar from each other.

3   Dicam idem iterum: habere hoc dilucidam illam divini hominis in dicendo copiam, ut existimanti se imitabilem praebeat, experienti spem imitationis eripiat. Fit enim undique ad eum concursus et quisque arbitratur illo modo se posse dicere. Homines enim natura suavitatis avidiores difficillimam rem voluntate, non facultate metiuntur. Itaque dum abundantiam sermonis et (ut ipsi aiunt) facilitatem imitantur, nervos et aculeos deserunt, et tum a Cicerone absunt longissime. Nec autem refert alieno ornatu et quibusdam luminibus ac quasi insignibus nostra scripta explere, nisi queamus id distincte apteque facere. Fit enim nescio quid monstrosum, cum membra cohaerentia male dissipantur.

4   Quare (ut de me loquar) nihil est, Politiane, quod me a Ciceronis imitatione deterreas, sed quod potius obiurges inscitiam, quod nequeam bene illum imitari, quamquam ego malo esse assecula et simia Ciceronis quam alumnus aut filius aliorum. Sed permagni interest utrum quis videatur quenquam velle imitari aut neminem. Ego autem statuo non modo in eloquentia, sed in aliis etiam artibus necessariam esse imitationem. Nam et omnis doctrina ex antecedenti cognitione paratur, et nihil est in mente quin fuerit prius in sensibus perceptum. Ex quo intellegitur omnem artem naturae esse imitationem, sed natura fieri ut ex eodem genere dissimilitudo nascatur. Homines enim, cum inter se dissimiles sint, similitudine coniunguntur, et quamquam alii coloratiores, alii pallidiores, alii venustiores, alii proceriores sint, una tamen est omnibus figura et forma. Illos autem quibus aut crus aut manus aut brachia desunt, non omnino ex hominum genere excludendos, sed aut mancos aut claudos appellandos putarem. Sic eloquentiae una est ars, una forma, una imago. Qui vero ab ea declinant, saepe distorti, saepe claudi reperiuntur. Aspice nunc eos homines qui sibi elegerunt

Let me add that to have available the brilliant richness[12] of the divine man's speech leads one to believe that it can be imitated, but snatches away all such hope from anyone that actually attempts it.[13] For everyone rushes to him and thinks he can speak that way. In fact men, being naturally greedy for sweetness, measure the most difficult matter by their desire, not their ability. Hence, while they imitate the abundance of his discourse and, as they say, his facility, they forgo his force and sharpness and thus depart far from Cicero. It is, moreover, inappropriate to fill our writings with another man's embellishments, brilliant passages and remarkable features,[14] unless we can do it with decorum[15] and distinction. One makes a sort of monstrosity[16] when the adjacent parts of one's discourse are badly integrated.[17]

So, speaking for myself, Poliziano, you have no reason to deter me from imitating Cicero; you should rather reproach me for my ignorance in that I am unable to imitate him well, although I prefer to be a hanger-on and ape of Cicero than the pupil or son of others.[18] But it is an important question whether one should wish to imitate someone or no one.[19] I maintain that imitation is necessary, not only in eloquence but in the other arts as well.[20] For all teaching is acquired from previous knowledge, and there is nothing in the mind except what has already been perceived by the senses.[21] It therefore is understood that all art is an imitation of nature,[22] but nature is so made that dissimilarity is born of the same genus. For while men are dissimilar to one another, they are also related by their likeness; and although some have more coloration, others are paler, some are more attractive and others taller, all still have a single shape and form. I would think that people lacking a leg, hand or arms should not be altogether excluded from the human species but that we should call them maimed or crippled. There is thus a single art of eloquence, a single form, a single image.[23] People that deviate from it are often found to be ill-formed, often limping. Consider the men who have decided to im-

Marcum Tullium imitandum, quantum ab eo distent, quantum etiam inter se dissimiles sint! Profluentem quandam sine modestia ubertatem Livius arripuit, acumen Quintilianus, sonum Lactantius, lenitatem Curtius, elegantiam Columella, quorum cum esset unum prope imitandi propositum, nihil est tam dissimile quam ipsi inter se, nihil tam distans (si comparentur) quam ipsi a Cicerone. Ex quo intellegi maxime et cum iudicio ponderandam esse imitationem, et eum ipsum hominem mirabilem fuisse, ex quo tam diversa ingenia, tamquam ex perenni quodam fonte defluxerint.

5   Omnino, Politiane, certis auctoribus insistendum est, quibus ingenia formentur et tamquam alantur. Relinquunt enim in animis semina quae in posterum per se ipsa coalescunt. Qui autem neminem imitari et sine cuiusquam similitudine laudem consequi videri volunt, nihil (mihi crede) roboris aut virium in scribendo prae se ferunt, et illi ipsi qui se niti dicunt ingenii sui praesidiis et viribus, facere non possunt quin ex aliorum scriptis eruant sensus et infarciant suis, ex quo nascitur maxime vitiosum scribendi genus, cum modo sordidi et inculti, modo splendidi et florentes appareant, et sic in toto genere, tamquam in unum agrum plura inter se inimicissima sparsa semina. Fieri enim non potest quin varia ciborum genera male concoquantur, et quin ex tanta colluvione dissimillimi generis inter se verba collidantur. Nec minus huius corruptae orationis asper concursus aures ferit quam ruentium lapidum fragor aut strepitus aut quadrigae transcurrentes. Quid enim voluptatis afferre possunt ambiguae vocabulorum significationes, verba transversa, abruptae sententiae, structura salebrosa, audax translatio nec felix, ac intercisi de industria numeri, quod necesse est his omnibus accidere qui ex singulis sensus et verba eruunt et neminem imitantur. Horum sane omnis oratio est tamquam Hebraeorum

itate Cicero – how much they differ from him, how much they differ even from each other![24] Livy took from him a certain unrestrained and flowing richness.[25] Quintilian adopted his sharpness, Lactantius[26] his sonority, Curtius Rufus his smoothness, Columella his elegance. Although these men had nearly one and the same goal in imitating him, nothing is so dissimilar as they are from each other, nothing so different, if they should be compared, as they are from Cicero. From this fact it will be understood that in weighing imitation we must use judgment, and that the man from whom such diverse talents flowed as if from a perennial spring was truly remarkable.[27]

To be sure, Poliziano, when a person's talents are being formed and nurtured, he should follow in the steps of reliable authorities. They leave seeds in his soul that later take root in and of themselves.[28] But when a man wants to look like he is imitating no one and pursuing praise without similarity to anyone, believe me, he demonstrates no strength or force in his writing, and someone who says that he depends on the support and power of his own talent cannot but pluck sentences from the writings of others and stuff them into his own. The result is a most vicious type of writing, since it now appears base and uncultivated, now brilliant and flowering, and so it is throughout, as though one had sown many types of seed, all extremely hostile to one another, in a single field.[29] It is unavoidable that various types of food digest together badly[30] and that, as a result of the impure mixture of dissimilar types of speech, their words clash with one another. The rough combination of this corrupt manner of speech assaults the ears no less than the crash of falling rocks or the uproar of a four-horse chariot running by.[31] What pleasure can result from ambiguous meanings, inopportune words, incomplete thoughts, an uneven structure, rash and fruitless metaphor and rhythms that are intentionally choppy? This happens inevitably to anyone who plucks his sentences and words from separate works and imitates no one.

5

domus, quibus sunt ad quoddam tempus diversorum hominum bona oppignerata. Nam ibi et lacernae et amictus et penulae et multorum saepe pallia suspensa internoscuntur. Ego autem tantum interesse puto inter eum qui neminem imitatur et qui certum ducem consectatur, quantum inter eum qui temere vagetur et qui recta proficiscatur. Ille devius inter spinas volutatur, hic autem ex proposito itinere ad constitutum locum sine lapsu et molestia contendit.

6   Praeterea, Politiane, sic habe neminem eloquentiae laudem consecutum qui non sit in aliquo imitationis genere versatus. Apud Graecos non modo oratores Demosthenes, Hyperides, Lycurgus, Aeschines et Deinarchus, sed etiam illi ipsi philosophi, virtutum magistri, alicuius imitatores esse voluerunt. De nostris hoc loco taceo, ne videar tibi uni omnium doctissimo quasi scholam quandam explicare. Nec item aliquid de Marco Tullio dicendum puto. Exploratum est iam illud omnibus, ut qui se ad Marcum Tullium effingendum contulerit, si minus aliquam imitandi gloriam assequatur, in eo tamen ornetur, quod illum sibi elegerit exprimendum, ut illud fuisse naturae et ingenii videri possit, hoc iudicii.

Vale.

Every speech of this sort is like the house of Jews where the goods of different men are pawned for a given time:³² one often finds hanging there the overcoats, cloaks, raincoats and traveling coats of many men.³³ I think that there is as much difference between a man who imitates no one and one who follows a sure leader as between a man who wanders aimlessly and one who sets out on a straight course.³⁴ While the one is tangled in thorns, the other follows a planned route to a designated place without error or difficulty.

Also bear in mind, Poliziano, that no one has won praise 6 for his eloquence who has not been versed in some type of imitation. Among the Greeks, not only the orators Demosthenes, Hyperides, Lycurgus, Aeschines and Dinarchus, but even the philosophers, teachers of virtue, were willing to imitate someone.³⁵ I say nothing here about men of our own time, lest I seem to give you, the most learned of men, a sort of lesson. Nor do I think I need say anything about Cicero. For everyone has already confirmed that whoever models himself on Cicero, even if he does not gain any glory for the imitation, still acquires distinction for his decision to write like him.³⁶ His failure to imitate Cicero successfully is ascribed to his nature and talent, while his decision to imitate him remains a credit to his good judgment.

Farewell.

Ad Petrum Bembum de imitatione libellus

1 Ioannes Franciscus Picus Petro Bembo salutem.

Utrum tibi cum antiquos imitanti scriptores, tum de imitatione mecum disserenti, assentiri an adversari deberem, nondum satis, Bembe, iudicavi. Quando ipsos etiam veteres qui proponuntur imitandi hac de re cum varios tum animi dubios fuisse plane comperiebam. Ipsa quoque ratio sese ita praebebat aequam utrique parti, ut quo vergeret non satis appareret.[1] Quamobrem, si quaereretur auctoritas, si ratio desideraretur, quibus quasi germanis ad veritatem indagandam viis utimur, lis adhuc sub iudice manere videbatur. Verum enimvero, dum cogitarem acrius ipsamque imitationem animo volverem, in eam sum adductus sententiam, uti non nihil quidem imitandum asseverem, usquequaque vero non putem;[2] imitandum inquam bonos omnes, non unum aliquem nec omnibus etiam in rebus. Quod tute ipse arbitrabare. Qua quidem in re ut ita sentiam multa me movent, eoque animus inclinat[3] uti adversus te standum facile existimem. Id ipsum tibi declarare tentabo conaborque quibus potero rationibus, ut, si non ego in te (quis enim in amicum et talem qualis est Bembus id faceret?) sententiam feram, ipse tamen fortassis litem secundum te dandam minime censeas.

2 Ac primum omnium satis constat imitatores a Platone vel inani vel nullo verius titulo notatos, ut qui proprio digni nomine non habeantur, nisi quod eis illa ipsa imitatio fecerit. Inhonesta vero Flacci nomenclatura damnatos et appellatos *servum pecus*. Hinc vi-

Gianfrancesco Pico, On Imitation, to Pietro Bembo

A Little Book on Imitation, dedicated to Pietro Bembo

Giovanni Francesco Pico sends greetings to Pietro Bembo.   1

I have not yet decided, Bembo, if I should agree with your way of imitating ancient writers and your discussion of imitation. For I have learned that even the ancients whom you propose to imitate held different and uncertain opinions on the matter. The argument itself favored both sides so equally that it was unclear which way it would swing. For this reason, whether there was an appeal to authority or a need for argument (for these are the twin paths we use to seek out the truth), the case has seemed to remain under adjudication right up to the present. But when I considered the quarrel more closely and pondered imitation itself, I was led to the opinion that some imitation is beneficial but not in everything. I say that one should imitate all good writers, not any one writer in particular and, furthermore, one should not imitate one writer in all things. This is what you yourself used to think. Many factors lead me to this opinion. I am leaning toward a position where I find it easy to oppose you. I shall try to explain this to you with whatever arguments I can muster in the hope that, if I may not cast my vote against you personally (for who would do that to a friend, especially one like Bembo?), you yourself may concede your case as lost.

First of all, it is commonly agreed that Plato brands imitators   2
for the emptiness or rather the nullity of their reputations.[1] They are considered worthy of no fame of their own except that which imitation by itself has made for them. In fact, Horace, using a dishonorable expression, condemns them and calls them a *servile*

deas omneis quicumque aliqua in re auctores celeberrimi extite-
runt, aliunde quam ex imitatione gloriam quae de rebus praeclare
gestis exurgit, easque[4] comitatur ut umbra corpus sibi ipsis quaesi-
visse. Ac potius vel intenta contentione adversatos prioribus vel
adnixos longo eos intervallo praeterire non sequi. Qui enim assecula cupit semper esse, primum sibi numquam vendicabit locum,
ad quem videtur vel naturae propensio vel nescio qua certe ambitio
totis viribus anhelare.

3   At imitatus dicitur Homerus Orpheum adeo ut carmen quod
hic poemati de Cerere composito praestituit, in Iliade duobus tantum nominibus exceptis oculatissimus caecus ille transtulerit. Nullus tamen inde honor est Homero partus, sed quoniam sonora
magis grandiorique tuba res Troianas cecinit, multa illum et unde-
quaque est gloria consecuta.

4   Obfuit magis quam profuit imitatio Vergilio, quoniam praecla-
rissimo vati (et, quoad[5] iudicium poeticum pertinet, omnium omnino praestantissimo), nihil fere magis vitio verti solet quam imitatio nimia veterum poetarum, a quo tamen vitio longe illum
abfuisse censeo: neque enim omneis aliorum imitatus est partes.
Suos ipse habet numeros, propria tenet lineamenta, dispositio-
nemque in primis peculiarem et maxime propriam (ut alia taceam)
quae non sunt ei communia cum ceteris; aemulator veterum verius
quam imitator: et quamquam mutuo si non furto quaedam hinc
inde quasi signa veterum atque toreumata carpsit ad ornanda suorum poematum aedificia: propriis tamen illa sunt ornamentis magis conspicua, atque omnino magis illustria.

5   Cicero quoque neutiquam Demosthenem, quod multis credi-
tur, enixius est imitatus; plerisque sane in rebus aemulatus suum
retinuit filum et instituta dicendi. Titus Livius Sallustio clarissimo
historiarum scriptori palmam vel aequam habuit vel praeripuit, di-

herd.[2] So you see, all men who have become famous authorities on any subject have sought from sources other than imitation the glory that arises from deeds performed with excellence and which accompanies those deeds the way a shadow does the body.[3] But whether competing vigorously with their predecessors or striving to far surpass them, they do not follow them. For the man who wishes always to remain a hanger-on or follower will never lay claim to the rank that either his natural propensity, or at least his ambition, seems to yearn for with all its strength.

Yet it is said that Homer imitated Orpheus, so that in the *Iliad* 3 that blind yet most visionary poet carefully copied a song that Orpheus included in his poem on Ceres, changing only two nouns.[4] Well, Homer received no honor for that. But since he sang of the Trojan war with a more sonorous and grander trumpet, he won great glory from all quarters.

Imitation hindered Virgil more than it profited him, for the 4 commonest charge against that most distinguished of poets (and as far as his poetic judgment is concerned, the most outstanding poet of all) is his excessive imitation of the ancient poets.[5] But in my opinion Virgil is completely free of that fault, for he did not imitate other poets in every respect. He has his own rhythms, his own features and above all an individual and distinctive arrangement (to name only a few of his qualities), which he does not share with other poets.[6] He is more truthfully an emulator than an imitator of the ancients.[7] Although he borrowed, if not stole, certain things to decorate the edifices of his own poems, as though appropriating images and reliefs from the ancients, those edifices are more remarkable for their own ornaments and in every way more brilliant.[8]

Cicero certainly did not imitate Demosthenes to excess, as 5 many believe.[9] Although he emulated him in several respects, he retained his own style and manner of speech. Titus Livy either won a palm equal to that of Sallust, the most famous of histori-

versam tamen cucurrit viam ipsius consequendae gratia. Debita quoque laude nec Cornelius, nec Curtius caruere, et primis illis et alter alteri dissimiles.

6   Quod si Graecam tractes historiam, quae maior quam inter Herodotum et Atheniensem illum cum ducem tum scriptorem rerum a se gestarum differentia stili? Utriusque tamen laudes amplissimae. Ad philosophos si deveniamus Graecos, Aristotelis eloquentia magnopere celebrata est cum Graecis tum Latinis qui Graece sciunt; Platonis vero numquam satis laudata, cum tamen illius stilus huius sit graphio dissimillimus, nec etiam Atticae similis Musae, quamquam celebratissimae, et Platonis plane dissimili cum scribendi ordine tum verbis, quibus hic ipse Xenophon κοινοῖς, Plato autem καλοῖς (ut Graeci dicunt auctores) utebatur. Non defuit autem Aristoteli facultas imitandi eum praesertim cuius auditorii limen viginti annos frequentissime contriverat. Non defuit eruditio, non iudicium; maluit tamen suo in calle praecedere quam in lata aliorum via vel secundus esse vel tertius.

7   Inter Latinos vero Ciceronem et Varronem quaenam quaeso loquendi differentia? Neque enim hunc ille, quamquam undecumque doctissimum, aut stilo imitatus est aut ordine rerum scribendarum et modo. Antiqui enim illi praeclarissimi viri numquam aliquorum imitationi studebant ita, ut in eorum verba membra circuitus iurarent, quasi semper infantes, quasi alitibus postponendi, quibus a parentibus extra nidum eductis, satis est si ter vel quater volanteis illos aspexerint.

8   Carpebant ex uno quoque quantum satis esse videbatur ad phrasim vel constituendam vel ornandam, quae tamen essent vel propriae cognata naturae vel accommoda materiae quae tractaretur. Sic et Celsus et Columella clari, nitidi, pressi et elegantes. In

ans, or snatched it from him, yet he ran a different course in order to achieve it.[10] Tacitus and Curtius Rufus also won well-deserved praise, though dissimilar to both of the aforementioned writers and to each other.[11]

If you turn to Greek history, what greater stylistic difference is   6
there than that between Herodotus and that Athenian who was both a general and the author of his own accomplishments?[12] Yet both received abundant praise. Coming to the Greek philosophers, both the Greeks and the Romans who knew Greek especially praised Aristotle's eloquence. And people never tire of praising Plato's style, though Aristotle's writing is very different from his.[13] Nor is it like that of the Attic Muse[14] who, though very famous, is clearly different from Plato in both order and language. While this Xenophon used the vernacular (koina), Plato used beautiful (kala) language, as the Greek critics say.[15] And Aristotle did not lack the ability to imitate, and imitated especially the man whose lecture hall he had entered so often for twenty years.[16] He lacked neither erudition nor judgment. But he preferred to lead the way on his own narrow track rather than come second or third in the broad avenue trodden by other writers.[17]

What a difference there is between the speech of the Latin au-   7
thors Cicero and Varro![18] The former did not imitate the latter, despite the latter's encyclopedic learning, either in style or in the order and manner of discussing his subject matter.[19] For the most famous ancients were never so eager to imitate anyone that they swore by their words, clauses or periods, as though refusing to grow up and develop their own wings.[20] After their parents had brought them out of the nest, they were satisfied to see their young flying three or four times.[21]

People used to pluck from any given author as much as seemed   8
sufficient for either composing or decorating a phrase.[22] Yet this was done either in accordance with the borrower's nature or with the material under discussion. Thus both Celsus and Columella

altero tamen egregia mundities, in altero flosculi fortasse crebrio-
res; imitationem in illis nihilominus vel nullam vel certe parvam es
deprehensurus; genium propensionemque naturae eorum quisque
sequebatur. Et si enim homo omnium maxime vim obtinet imitandi, ut hinc et multa et varia discere possit, quod scribit Aristoteles in *Problematibus* (eaque de causa poeticam homini naturalem
esse, primo quem ea de facultate libro scripsit, est aperte testatus)
proprium tamen et congenitum instinctum et propensionem animi
nactus est ab ipso ortu, quam frangere et aliorsum vertere est ipsam plane violare naturam.

9   Itaque cum nostro in animo idea quaedam et tamquam radix
insit aliqua, cuius vi ad quodpiam muneris obeundum animamur
et tamquam ducimur manu atque ab aliis quibusdam abducimur,
colere illam potius quam incidere, amplecti quam abalienare,
operae pretium est. Nihil enim nostrae consulens felicitati aut a
virtute alienum aut noxium nobis impertiit ipsa natura. Ideam igitur ut aliarum virtutum ita et recte loquendi subministrat, eiusque
pulchritudinis affingit animo simulachrum, ad quod respicientes
identidem et aliena iudicemus et nostra. Neque enim eam quisquam adhuc perfecte attigit, ut hac in re illud etiam possit dicier,
nihil omni ex parte beatum.

10   Quandoquidem non uni tantum, sed omnibus et universis dis-
tribuit praeclara sua munera, ut ex ipsa varietate totius universi
pulchritudo constituatur: an putas frustra prudentem illum picto-
rem censuisse omnia se uno in femineo corpore reperire non posse
ad venustatem? Et incassum putas prudentissimum oratorem eius
industriam secutum, longe etiam illum praeterisse iudicio? Qui ut
imaginem illam pulcherrimi eloquentiae corporis effingeret omneis
delegit viros facundia praestantes, cum ille quinque solum Croto-
niatas selegisset virgines pulchritudine celebratas. Nec satis illis
fidens formam ipsam seu speciem absolutam eloquentiae, nulli

are clear, brilliant, articulate and elegant.[23] Still, in the one there
is a remarkable polish, in the other little flourishes are perhaps
more common. But you will detect in them either no imitation or
very little. Both followed their own genius and natural propensity.[24] For even if man is the greatest of all in asserting his power
of imitation in order to learn many different things, as Aristotle
writes in the *Problems*[25] (which is why he openly states that poetry
is natural to man in Book I of his work on that ability),[26] he has
from birth his own hereditary instinct and intellectual propensity.
To wreck this and twist it in another direction is clearly to violate
one's very nature.

Since in our soul there is a certain idea and root, if you will,   9
whose power inspires us to achieve any reward, leads us by the
hand, and helps us avoid certain other things, it is important to
cultivate that root rather than sever it; to embrace it rather than
cast it aside.[27] For nothing that nature itself imparts for the sake
of our happiness is foreign or injurious to us. Thus it subserves
the idea of correct speech, as it does our other virtues, and pro-
duces a likeness of its beauty in the soul. By gazing on this likeness we may judge the works of others as well as our own. For certainly no one yet has perfectly grasped that idea, so one could even
say that no one is entirely fortunate in this sense.[28]

In fact Nature distributes its own splendid gifts not just to   10
one person but to each and every one, and it is from this very variety that the beauty of the entire universe is constituted. Or do you
think that that wise painter was wrong to believe that he could not
find all beautiful qualities in the body of a single woman?[29] Do
you think that the wisest of orators imitated the painter's diligence in vain, though he far surpassed him in his powers of judgment?[30] To form his image of the most beautiful body of eloquence, he chose to copy everyone who excelled in fine and fluent
speech, whereas the painter had selected only five Crotonian maidens who were celebrated for their beauty. And because he was not

23

prorsus addictam sola imitatione dignam existimarit. Imitari itaque eam debemus quam animo scilicet gerimus dicendi perfectam facultatem, qua et aliorum et nostra cum errata in obeundo loquendi munere, tum virtutes etiam metiamur, sive ea ipsa penitus innata sit idea atque ab ipsa origine perfecta, sive tempore procedente multorum auctorum lectione consummata. Ea fiebat ut Marcus Ciceronis aures semper Demosthenes non impleret; ea ipsa patavinitatem in Livio causabatur Asinius; ipsa eadem et Brutus elumbem Ciceronem quamquam amicum praecipuum iudicabat. Alii Asianum, tumidum, redundantem, nimium viro molliorem. Qua etiam factum opinor ut nec aliquem unum scrupulosius imitandum vel Celsus vel Fabius praeceperint. Neque etiam ipsi fuerant Ciceronem, quem maxime laudant, imitati. Quid enim causae fuit, ut tot illos variis non solum in rebus, sed una eademque in facultate diversos dicendi artifices posuerint in medium, nisi ut vel ab hoc vel ab illo quod placeret magis decerperemus, sive impulsu acti naturae sive iudicio?

II   Nam qui non ita censent illud oro dissolvant, cur ii qui Ciceronem tam laudant quam qui maxime, illum ipsum tamen non sunt imitati, stilo scilicet et figura dicendi. An id scilicet facile[6] non potuerunt[7] Celsus, Caecilius, Plinius, Fabius, alii Ciceronis saeculo proximi, cum restarent adhuc tamquam reliquiae et inviolatae illae quidem puri Romanique sermonis, ipsamque latinitatem sugerent cum lacte nutricum? An ignorarunt imitandum esse magno scilicet et excellenti ingenio viri qui et aliis de imitatione praecipiebant? Dicendum potius videtur eos noluisse, ne, si voluisse quod non potuerant afferamus, vel tacito nos eorum opponamus gloriae, qui, quod illi non potuere viri clarissimi, nos ipsi vel obtinuerimus vel speremus.

confident enough in them, he thought that the very form or abstract notion[31] of eloquence, which was consigned to no one in
particular, alone warranted imitation. So too should we imitate
that perfect capacity of speech that we bear in our mind.[32] Using it
we may measure both others' errors and our own in practicing
the gift of speech; but we may also estimate our virtues, whether
the idea is itself innate in us and perfect *a priori* or gradually ab-
sorbed by reading many different authors. That is why Cicero did
not always fill his ears with Demosthenes;[33] that is why Asinius
criticized Livy's provincial tone;[34] that is why Brutus considered
Cicero bland, though a very special friend.[35] Others thought him
Asiatic, bombastic, redundant and too soft for a man.[36] It was for
the same reason, I think, that Celsus and Quintilian taught us not
to imitate anyone with too much nicety.[37] Nor had they themselves imitated Cicero, though they praised him more than anyone
else. Why did they place before us so many artists who differed
not only in the variety of their subject matter but even in one and
the same faculty of expression, except to encourage us to pick and
choose whatever we please from each one, whether it is our natural
impulse or judgment that directs us?

Those who do not agree should explain why the men who give   11
Cicero the highest praise did not imitate him in style and figure
of speech. Surely Celsus, Caecilius, Pliny, Quintilian and others
who lived in the period just after Cicero's could easily have imitated him, since there survived still inviolate the remnants, as it
were, of pure Roman speech, and they sucked that pure Latinity
with their nurses' milk?[38] Did the men who taught others about
imitation not know that a great and excellent talent must imitate?
Rather, it seems, we should say that they simply did not want to
imitate, lest by affirming that they could not do what they wanted
we tacitly place ourselves in opposition to their glory — we who either have obtained or hope to obtain what those most famous men
could not.

12   Dicturus est fortasse quispiam eos qui magis nobis placent esse
magis imitandos, quod ego quidem non condemnarim. Placeat
prae aliis Plato, placeat Cicero, non opinione solum sed stilo Pla-
tonicus: eos sequamur. Nam quamquam sua est cuique propria facies animi, sicut et corporis, ut duos omnino similes non facile sit
invenire, minor tamen in animo nostro cum aliquibus prae aliis est
dissimilitudo, atque per hoc facilius erit nobis uti similes evada-
mus. Meminerimus tamen nos simias non esse oportere quae dete-
riora sibi deligunt ad imitandum. Sunt enim qui nevos, qui cicatrices, qui maciem, qui excrementa etiam effingere velint, vel nulla vel
minima ratione habita et lacertorum et vividi roboris et gratiae. Ab
iis non dissimiles quibus magna est cura ut rara quaepiam voca-
bula, quae forte aut Ciceroni exciderunt multa scribenti aut vitio
temporum fuere in eius libros introducta, adeo ut si ab inferis exci-
taretur a se prompta negaret, gestientes surripiant, vel etiam quae
mancipes librarii integritatem lectionis dum passim corrumpunt
edidere, ipsi observent magna cum diligentia.

13   Superfluum praeterea vanumque existimari debet, si ad omnem
rhetoricam portionem imitatio adhibeatur. Inventio enim tum lau-
datur magis cum genuina est magis et libera, explodique solet quae
repticia iudicatur, nedum accersita. Unde nam quaeso illud *furem
non poetam fabulam dedisse?* An etiam aliunde prodiit, ut illi omnes
damnarentur, qui dum Musarum et Apollinis haberentur ludi,
aliorum imitatione sibi quaesivissent unde probarentur, et soli re-
lata sit a criticis palma, qui ex sese et ex propria penu eruditi
prompserat obsonium animi, tametsi eo non ita convivarum gus-
tus oblectaretur?

14   Dispositio vero sequitur inventionem ita, ut haec[8] qualis fuerit,
talem quo rite disponatur ordinem expetat, ne id quod effingis,

Perhaps someone will say that we should concentrate on imitat- 12
ing those who please us the most.[39] I would not disagree with this
advice. Plato may please you more than others; so may Cicero,
who is Platonic not only in his views but also in style.[40] We should
follow them. For although the features of each person's soul, like
those of his body, are so proper to him that it is difficult to find
two that are completely alike, our souls are still less dissimilar to
some than to others, and it will therefore be easier for us to become like them.[41] Yet we should recall that it is improper for us to
be apes who choose to imitate inferior qualities. There are people
who wish to copy moles, scars, emaciation and excrement, though
they give little or no attention to their subject's muscles, living
strength and grace.[42] They are not unlike people who take great
care to pilfer with cries of joy any rare terms that Cicero may have
used once in his many writings or that were introduced into his
books by the ill effects of time. If Cicero were revived from the
dead, he would deny that they had taken these words from him.[43]
Or they pay careful regard even to what mercenary booksellers
have published, who corrupt the integrity of the text throughout
in the process.

We should also think it superfluous and vain if imitation were 13
applied to every part of rhetoric.[44] For invention receives greater
praise when it is genuine and free. [45] And it is common to dis-
praise what is judged to have crept — not to say forced — its way
in. Where, pray, did the saying *a thief or a poet told this tale* come
from?[46] Wasn't it put about to condemn all those people who, during contests of the Muses and Apollo, tried to win approval by imitating others, while the critics awarded the palm of victory only to
the speaker who had produced the food of a learned mind on his
own and from his own stock of provisions, even if he did not
please the taste of his dinner-companions that way?

Arrangement follows invention in such a way that the type of 14
invention employed determines the order in which it is arranged.

quasi intellectile corpus orationis, aut vasta nimis aut pusilla nimis[9] aut omnino praepostera membra deforment. Tua autem haec[10] ut sit, necessarium dubio procul omni futurum arbitramur, eoque maiori tibi fuerit adnitendum diligentia—a te ipso videlicet, non ab aliis petenda—quo maioribus ingenii viribus in ea perficienda opus est—si Plinio maxime crediderimus, affirmanti et barbaros etiam invenire magnifice et enuntiare, recte vero disponere et figurare non nisi eruditis concessum esse.

15   Elocutio vero num et ipsa sequitur inventionem, quando diversam ad materiam diversa phrasis adhibenda est? Num et ipsa quoque dispositionem comitatur? Huic enim alia, illi alia tribuenda est, ita ut a te ipso omnis tandem pendeat oratio.

16   Nam de memoria et pronuntiatione tacendum puto, quando earum neutra chartis mandetur, et alteram nulla ex imitatione[11] tibi compares, sed ex matris (ut inquit Lucilius) bulga tecum feras. Ut autem haec[12] exercitatione perfici solet, ita exempla maiorum aliis partibus, quae referri litterarum monumentis queunt, opem ferre non mediocrem iure affirmaverim. Poteris enim inventionem quapiam de re ab aliis traditam vel aemulari vel superare; poteris disponere melius, eloqui etiam ornatius.

17   Neque enim quasi vetula mulier suis est viribus parens effeta natura, ut nostro scilicet hoc saeculo quasi nimio partu lassata defecerit. Nec deus optimus maximus nostrae aetati non est largitus ingenia. Utinam tam bene excolerentur quam bona sunt edita, et non inanibus nugis ac fabulis quasi glande et siliquis edendis dedita, sua alimonia fraudarentur! Ita enim macerata sunt nonnulla

In this way you don't distort your composition, the intellectual body of your speech, with parts that are too grand, too trivial or completely absurd. I believe it will be necessary, beyond all doubt, that this arrangement be yours. And you will have to strive with that much more diligence — which of course must be sought from yourself and not from others — in that greater powers are required to perfect that arrangement, assuming we place the utmost trust in Pliny, who claims that even uncivilized people invent and express things magnificently, but the ability to arrange and shape discourse correctly has been granted to none but the well-educated.[47]

Isn't it the case that style is logically posterior to invention, since different materials call for different kinds of diction? Doesn't style also go together with arrangement? For different types of speaking should be assigned to different types of arrangement. In short, the whole art of speaking ultimately depends on you yourself.

I don't think there is any need to talk about memory or pronunciation, since neither of these is set down on paper. You don't get the second of these from imitation; you bring it with you, as Lucilius says, from your mother's "pouch."[48] But while one usually perfects this [last] part of rhetoric by practice, I have rightly claimed that the examples of our ancestors give no small aid to the other parts of rhetoric which can be preserved in literary form. You will thus be able either to emulate or to surpass the invention handed down by others on any matter at all. You will be able to arrange your material better and even speak more artfully.

Nature is not like a poor old woman, a mother exhausted of her powers, so that it has faded in this age of ours, weary from too much childbearing, as it were.[49] Nor has God Almighty ceased to bestow natural talent on our age. Would that those talents had been as well cultivated as they were bestowed! If only they had not been cheated of their proper nourishment, addicted as they are to empty trifles and fables, as though feeding on nuts and shells.[50]

et quasi tabe consumpta — alioqui suapte natura formosa — ut simulachri et evanidae umbrae magis quam vivi animi effigiem prae
se ferant. Crescunt (ut mea fert opinio) verius quam decrescant ingenia. Multa enim quae ad rerum spectant notitiam et nostrum
saeculum, et huic proxima novere quae docta illa ignoravit antiquitas.

18   Lingua certe veteribus illis cum Graeca tum Latina quasi nativa
adfuit, quam ab eorum libris petere nos oportet, quibus maior ea
de re fit legitimae laudis accessio. Illi enim vel nolentes et in Hel-
lade Graece et in Italia Latine loquebantur; nobis Italis qui Latine
loquamur, nedum Graece, id nostra est partum et elaboratum industria. Inde fiet aequum rerum aestimatorem si sortiatur nostra
aetas, posse eos qui nunc mediocriter loquuntur praecipuis illis et
antesignanis iure praeferri, qui scilicet inter Gothos, Vandalos,
Hunnosque versati priscam illam et tot saeculis abolitam dicendi
rationem aut teneant aut tenere conentur imitatione continua, qua
etiam in re mira subtilitas et forte nimia.

19   Nam nec cursu solum veteribus similes nec gressu vel esse vel
videri volunt quidam, sed ita incedere, ut eorum in vestigiis po-
nant vestigia. At si veterum maiora vestigia fuerint ut etiam corpora, num in illis minor pes firmabitur an labascet si solum
maxime subudum fuerit? Si vero illa nostris minora extiterint,
num excludentur curiosi pedes et frustrabuntur voto? Aequum
enim vestigium quod omni ex parte quadret quis invenerit? Ni cal-
ceorum fortassis officina quaepiam e Romanis eruta ruinis formulas nobis quasdam subministraverit. At quot veterum pedes tot
calcei. Nec ambigas, Bembe, etiam si antiqua sandalia in abscondi-
tis thesauris inveneris et aptaveris tibi, te umquam propterea posse

For some talents have been so wasted and devoured as if by disease (though otherwise they are beautiful in their own nature) that
they present themselves more in the likeness of a phantom and
vanishing shade than in that of a living soul. In my opinion, natural talents are really increasing more than decreasing. Many inge-
nious people who have studied the world, both in our time and in
recent ages, have known things that learned antiquity did not.[51]

To be sure, a knowledge of both Greek and Latin were almost   18
innate in the ancients. It is proper that we learn these languages
from their books; and the legitimate praise we get for this should
be even greater [than the ancients earned].[52] For whether they
wanted to or not, people naturally used to speak Greek in Greece
and Latin in Italy. We Italians who speak Latin, let alone Greek,
have acquired and developed that skill by our own industry. So if
our age were allotted a fair judge in such matters, he would be
right to prefer to those great men and champions of yore the mediocre speakers of today, namely those who, though surrounded by
Goths, Vandals and Huns, keep to that ancient pattern of speech,
wiped out so many centuries ago — or who try to keep to it
through continual imitation, showing in this matter remarkable
and perhaps excessive subtlety.

For certain men wish neither to be nor to seem like the ancients   19
either in the way they run or the way they walk alone, but to advance by stepping in their predecessors' tracks.[53] If the ancients'
steps are bigger, even as their bodies were, will the smaller foot
step surely in those tracks or will it slip if the ground there is
soaked? But if the ancients' steps turn out to be smaller than ours,
will careful feet be kept out of them and be frustrated of their
wish? For who will find a footprint of the same size that fits him
exactly? That is, unless some shop is unearthed from the ruins of
Rome to provide us with some shoemaker's lasts. But the ancients
had as many shoes as they had feet.[54] Don't think, Bembo, even if
you discover ancient sandals among some hidden treasures and get

a criticis impetrare ut antiqua credantur. Efficiet hoc invidia. Semper simultas erit in causa, quoad illam ipsam dies longa praescripserit. Neque enim alia habebuntur quam nova, hoc est non absoluta, nec omnibus perfecta numeris.

20   Quod quidem in signis evenire persaepe sumus contemplati, quae et si quando praestantiora fiunt quibusdam quae vetustis illis saeculis exculpta fuere, nihilominus cum ut nova circumferuntur, imperfectioribus posthabentur, tantum vana illa mille annorum imago quasi pestis invasit hominum iudicia. Nam si vetera creduntur esse, si etiam spectator est animi dubius antiqua ne sint an minime, mira laus; nulla insurgit censura rigidior. At si compertum fuerit recenter edita, prodaturque etiam nomen opificis, tum mille Aristarchi, tum et sibila quandoque erit audire. Tum non tertius modo cadet de caelo Cato, sed et Timon atque etiam Momus exurget ab inferis.

21   Novimus hominem scripsisse epistolas sub Ciceronis nomine, quae non laudi solum, verum etiam admirationi maxime fuerint, eundemque ipsum epistolis Ciceronis suum adscripsisse nomen, demptis tantummodo iis vocabulis quae prodere fallaciam possent. Es ne, Bembe, crediturus? Quod illae ipsae Ciceronis epistolae et rubras ceras et virgulas et asteriscos et obelos et sexcentas censorias notas perpeti quiverint novae inscriptionis causa; quae tamen antea sub veteri titulo fuerant numquam satis laudatae et celebratae. Incassum igitur sategerat ille prioribus in epistolis dum verba rimabatur, dum caesa metiebatur et membra, dum circuitus deligebat, dum numeros mandabat memoriae, dum observabat lineamenta, ut quae scribebat Ciceronis esse viderentur; poterat enim parvo impendio et labore id praestare titulum[13] et auferre.

22   Sed illud quoque ad nimiam aviditatem imitationis compescendam facere potest, quod mediocris etiam auctoris scribendi genus,

them to fit, that you can ever get the critics to reckon them ancient. Envy will make sure of this. Dissent over a given case will
always be relative to how long the precedent has stood. They will
not be considered anything but new, that is, incomplete and imperfect in every category.[55]

We have often seen this happen in the case of statues. Even 20
when people produce better sculptures than certain ancient ones,
nonetheless when they come into circulation as modern statues
they are considered inferior to their more imperfect predecessors
because that empty image of a thousand years has so infested people's judgment, like the plague. If they are believed ancient, even if
the viewer doubts their antiquity, it's wonderful the praise they get
and how they escape tough criticism.[56] But if someone discovers
that they were recently produced and even discloses the artist's
name, there will be a thousand Aristarchuses;[57] sometimes you
will even hear hissing. Not only will a third Cato fall from the
skies, but Timon and Momus will rise from the dead.[58]

We know a man who wrote letters under the name of Cicero 21
which people greatly praised and admired; that same man put his
own name on letters of Cicero, removing only those words that
might betray his trick.[59] Would you believe it, Bembo? Because of
the new superscription, those same letters of Cicero were sub-
jected to red ink, indications of spurious, defective and suspect
passages, and six hundred critical marks.[60] Yet under the old title
people could not praise and celebrate them enough. The man had
wasted his time in his earlier letters digging up words, counting
phrases and clauses, selecting periods, memorizing rhythms and
studying Cicero's features to make people think that what he had
written was Cicero's. Adding and taking away a title could have
done the same thing with little cost and effort.

But the following consideration can also make you curb your 22
excessive desire to imitate. If you remember what we said above
about the interrelationship among the elements of composition,

nedum Ciceronis, non imitabile videtur omni ex parte, si quae de complexu illarum muneris loquendi partium supra diximus ad memoriam revocentur. Ubi enim inventio, quae quasi materia orationis est, eadem non habetur, nec forma, nec quae illam nexu inseparabili sequitur, dispositio, eadem prorsus habebitur; si autem similis quoquomodo, si dissimilis nullo pacto conveniet. Quotum[14] autem quemque[15] reperias, etiam si accersas Aesopi gracculum pennis ornatum alienis, qui quae[16] aliorum sunt propria eadem prorsus et impudenter cogitet expromere, et impudentius disponat et effutiat impudentissime? Sed fac eadem esse omnia. Mox dimove lineamentum, verte membrum, varia numerum, tolle circuitum: omnem orationis integritatem sustulisti. Adeo constant[17] illa coagmenta nexis[18] omnibus quae sibi propria peculiariaque adsciscit, ut ex illis ipsis eisdemque solis, non alienis, non mixtis, non permutatis, confleatur[19] atque dissultet.

23   Huc accedit scripti genus varium, quod variam quoque sibi vendicat phrasin. Ciceronis enim orationes, libri *De oratore ad Quintum fratrem*, *De claris oratoribus* et alii plerique magno eloquentiae inundantur flumine, si non potius Oceano, sed ille ipse tam vastus fluvius vix irrigat rhetoricos libros et eos qui *De universitate*, et *De fato* inscribuntur, idemque ipse vix stillat in *Topicis*. Mutatur quoque aetate mutata, et ab eodem Cicerone dicta est canescere oratio, quae alia itidem est dum monet, alia dum respondet, diversa quoque dum deprecatur, dum interpretatur, dum invehitur. Varia item pro variis animi affectibus et saepe corporis, nedum rebus, quae ipso sunt explicanda sermone.

the type of writing used even by a mediocre author, not to mention a Cicero, does not seem to be imitable in every respect. For when invention, which is (so to speak) the matter of a speech, does not remain constant, neither will the speech's form nor its arrangement, which are inseparably linked with each other. The speech being imitated will be suitable in some degree if it is similar to the imitation; if it isn't similar, it won't be suitable at all. How many people would you find, even if you called in Aesop's jackdaw adorned with the feathers of others,[61] who would be so utterly shameless as to think of putting out as their own what belongs to others, or even more shamelessly, would circulate it, or most shamelessly of all, blurt it out aloud? But grant that all the circumstances are the same. Now take away a feature, change a clause, vary the rhythm, remove a period: you've completely spoiled the unity of the speech.[62] The parts joined together, in all the interrelations, proper and peculiar to themselves, which the speech has imposed on them remain constant, so much so that the speech runs together and flies apart from those original elements alone, and not from the foreign, mixed or altered elements.

There are, moreover, variations in the type of writing to consider, because each type calls for a different kind of diction. Cicero's orations, his books *On the Orator, Brutus* and several others are flooded with a river, if not an ocean, of eloquence.[63] But that vast river hardly even moistens his books on rhetoric,[64] *On the Universe*[65] and *On Fate*, and it leaves hardly a drop in the *Topics*. It also changes with his age, and this same Cicero said that his rhetoric "was growing old."[66] Likewise, his rhetoric was one thing when he gives advice, another thing when he is responding to someone, something else again when he is pleading, explaining or on the attack.[67] It likewise often varies with various mental and bodily states, not to mention how it varies in response to different subjects. All of these variations should unfold from the discourse itself.[68]

23

24 Hunc igitur unum dices imitandum quem natura produxerit ut in eo suas vires omnis experiretur eloquentia, eoque fieri ut miscere, cum ipse sit etiam varius, ipsum Ciceronis filum queas, et quaque de re quae tibi dicenda tractandaque fuerit, possis ipsius more et (ut sic dixerim) Ciceroniane loqui. At forte veritas esset in connexo, ni duo illud aperte distraherent. Primum, quod propterea quispiam non esset Ciceroni similis. Huius enim verba, etiam si loca mutent, erunt tamen verba Ciceronis, non autem Ciceronis ea constructio, quam ipse non struxerit, sed tamquam ex lapidibus illius alius murum confecerit. Cui si quidpiam alienae calcis et intriti misceatur, ne vero misceatur fieri nequaquam poterit, sed etsi lapidem lapidi iunxerit haerentius aut minus nimiove plus in dolio mersaverit, nequaquam Tullianus paries ille futurus est.

25 Alterum est quod tacito videris existimare, ut ceteri auctores legitimi non sint naturae partus, sed tamquam abortivi, ac ut cum eis praeclare agatur veluti octimestres infantes habendi. Si ita reris, si ita censes, dabitur provocatio ad eloquentiae magistros antiquos illos quidem et probatissimos. Ipsum etiam appellabo Ciceronem. Proposuerunt enim non unum quempiam, sed multos imitandos. Nec id satis: ad ipsam ideam filum esse dirigendum praeceperunt. Num igitur mihi quaeso licebit, num et expediet vim Demosthenis, quamquam eam expressisse Cicero dicitur, in ipso potius Demosthene, ubi inesse illam non ambigitur, et demirari et imitari? Sic et copiam Platonis et iucunditatem Isocratis, a fonte puro, non a decurrentibus rivis, ubi ipsa miscetur eloquentiae lympha, combibere.

26 Adde quod alio hic, alio ille charactere delectabitur et alia afficietur figura dicendi, ut nec frustra nec inconsulto varios eiusdem

You will then say that we should imitate this one man, whom   24
nature produced so that all eloquence might test its powers on
him; that, since he is also varied, you can make a blend from
Cicero's own style; and that, whatever it is you have to say, whatever the subject you are treating, you can speak in his manner and
(if I may use the expression) "Ciceronianly."[69] There might perhaps be some truth in your inference, if two things did not obviously break it apart. First, no one could be like Cicero. The words
will still be Cicero's words, even if they change position, but the
construction won't be Cicero's since he didn't construct it. Some-
body else will have built a wall, as it were, from his stones.[70] If any
non-native lime and paste is mixed in, it is impossible to avoid a
mixture, but even if the man fits stone to stone very tightly or
makes the mortar thicker or makes it thinner, the wall is still not
going to be at all Tullian.

The second reason is that you seem to assume tacitly that other   25
authors are not nature's legitimate offspring, but are like prema-
ture infants, and that one may deal with them as if they were
eighth-month-old fetuses.[71] If this is what you think, if this is
your opinion, this will be a challenge to those ancient and excellent masters of eloquence. I shall even call Cicero himself to wit-
ness. For they proposed that we imitate not any one person but
many. And if that was not enough, they taught that we should
guide our style by the idea itself. Shall I not, if you please, be
permitted to imitate, won't it be profitable to imitate the power
of Demosthenes, when Cicero is said to have imitated it, when
Cicero admired and modelled himself on Demosthenes, of whose
power he had no doubt? So too in the case of Plato's richness and
the delightfulness of Isocrates, it will be licit and profitable to
drink from the pure fount, not downstream but where the very
waters of eloquence mix and mingle.[72]

Also consider that different people will enjoy different styles   26
and are affected by different figures of speech. It therefore is nei-

rei dicendae modos, quae chriae dici solent veteres illi qui eloquentiae tradidere praecepta, excogitaverint. Nec nequicquam ha-
buerunt diversa genera dicendi probari diversitate videlicet iudi-
ciorum, a diversa humani temperamenti proprietate manantium.
Hinc amplum et augustum dicendi genus, hinc exile et tenue, hinc
ex utroque permixtum, in quibus qui excelluerint diversi diversam
quoque sibi gloriam paraverunt. Hinc et siccum et nudum, hinc
succulentum et vario eruditionis colore vestitum. Et haec omnia
introducta sunt duce natura. Erit enim ille suopte ingenio, Laco-
nicae brevitatis amator, alius Asiaticae fertilitatis avidus. Hic
Atticae illius et aureae mediocritatis aestuabit desiderio, Rhodio
ille temperamento delectabitur. Tot sunt variae animi voluptates,
ut etiam de numeris terminandae clausulae et pedibus multa sit
inter antiquos atque inter Aristotelem et Ciceronem orta dissensio. Induebant animum illi variis habitibus, ceu ipsis quoque vesti-
mentis induimus corpora. Atque ut in his, non secus in illis varia
materies, variae figurae, variique colores et placebant olim et nunc
etiam placent; sunt enim nostra tempestate plurimi qui panno ves-
tiantur libenter qui sit contextus ex lato illo Ciceronis stamine et
presso Plinii subtegmine; admittunt etiam tramam Celsi et Columellae. Alii, quia frigus fortasse metuunt, conantur ut evolvant
scrinia Carmentae, unde peplum surripiant aptandum sibi. Nec eo
contenti vetustos illos et cariosos Romanorum augurum et Mar-
tiorum fratrum cophinos adeunt. Atque cum resciverint Catonem
et Ennium ditasse patriam, in eorum etiam supellectilem praeda-
bundi et populabundi penitus irruant; nec desunt qui asinum,
cum existiment bellum animal et aureum, de illius pilis sibi lacernam conficiant. Qui vero abalienati sensus haec signa ducerent, ar-

ther in vain nor without reason that those ancient authors who
handed down the principles of eloquence conceived of different
ways to discuss the same matter, which they usually call *chriae*.[73]
Nor was their belief vain that different styles have won approval
because of the diversity of judgments springing from the individu-
ality of the human temperment.[74] Hence the full and august type
of speech, hence the meager and thin, hence the type mixed from
both.[75] The different men who have excelled in these have also
won different forms of glory. Hence both the dry and bald style,
hence the rich style dressed in the varied coloring of erudition. All
of these have been introduced under the guidance of nature. Because of his own natural bent, one man will love Laconic brevity,
another will be eager for Asiatic richness. This man will burn for
that golden Attic mean, that one will prefer Rhodian moderation.[76] So many and varied are the forms of mental pleasure that a
great deal of dissension arose among the ancients, including Aristotle and Cicero, even about the rhythms and meters to be used at
the ends of sentences.[77] They used to dress the soul with different
habits just as we dress the body with clothes.[78] And habits are no
different from clothes in the sense that different material, different
figures, different styles once gave pleasure and still do. Many people of our time willingly dress in garments woven from Cicero's
broad warp and Pliny's tight woof.[79] They even use the web of
Celsus and Columella. Others, perhaps because they fear the cold,
try to open up the writing-desk of Carmenta, whence they pilfer a
robe to suit themselves.[80] Not content with that, they have recourse to those ancient and withered baskets of the Roman augurs
and the twin sons of Mars.[81] And when they learn that Cato and
Ennius enriched their country, they may make an attack on their
wardrobe too, to loot and plunder it.[82] There are even some who
consider the ass a beautiful and golden animal and make themselves a coat from its hair.[83] Those who think these are the signs of
a madman should rely on the principles of medicine and listen to

tis medicae regulis freti, audiant Hippocratem aetati, tempori, consuetudini quidpiam dandum esse praecipientem.

27   Sed ut in summa dicam: ut varii sunt auctores et in suo quique genere probati, varia quoque humani animi propensio, atque adeo diversae in eadem etiam facultate ideae speciesve dicendi—lata, pressa, mediocris, austera, dulcis—diversaque quasi fila diversae texendae apta orationi (quibus de rebus apud probatos auctores cum alios, tum maxime Dionysium et Hermogenem praecepta dantur), ad unam haec omnia quam in mente gerimus ideam referenda sunt, et habenda est in consilio ratio mixtioque paranda talis, ut una ex omnibus quae nulla sit illarum, sed perfectissima tamen illa quidem, quoad fieri possit, et confletur et coalescat oratio. Tantum abest ut quispiam unus usquequaque sit imitandus, quasi ille Deo praestaret optimo maximo, qui nobis usquequaque imitandus non proponitur, neque enim potentiam eius possumus, nec sapientiam aut debemus aut possumus omnino imitari. Sed quam ille voluit ex sole illo intellectili nostris mentibus illucescere eam ipsam excolere operae pretium est, ad ipsius dei manifestandam gloriam, ad accendendum nostris in pectoribus amorem divinae bonitatis, quae quidem nobis, quoad vires nostrae queunt efficere, proponitur imitanda amore intentissimo et officiis quae[20] de illo prodeunt. Quibus et boni ipsi efficimur et umbratilis huius vitae peracto cursu omnino felices.

28   Haec habui ad praesens, Bembe, de imitatione quae dicerem, sex (ni coniectura fallor) aut septem horarum spatio, eoque interrupto ac sine libris, stilo et memoria usi, quicquid sese obtulit, arripuimus atque compegimus. Scis enim me more tabellarii, mutatis etiam ad celeritatem iumentis, hucusque cucurrisse. Sed neque inficias ivero, me deprecari culpam, si qua occurrerint errata.

Hippocrates, who teaches that a person should be given medicine to suit his age, the season of the year and the person's habits.

In short, I would say that, just as there are various authorities 27 and each has won approval in his own genre, so too is the propensity of the human soul diverse. So different are the ideas or species of eloquence even in the same mental faculty — broad, compressed, moderate, austere, sweet — and so different are the styles that are suitable to weaving different speeches (and precepts are given on these matters in respected authors, principally Dionysius and Hermogenes among others), that all these stylistic choices should be considered in relation to the one Idea we hold in our mind, and we must use reason in making up our minds and put together a mixture such that a single eloquence is forged of all those elements but identical to none of them, an eloquence which is as perfect as possible. Heaven forbid that we should imitate one person in all respects, as though the man excelled God Almighty, for even He is not proposed to us for imitation in all respects; we can't imitate His power and we cannot and should not imitate the fullness of His wisdom. But it is worthwhile for us to cultivate the wisdom that He wished to shine down from the intelligible sun into our own minds in order to proclaim the glory of God himself, to kindle in our hearts the love of divine goodness, which indeed *is* ours to imitate, insofar as we can, with the most intense love, and the obligations which that love creates. In the process we ourselves become good and, once the course of this shadowy life is run, absolutely happy.

This is what I have to say about imitation for the present, 28 Bembo. Using pen and memory but no books, I have gathered up and put together whatever presented itself in the space of six or seven interrupted hours, if my guess is correct. You know that I have run here and there like a courier, even changing horses for speed. But do not use your red pen on me, I pray, if I have made any mistakes. If my composition seems more disjointed and

Quare si hiulca magis et divulsa quam sonora et pressa composi-
tio, si fracta et stridula quam aequabilis aut numerosa videbitur,
veniam praestes oro, sicut et poeticae venae in edendis inter expel-
lendam Venerem atque Cupidinem carminibus arescenti nuper, ut
arbitror, praestitisti. Qui enim fieri potest, ut praeter haec etiam
ab aequo non absolvar iudice, qui inter theologos atque philosophos nostrates istos recentiores mente quidem plusquam subtiles,
sed rubiginosa et plusquam barbara lingua diutissime versatus, ad
mansuetiora studia, ad rhetorica delinimenta numerosque poeticos
interdum quodam quasi postliminio revertor? Quibus in numeris
et exculta illa phrasi, a priscis illis ducta temporibus, si nostro hoc
seculo inter eos qui nunc vivunt et nobis noti sunt, ipse tibi palmam non vendicasti (quod ego nequaquam obstinate negaverim)
propior tamen aut es aut iam brevi es futurus primo quam tertio.

Vale. Romae, tertiodecimo Kalendas Octobres MDXII.

choppy than sonorous and tight, if more broken and strident than even or rhythmical, I beg your pardon, just as you recently pardoned, I think, my withered poetical skills in the poem I am publishing *On the Expulsion of Venus and Cupid.*[84] Apart from this, how could a fair judge not acquit me, when I have been associating for so long with those modern theologians and philosophers of ours who are certainly exceedingly subtle, though rusty and exceedingly barbarous in their language, but return from time to time to gentler studies, to the charms of rhetoric and poetical rhythms, as though coming home again? If you yourself have not laid claim to the palm of victory in numbers and polished phrase drawn from ancient times, among those who now live in our time and are known to me — something I would by no means obstinately deny — you are nevertheless nearer, or shortly will be, to first place than to third.

Farewell. Rome, September 19, 1512.

1 Ioanni Francisco Pico Mirandulae Petrus Bembus salutem plurimam dicit.[1]

Recte atque amanter factum abs te est quod eius sermonis tuas partes, quem una de imitandi ratione nuper habueramus, etiam tuis ad me perhumaniter scriptis literis perferri voluisti. Quamquam enim propter eximiam tuam in omni genere doctrinarum praestantiam et meum summum erga te amorem singula tua dicta inhaerescere penitus in sensibus consueverint atque memoria mea, tamen ea ipsa prodita literis et stabilius atque diutius permanent et facilius repetuntur. Tum accidere etiam illud solet, ut ea quae chartis mandantur pleniora uberioraque sint quam quae homines inter se colloquuntur. Addit enim semper aliquid stilus et scribendi mora, crescitque cogitatione ipsa oratio. Itaque sermo ille tuus, qui me mirifice delectabat cum te loquentem audiebam, idem perlectus in tuis literis mihi sane multo iocundissimus fuit. Quibus omnino literis, quoniam me amantissime provocas, respondebo, non tam quidem adversandi tibi studio quam tuendi mei, neque tam refellendae tuae sententiae causa quam ut,[2] quae me rationes impulerunt ut eos laudarem, qui quidem quem scirent in eo scribendi genere, in quo sibi elaborandum esse duxissent, excellere ac praestare ceteris, illum sibi unum ad imitandum proponerent, eas tu rationes cognosceres, quas tibi coram explicandi mihi sane otium non fuit.

2 Sed antequam illo veniam, peto abs te, quoniam initio literarum tuarum ita scribis, videri tibi imitandos esse omnes bonos, cur in reliquis earum ipsarum literarum partibus eos, qui aliquando imitati sunt, universos vituperes, laudes nullum? Hoc, si te propterea dices facere quia malos quidem habeas quos repre-

Pietro Bembo to Gianfrancesco Pico

Pietro Bembo wishes Gianfrancesco Pico della Mirandola excel-   1
lent health.

It was right and kind of you to have wished to send, in the literary work you generously dedicated to me, your part of the discussion that we recently had of one method of imitation. Because of
your remarkable learning in every area and my high regard for you,
your every word usually makes a deep impression on my senses
and memory. Yet, when presented in literary form, these same
words last longer and more firmly and are more easily recalled.
Then too it often happens that what is entrusted to paper is fuller
and richer than the things men exchange in conversation. For the
pen and the time required for writing always add something, and a
speech grows from the process of thought itself. Hence that discourse of yours, which gave me great pleasure when I heard you
speaking it, pleased me even more when I read it in your letter.
Since you offer me this friendly challenge, I will by all means respond to your letter, not so much out of the desire to oppose you
as to defend myself, and not so much to refute your opinion as to
make you understand the reasons (since I did not have time to explain them to you in person) that compelled me to praise those
who propose to imitate only that man whom they know excels and
surpasses all others in the sort of writing that they believe they
should cultivate.

But before I come to that, I ask you, since at the beginning of   2
your letter you write that you think we should imitate all good authors, why in the rest of that same letter do you criticize everyone
and praise no one who has ever imitated? If you say that you did
this because you have bad writers to criticize but have no good

hendas, bonos quos ornes non habeas, primum id quidem verisimile non est, imitandi artem esse aliquam, quae laudabilis sit, ea vero arte qui sit recte usus neminem unum inveniri, praesertim in tanta imitatorum frequentia, quantam necesse est et esse nunc, et fuisse antea omni tempore, et deinceps semper futuram. Imitandi enim vim atque sensum ac aemulatione quadam mixtam cupiditatem natura omnibus hominibus tribuit, quae sedari et comprimi ratione quidem potest, evelli prorsus extirparique non potest. Deinde si tibi concedatur imitatum fuisse recte neminem — video enim tibi etiam Maronem ipsum bonum imitatorem non videri — cur eam probas artem, in qua tametsi innumerabilia se clarissima ingenia exercuerint, laudem tamen boni artificis atque nomen tuo iudicio nullum est eorum consecutum? Ac plane cur non potius ad eorum te sententiam contulisti qui affirmaverunt imitari non oportere damnaveruntque quicumque id facerent et quoquo modo? Aequius enim fuerat vel in illos te non invehi quorum artem antea probavisses, vel eam artem non probare cuius amantis et studiosos homines tantopere fueras tamque multis verbis improbaturus. Nam id quidem (quae tua est in scribendo vis ac eloquentia) facillime assequeris, ut illos acriter ac vehementer insectere.

3   Quam tu sententiam si esses secutus et tibi campum liberiorem disputandi patefecisses, et mihi laborem respondendi tuis litteris non attulisses. Reiecissem enim te ad Pauli Cortesii epistolam bellam illam quidem et cum argutulam tum etiam gravem, qua is Politiani, vicini sui docti mehercule ac ingeniosi hominis, sed (ut mihi quidem videtur) non multum prudentis levitatem fregit. Qui profecto[3] Ciceronianam illam scribendi rationem atque formam, a qua longiuscule abfuit, sese assequi nullo modo posse cum videret, ad eos damnandos qui sibi illum exprimendum sumpsissent quique omnino stilum imitatione aliqua colerent, se convertit.

ones to commend, it is first of all unlikely that there exists some praiseworthy art of imitation but that not one person can be found who has used that art correctly, especially in such a great throng of imitators as now necessarily exists and has existed in all times past and shall always exist hereafter. For nature has given to all mankind the faculty and disposition and yearning to imitate, mixed with a certain sense of rivalry, and nature can certainly be checked and controlled by rational means, but it cannot be entirely eradicated and stamped out. Moreover, if I grant you that no one has imitated correctly (in fact, I see that you do not even consider Virgil himself a good imitator), why do you approve of an art in which, although countless brilliant talents have practiced it, none of them in your judgment has achieved the renown and reputation of a good artist? Why haven't you rather sided with those who assert that one simply should not imitate and reject whoever does so in any way at all? It would have been more consistent either not to criticize those men whose art you had just commended, or not to commend an art whose most ardent practitioners you were about to reject so completely and in so many words. For you succeed with the greatest facility (such is the power and eloquence of your writing) in bitterly and vehemently attacking them.

If you had adopted this view and opened up for yourself a freer 3
field of contention, you would not have given me the trouble of responding to your letter. I would have simply referred you to Paolo Cortesi's beautiful, subtle and serious letter wherein he destroyed the shallow argument of Poliziano. The latter was, by Hercules,[1] his like in learning and talent, but not a very wise man, I think. Indeed when he saw that he could never catch up with that Ciceronian method and form of writing and was quite far behind, he turned around and criticized anyone who had undertaken to write like Cicero and who was entirely devoted to imitating his style. Thus Paolo could have satisfied even you with his learned

Itaque Paulus docte sane ac prudenter illius dissimulationem reii-
ciens tibi etiam satisfacere potuisset, si cum illo sensisses.

4   Nunc autem cum affirmes imitandum quidem esse, verum non
unum aliquem sed omnes bonos, hoc quemadmodum accipias non
intellego. Nam si omnes ii, qui aliquo uno in genere boni scribendi
magistri sunt habiti, pares inter se stili nobilitate, scriptorumque[4]
elegantia extitissent, concedi tibi fortasse poterat id quod dicis:
non uni eorum operam a nobis esse dandam sed plane omnibus.
Nunc vero, cum uniuscuiusque ratio vel ingenii vel artificii uniuscuiusque cum ingenio tum artificio dispar esse dissimillimaque reperiatur sitque alius alio praestantior, quid esse causae potest,
quin, si melioribus operam dederimus, eos, qui minus boni sunt,
negligamus? An si inter illos quicumque boni dicuntur esse, unus
est omnium longe optimus longeque praestantissimus, ut quae singula insunt in ceteris, ea universa in uno illo splendidiora etiam
ornatioraque conspiciantur, eum unum multo omnium maximum
atque summum recte imitati cum fuerimus, nisi illos etiam, qui
boni mediocriter habentur, imitabimur, nihil proficiemus? Quasi
necesse sit qui Apellis more pingere didicerit, cuius artem reliqui
pictores admirati primas ei partes sine controversia tribuerunt, illum etiam Polygnoti et Thymantis tabulas, a quibus doceretur,[5]
adhibuisse, aut eum qui Lysippi excellens ac praeclarum fingendis
imaginibus artificium expresserit, Calamidis signa rigida vel etiam
magis rigida Canachi fuisse contemplatum. Atque illi artifices,
cum Alexandri vultum imitari suis artibus cuperent, neminem
alium intuebantur; mentem in eum unum suam atque oculos in-
tendebant. Nos, qui eius scripti simulachrum quod sit pulcherrimum et perfectissimum nobis proponere debemus, in quo effingendo studium et diligentiam adhibeamus, cum illud ante oculos
habeamus, ad eorum etiam, quae non ita pulchra sunt exprimen-
das imagines, curam atque animum traducemus? Mihi quidem
falli, Pice, videtur, qui sic existimat, neque enim ita formati a diis
immortalibus sumus ut cum suppeditare nobis ea quae prima sunt

and prudent exposure of Poliziano's pretense, if you had sided with Poliziano.

As it stands, however, I don't understand how you can assert 4 that we should engage in imitation, but of all good authors, not of any one in particular. For if all those who are considered masters of good writing in any one genre were equal to all the rest in nobility of style and in the elegance of their writings, it might be possible to grant what you say — namely, that we should direct our attention not to one but to all of them. But in fact, since the pattern of everyone's talent and art is found to be very different, every author being unequal in talent and artistry and one author being superior to another, what could prevent our neglecting inferior authors, if we devote study to the better? Or, if one author is by far the best and most excellent of all those we consider good, such that all the qualities each of the others has are even finer and more splendid in that one writer, will we gain nothing by rightly imitating the greatest and best of all, unless we also imitate those that we consider only moderately good? It is as if an artist who has learned to paint in the style of Apelles — whose skill the other painters so admired that they awarded him first place without contest — also was made to consult the paintings of Polygnotus and Timanthes by whom Apelles was taught; or a sculptor who imitated Lysippus's excellent and famous art of statuary also had to contemplate the stiff figures of Calamis or the even stiffer ones of Canachus.[2] When artists wanted to apply their skills to imitating Alexander's face, they looked to no other; they directed their mind and eyes to him alone.[3] Shall we, who should give ourselves the most beautiful and perfect pattern of writing, applying persistence and diligence to reproduce it — shall we disgrace our energy and intellect, when we have that pattern before our eyes, by copying images of things that are not so beautiful? Whoever thinks thus, Pico, seems to me to be mistaken. For the immortal gods have not so formed us that, when we can supply ourselves in abundance

valeamus, sectemur quae secunda sunt, multo minus quae sunt infra secunda. Animus enim noster summum quiddam semper atque altissimum suspicit. Itaque, ut dixi, valde miror te non ita potius sensisse ut alterum eorum statueres: vel omnino imitari non oportere vel, si imitandum quidem esse duceres, non ad ea quaecumque bona essent, sed ad illa tantummodo quae optima quaeque perfectissima haberentur, imitationis esse nostrae omnes nervos intendendos.

5   Nam de Ideis quod scribis, difficile quidem est tibi, homini doctissimo et in omnium philosophorum disciplinis et scholis multa cum laude atque gloria diu versato, aliquid affirmanti non credere. Sed quam tu esse in animo tuo insitam atque a natura traditam scribendi ideam atque formam sentias, de eo ipse videris. De meo quidem animo tantum tibi affirmare possum nullam me in eo stili formam, nullum dictandi simulachrum, antea inspexisse quam mihi ipse mente et cogitatione legendis veterum libris multorum annorum spatio, multis laboribus ac longo usu exercitationeque confecerim. Ad quod nunc, cum aliquid scribendum est, me converto.

6   Videoque quasi oculis, sic cogitatione, quae conficiendo scripto opus sunt, unde sumam. Ante autem quam in iis quas dico cogitationibus magnopere essem versatus, inspiciebam quidem in animum meum nihilo sane minus, quaerebamque tamquam a speculo effigiem aliquam, a qua mihi sumerem conficeremque quod volebam. Sed nulla inerat in eo effigies, nihil se mihi offerebat, nihil conspiciebam. Itaque si quid calamo uterer, si quid molirer, non lege, non iudicio quo volebam, sed temere inconstanterque ferebar; nulla me earum quas commemoras idea speciesque moderabatur. Neque vero sum nescius, te id cum diceres, de Platonicorum sententia dicere, qui quae prima quaeque praestantia in natura rerum sunt vel esse aliquo modo possunt ad divinas illas imagines speciesque referebant. Ac ego quidem sic existimo in ipso mundi ac rerum omnium auctore et effectore deo ut iustitiae, ut tempe-

with the best things, we pursue what is second-best, much less even worse things. Our soul always looks up to the thing that is highest and loftiest. So as I said, I am really amazed that you did not rather adopt one or the other of these views: either that we should not imitate at all, or, if you believe we should, that we should direct all our powers of imitation not to whatever is good but only to what we consider best and most perfect.

It is difficult not to believe what you assert about the Ideas, considering your great learning and what a long time you have spent with the teachings and schools of all the philosophers, to your great praise and glory. But it's your business if you see in your soul an idea and form of writing planted there and handed down by nature. I can speak to you only of my own soul. I saw no form of style in it, no pattern of discourse before I developed myself in mind and thought by reading the books of the ancients over the course of many years, by long labor, practice and exercise.[4] Since something should be said about this, I now turn to that topic.

I see by thought, as though with my eyes, from what source to take the highest example which I need to compose some piece of writing. Yet, before I engaged in the thoughts I mention, I too used to look no less into my soul and to seek, as in a mirror, some likeness I might use to compose what I wanted. But there was no likeness in my soul, nothing presented itself to me; I saw nothing. Therefore, if I used the pen at all, if I composed anything, I was taken where I wanted to go not by law or the faculty of judgment but randomly and inconsistently. None of the things that you mention — the Idea and form — guided me. I am aware that you were speaking here about the opinion of the Platonists who used to compare what is best and most excellent in nature (or can be in some way) with these divine images and types. I for my part believe that in the Author of the entire universe and in God the

rantiae, ut aliarum virtutum, sic etiam recte scribendi speciem quandam divinam illam quidem et cui nihil desit atque omnino beatissimam[6] existere, ad quam et Xenophon et Demosthenes et ipse imprimis Plato, tum et Crassus et Antonius et Iulius et maxime omnium Cicero, cum dictarent aliquid et scriberent, quantum consequi cogitatione poterant, respiciebant, atque ad illius, quam animo conceperant imaginem, stilum mentemque dirigebant. Idemque nobis faciendum arbitror conandumque modis omnibus, ut ad eius formae simulachrum scriptis nostris, quoad fieri potest, quam rectissime[7] quamque proxime accedamus.

7   Quod si in animis etiam nostris Ideae illae insident quas dicis, singulae in singulis, tum diversae inter se atque variae, prout[8] illas a natura ipsa ego pro mea, tu pro tua, pro sua quisque animi corporisque temperatione initio nascendi est sortitus, ab iis si cura diligentiaque nostra stilum flectere in quamcumque volumus partem nobis licet, cur non tu eum unum, qui sit omnium maximus atque summus, imitari nos tantummodo statuis oportere? Si non licet, cur omnes[9] bonos? Nam et invidiosum quidem est, quod homines possunt assequi aliquo in genere optimum, id omnibus non proponere, et supervacuum omnes illis bonos imitandos esse dicere, quibus animum a sua scribendi specie atque forma, quam a natura traditam possident, facultas revocandi non est data.

8   Sin vero, quod est tertium atque ultimum, in quorundam animis ideae illae atque species eiusmodi insunt, ut, si quis studium adhibeat, verti atque inflecti facile possint, in quorundam autem eiusmodi, ut nullo modo possint, eodem tamen decidas, eodem labare necesse est. Nam neque ii, quibus negatum est aliquo progredi, ad ullum imitationis genus invitandi sunt, neque non ad optimum, qui quo libuerit si volent progredientur, sunt incitandi. In alteris de facultate, ne quid detrahatur, adhibenda cura est; ab alte-

Creator there exists a certain divine form of correct writing which is perfect and blessed in every way, as there is of justice, temperance and all the other virtues. It is to this that Xenophon, Demosthenes and especially Plato himself looked, that Crassus, Antonius, Julius Caesar and most of all Cicero looked, insofar as they could reach it in their thought, whenever they spoke and wrote.[5] It is to this image which they had conceived in the soul that they directed their mind and style. I think that we should do the same and try by all means to come as close and as correctly as possible in our writings to the image of that form.

But if these Ideas of which you speak reside in our souls too, individual ones in individual souls, each different from the others and varied—I being allotted them from nature itself according to my temperament, you according to your temperament, each according to his own temperament of body and soul at birth—and if through care and diligence we may use these ideas to inflect our style in whatever direction we wish, why don't you conclude that we ought to imitate him alone who is the greatest and best of all? If we may not do this, why do you say we should imitate all good writers? For it is certainly invidious not to propose to everyone the best model they can pursue in any genre, and it is useless to recommend for imitation every good writer to people who have not received the ability to summon back their soul from the notion and form of writing with which nature has endowed them.[6]

But if (and this is the third and last possibility) in the souls of some men these ideas and forms are such that, if a man should apply himself, he may easily change and alter them, but in the souls of others they are such that they can in no way be changed, you are bound to be mistaken however you decide. For people who have somehow been denied the ability to improve should not be invited to engage in any type of imitation, and people who will improve as much as they like should be urged to follow the best model. In the case of some people, we must take care lest anything

ris, ut inepti esse desinant, non est requirendum. Ac ego illis nec imitandum esse quenquam statuo, nec vero ullo in genere quicquam conandum, qui pravo, qui tenui, qui inerti ingenio sunt, qui duram atque implacabilem naturae suae quasi faciem prae se ferunt. Scribant ii mihi libros, necne; vigilent, dormiant, nihil moror. Eos volo, eos alloquor, qui si operam dederint, si animo non frangentur, nihil non assequi poterunt, et quorum ingenia, si excolantur, fructus uberes atque magnos ferent.

9 Neque illud me movet quod existimem, qui ita formati sint[10] ut quibus artibus animum intenderint, quo in genere scribendi elaboraverint, sua illos spes non sit frustratura esse, non multissimos. Neque enim aut Ciceronem a scribendo deterruit pulcherrimos illos *De oratore* libros, quod qualem in iis[11] statuerit oratorem esse oportere, talem fortasse neque legerit ipse umquam fuisse[12] neque audiverit, aut Plato *Reipublicae* suae leges propterea non perscripsit, quod eas ab usu atque consuetudine gentium longius abesse arbitraretur, quam quibus ullos populos, ullam civitatem esse usuram confideret. Qui enim artem aliquam recte praecipiunt, non id cogitant ut omnes assequi eam possint, sed id potius, ut qui potest, ita assequatur, ut nihil possit esse eo in genere praestantius. Quicquid autem est eiusmodi, qui praestanti ingenio non sit, aggredi fortasse potest, assequi atque perficere nequaquam potest. Itaque mediocritatem ingeniorum reiiciunt; nihil enim mediocre idem atque praestans est. Quod cum fit, pusillum ad numerum res redigatur, necesse est; praestantia enim quae sunt eadem, perrara esse consueverunt, rarioraque quo praestantiora. Praestantium autem rerum paucitas mediocrium multitudini non modo non posthabenda, sed longe etiam anteponenda est. Placetque Nautes ille mihi Virgilianus, qui Aeneam admonet, quo in Italiam transmittere facilius possit:

diminish their ability; in other cases one need not stop them from being inept. In my opinion they should not imitate anyone, nor should people who have a corupt, shallow or weak talent, who make manifest the hard and implacable face, if you will, of their own nature, attempt anything in any genre. As far as I am concerned they may write books, or not write books. Let them spend long nights at it, let them fall asleep, I don't care. The ones I want, the ones I'm addressing, are those who, if they apply themselves, if their spirit is not broken, will be able to accomplish something; whose talent, if cultivated, will bear large and rich fruits.

I am not influenced by my belief that there are only a very few 9
men who have been so formed that to whatever arts they apply themselves, in whatever literary genre they work, their expectations will not deceive them. Cicero was not deterred from writing his beautiful books *On the Orator* by the fact that he himself probably had never read nor heard the kind of orator that he there prescribed.[7] Nor did Plato refrain from writing down the laws of his *Republic* because he believed that they were further from the use and custom of nations than those he trusted any peoples or states to use.[8] For whoever teaches any skill correctly does not plan for everyone to acquire it, but rather intends that whoever has the capacity may learn it so well that nothing more excellent in that type of skill could be accomplished. A person who does not have the finest talent can perhaps get closer to that skill, but he can never acquire and perfect it.[9] That is why teachers reject mediocre talents, for no talent is mediocre and at the same time excellent. When a talent is excellent, it is necessarily restricted to a very small number. For excellences that are alike are usually very rare, and the more excellent they are the rarer they are. But the rarity of excellent things should not be esteemed less than the multitude of mediocre things, but much more. I like Virgil's Nautes who advises Aeneas on how they may cross over more easily to Italy:

quicquid invalidum ac metuens pericli est, esse reiiciendum;

quod cum esset factum, poeta statim intulit:

exigui numero, sed bello vivida virtus.

Ex quo apparet, poetarum sapientissimum non virtutem modo in illis, quos commemorat, requisivisse, sed etiam *vividam*, hoc est, praestantem.

10 Quamquam quidem non ego ulla simulachra quae nusquam sint quaeque vix animo percipi possint, quemadmodum illi duo quos dico fecerunt, nostris hominibus ad imitandum propono, cum eum unum, qui sit omnium optimus atque praestantissimus, illis propono. Quod si facerem, numquam me tamen illorum defenderem exemplis. Potest enim quilibet cum oratoriae ac rerum publicarum ratione atque modo constituendarum, tum aliarum plane rerum artes et disciplinas ita tradere, ut ad excellentiorem statum atque formam velit earum[13] cupidos progredi, quam cuius simulachra oculis cernantur manibusque contineantur. Imitatio autem, quia in exemplo tota versatur, ab exemplo petenda est. Id si desit, iam imitatio esse ulla quae[14] potest? Nihil est enim aliud totum hoc, quo de agimus, imitari, nisi alieni stili similitudinem transferre in tua scripta, et eadem quasi temperatione scribendi uti, qua is est usus, quem tibi ad imitandum proposuisti.

11 Sed redeo ad illud quod ais, imitandos esse omnis bonos, quaeroque iterum[15] abs te, velisne nos ita bonos omnis imitari, ut eorum cuiuslibet universam scribendi rationem exprimamus, an satis habeas, qua quisque in rationis suae parte maxime bonus est habitus, eam nos tantummodo ab uno quoque mutuari? Atque ita multis ex rationum partibus, quibus rationibus sunt alii permulti usi, unam conficere rationem integram, qua utamur? Utro modo

we should cast off the weak and those afraid of danger.[10]

As soon as they had, the poet said,

Small was their number, but lively their virtue in war.[11]

It thus is apparent that the wisest of poets did not simply demand virtue in the men whom he mentions, but "lively," that is, excellent, virtue.

Although I certainly do not propose that our men imitate any images that nowhere exist and that can hardly be perceived by the soul, as the two whom I mention [i.e., Plato and Cicero] have done, I do propose to them that one writer who is the best and most excellent of all—and if I were to do the former, I would never defend myself by citing their example. For anyone can, using the method and manner of the disciplines of rhetoric and political theory, pass down other arts and sciences in such a way that he wishes those desirous of them to advance to a higher level of abstraction than the level wherein images may be seen with the eyes and held in the hands. Imitation, however, because it has to do entirely with example, must be sought from example. If that is missing, how can there be any imitation? For this entire matter of imitation which we are discussing is nothing but transferring the likeness of another's style into your own writings. It is to use the same temperament of writing, if you will, that the person you have decided to imitate used. [10]

But I return to your statement that we should imitate all good writers. I again ask, do you want us to imitate all the good ones in such a way that we copy the general method of each of their styles, or do you consider it sufficient to borrow from each only that part of his method where he is considered good by most people? And do you want us in this way to construct one complete method of our own from the many parts of the methods that many different men have used? Look, in which of the two preceding ways would [11]

accipi dogma istud tuum malis, vide. Sed priore velle te non est
existimandum. Quid enim esse potest absurdius, quam quas multi
species scribendi atque formas diversas, illas quidem inter se mul-
tumque saepe differentes, sunt assecuti, suis eas membris omnibus, suis partibus praeditas, una in scribendi forma ac specie velle
universas exprimi atque contineri? Quasi existimes exaedificandis
unis aedibus multa aedium exempla variarum imaginum atque
operum omni ex parte posse repraesentari. Altero modo si te dices
velle, primum iam id quidem imitari non est plurimis ex partibus,
quae stilum singulorum conficiunt, aliquam unam tibi sumere, ut
cum id saepius feceris, sumere autem ex multis potes, stilum inde
conficias tuum. Excerpere id quidem potius dicendum est aut, si
libet, etiam mendicare; ita enim degere homines invictus mendici-
tate consueverunt, ut quae sibi opus ad vitam sunt, non ab uno,
sed a multis petant.

12   Imitatio autem totam complectitur scriptionis alicuius formam,
singulas eius partes assequi postulat; in universa stili structura
atque corpore versatur. Neque enim qui Sallustianam brevitatem
assecutus sit, verbis autem illam aut obsoletis aut popularibus,
structura etiam inconcinna conglutinaverit, Sallustium imitari est
dicendus. Neque qui Iulii Caesaris in enarrandis rebus temperan-
tiam expresserit, sermone vero plane rudi in illa exprimenda sit
usus, is erit propterea dignus existimandus quem Caesaris imitatorem vocemus. Totam[16] mihi oportet eius stili faciem exprimat
cuius se imitatorem dici vult, quem eo nomine dignum putem.

13   Itaque Cicero, cum eius verbi definitionem traderet, 'imitationem esse,' dixit illam, 'qua impellimur cum diligenti ratione ut aliquorum similes in dicendo esse valeamus.' Sunt ne ista,[17] Pice,
Tulliana verba singula quae commemoro? Qui autem fieri potest,
ut aliquorum similes esse valeant ii qui de singulis sumunt quod

you like us to understand this dogma of yours? We shouldn't think you mean the former. For what can be more absurd than for you to desire that all the many different types and forms of writing men have pursued, which often differ greatly from one another, each being endowed with its own members and its own parts, be expressed and embraced all at once in a single literary form and type? It is as if you thought that in constructing a single building you could represent on every side many examples of buildings of various design and workmanship.[12] If you support your position in the second way, [our response is as follows]: first, imitation is certainly not appropriating one of several parts that make up the style of an individual author in order to make your own style out of elements borrowed on numerous occasions from many authors. We should rather call this excerpting or, if I may, even begging.[13] People who have become accustomed to live in this way, by begging, seek the necessities of life not from one person, but from many.

Imitation, however, embraces the entire form of any piece of writing and demands that one follow the individual parts of that form. It involves the entire structure and body of the style. For someone who followed the brevity of Sallust but has pasted it together with obsolete or vulgar language or in a disorderly way cannot be said to be imitating Sallust.[14] Nor should we think that anyone who copies the restraint of Julius Caesar in narrating events but uses unpolished diction merits being called an imitator of Caesar. The man I would consider worthy of that name should copy the complete stylistic effect of the writer whom he wishes to be said to imitate.

Thus according to Cicero's definition, "imitation is the process that leads us by exact method to succeed in assimilating our speech to that of others." Am I not citing Cicero's own words, Pico?[15] How can it be that those who borrow what they express from individuals succeed in becoming like some of them, but those who take something from everyone achieve nothing? Furthermore,

exprimant, de omnibus ut nihil assequantur? Deinde, si tibi etiam de verbo concessero (ambitiose enim tecum agere nihil volo), nae tua ista imitandi multos ratio optari potius quam sperari, fingi quam teneri, ore dici quam re perfici facilius potest. Nam neque qui eodem tempore imitari plures vult, quicquam ab ullo proficiet; distrahit enim mentem atque sensum copia, neque haerere animum sinit; cuius autem in nullo haeret animus, is omnino recte conficere nihil potest.

14   Neque qui alium post alium aggreditur, ei quam in uno curam intenderit, non in alio saepe remittere necesse est. Capimur enim plerique omnes novitate, a qua ita oblectantur quidam ut etiam illa damnent, a quibus recesserunt. Accedit eodem scriptorum diversitas et dissimilitudo. Itaque dediscendae plerumque sunt veteres perceptiones ut novis perceptionibus curam atque animum adhibeamus. Placet enim in illo[18] cum dignitate quaedam quasi severitas orationis; hilaritas in alio, comitas, lusus ipsi multum probantur. Horum cum imitari alterum didicerimus, alterum doceri aggrediamur, reiicere multa cogimur eorum quae paulo ante summa industria, summo nostro labore sumus consecuti. Quamobrem frangitur studium, debilitatur diligentia, contentio illa nostra ardorque omnis animorum elanguescit atque restinguitur, dum huc illuc tamquam a fluctibus, sic in exemplorum varietate iactamur.

15   Postremo, quod tu singulas uniuscuiusque bonas partis imitandas esse tantummodo existimas, id si recte considerabis, quomodo assequi possis, non invenies. Omnibus enim ex partibus uniuscuiusque scriptoris conflatur coalescitque id quod in quoque bonum atque praestans est; omnes eius virtutes, et vero etiam vitia, si qua insunt in illo vitia, eam conficiunt. Nam ut hominum vultus, alius morum benignitatem, alius alacritatem naturae, animi alius fortitudinem, alius ingenii fertilitatem, alius maiestatem, alius ve-

even if I grant your definition of "imitation" (I don't want to argue any issue with you out of personal ambition), surely your method of imitating many authors can more easily be desired than hoped for, sketched out than adhered to, spoken of than accomplished in fact. For whoever wishes to imitate several writers at the same time will fail utterly to profit from any of them. Too much material distracts the mind and senses and does not permit the soul to focus.[16] But if a man's soul focuses on nothing he cannot accomplish anything that will be correct in every respect.

Someone who passes from one model to another necessarily 14 relaxes the attention he pays to the one while he is occupied with the other. Most of us are taken with novelty, and some men are so delighted by it that they even despise what they have left behind. Diversity and dissimilarity among writers only intensifies the tendency. Thus we must generally unlearn old concepts in order to apply one's mind and effort to new ones. One writer pleases us with his serious and dignified tone; another writer we like for his good humor, friendliness and playfulness. When we've learned to imitate one author and then start to learn from the other, we are forced to reject much of what we pursued a little while earlier with the greatest industry and effort.[17] That is what breaks our enthusiasm, weakens our energy, causes to flicker and go out all our striving and spiritual ardor: being tossed about hither and yon, as though on the waves of the sea, by a wide variety of literary models.

Finally, regarding your view that we should imitate only the 15 good parts of any writer: if you consider the matter correctly, you will find it impossible to do this. What is good and excellent in any writer flows together and coalesces from all the parts of his work. All his virtues, but also his faults (if he has any) go together to make up his style. If we consider the faces of men, one reflects a kind character; another, a lively nature; another, courage; another, a fertile intelligence; another, grandeur; another, charm. Yet these

nustatem prae se ferunt, eae autem singulae indoles non ex oculo-
rum aut ex superciliorum solummodo forma aut oris aut genarum
aut ceterarum ex aliqua partium qualitate, verum ex omnibus sui
quaeque vultus partibus atque membris sunt constitutae, ut si quis
aliquam pictor imitari coloribus velit, is singulas eius faciei partes
cuius est ipsa indoles ante exprimere cogatur. Ita mehercule in
scribendi rationibus insunt eae quas laudamus, sive virtutes sive
lumina scriptorum singulorum, quas profecto virtutes praestare
nostris in scriptis minime possumus nisi etiam universas illas, quarum sunt ipsa lumina, scribendi rationes praestemus.

16   An tu candorem illum puritatemque sermonis, quam in Iulio
esse maximam atque mirificam videmus, imitari te posse existima-
bis, nisi et temperamento fueris usus tanto, quanto ille maiore
usus est, quam umquam alius propterea, quia ipse de se scripsit ne
aut odio in scribendo videretur aut cupiditate ulla duci? Et neglec-
tum eundem elocutionis expresseris qui est ab illo vel necessitate
institutus, quoniam plurimis agendis, maximis difficilimisque rebus occupatus diligentiam in scribendo maiorem adhibere non
potuit, vel accersitus industria, ne plane crederetur potuisse, ut
existimarent homines, multo plus illum gratiae scriptis fuisse ac-
quisiturum suis, si plus ei temporis ad scribendum bellicarum rerum occupatio suppeditavisset? Atque ipse quidem candor non ex
sese, sed cum ex aliis, tum ex his duabus praecipue partibus con-
stare mihi videtur, quas dico. Has si tu duas partis non praestabis,
candor iam ille tantopere laudatus numquam mediusfidius ex-
primetur; sin praestabis, voles autem etiam Ciceronianam illam
maiestatem scribendi assequi, quam omnes laudibus usque ad cae-
lum ferunt, neque hoc quemadmodum optabis, efficies, et illud
quod effectum iam erat,[19] perturbabis. Quantum enim addes ad
alterum, tantundem ex altero adimas necesse est. Ita quae per se
atque seiuncta eximia utraque praeclaraque habentur, eorum neu-

individual characteristics come not only from the shape of one's eyes, eyebrows, mouth, cheeks or the quality of any other part, but each is constituted of all the parts and members of its own face. So if any painter should wish to imitate one of them, he would first have to copy the individual parts of the face that bears the desired characteristic. It is in this way, by Hercules, that the characteristics we admire are implied in our compositional methods, whether they be virtues of style or brilliant passages in individual writings, which we certainly cannot evince in our own writings unless we also evince the general compositional methods to which the brilliant passages themselves belong.

Do you think that you can imitate the clarity and purity of 16 speech we see at its finest and most wonderful in Caesar unless you too employ as much restraint as he did? — And he used an unprecedented degree of restraint because he was writing about himself and did not want to appear to be influenced by hatred or cupidity. Do you think you can achieve it without copying that same disregard for eloquence that Caesar, or rather necessity, dictated, since he was occupied with many important and challenging affairs and therefore was unable to apply greater diligence to his writing? Or did he produce this effect intentionally so that it might be believed, as people do think, that he was capable of having written far more gracefully if the business of warfare had allowed him more time to write?[18] Even his clarity seems to me to stem not from itself but from other features of his style, especially the two that I mention above.[19] If you do not manifest these two features, you will never, by Jove, produce that clarity which has received such praise. But if you do capture it, and you still want your writing to achieve that Ciceronian grandeur that everyone praises to the skies, you won't achieve the latter effect in the way you wish and you'll ruin the former effect that you've already achieved. For you must necessarily diminish the one effect to the degree that you

trum, si permisces, suam pristinam faciem dignitatemque retine-
bit. Quod si et candorem Caesaris et maiestatem Ciceronis, tum[20]
et Sallustii brevitatem et ubertatem Livii, et nitorem[21] Celsi et diligentiam Columellae, si denique quod in unoquoque scriptorum
egregiorum proprium esse lumen, tamquam in vultu indoles conspicitur, ea omnia praestanda esse statues scriptis tuis, vereor ne
non tam quidem imitari illos voluisse quam illudere, neque tam assequi quam pervertere videare. Quam tamen si effugies calumniam
voluntatis tuae, illud certe non evitabis quin appareat, neminem te
illorum, non dicam recte assequi, sed etiam effingere mediocriter
potuisse.

17   Denique si quis deus id, quod sponte nostra facere nullo modo
possumus, te doceret, artem videlicet quandam novam ac plane divinam, qua imitari multos calleres quemadmodum praecipis, tamen esset verendum, num illa sane arte tibi esse utendum statueres. Qui enim fieri potest ut qui multos assequi una scribendi
ratione vult, eius oratio non dissimilis, non impar, non sibi diversa
inconstansque sit, non inconcinna, non parum cohaerens, dum
huius lenitatem, illius vero ardorem, alterius ornatum, alterius ne-
gligentiam (quae quidem interdum ut in muliere non fucata facies,
sic in scribente gratior est), sexcenta praeterea alia varia, mul-
tumque differentia scribendi genera qualitatesque complectitur?
Ac mihi quidem vetustissimi poetae finxisse Protea videntur, cum
illum modo aquam fieri, modo ignem, modo belluam dicerent,
numquam tamen eodem aspectu plus unam formam prae se tu-
lisse, non solum quia id posse fieri non existimabant, sed etiam

add to the other. Thus neither of these features, which by themselves and separately are each considered extraordinary and brilliant, will retain its pristine appearance and dignity if you mix
them up. But if you decide that the clarity of Caesar and the grandeur of Cicero, the brevity of Sallust and the richness of Livy, the
brilliance of Celsus and the thoroughness of Columella, if finally
you decide that the individual marks of distinction found in every
outstanding writer, like the natural character seen in his face, are
all to be displayed in your own writings, I am afraid it may look
like you want not so much to imitate as to mock them, not so
much to equal as to pervert them.[20] And even if you do escape a
charge of calumny with respect to your intentions, you will certainly not avoid giving the impression that you have not been able
to copy any of them even in a mediocre way, to say nothing of imitating them correctly.

Finally, if some god were to teach you something we can't learn 17
to do of our own accord—that is, some new and obviously divine
art that gave you the knowledge to imitate all those authors you
recommend—it would still be a fearful decision whether or not
you should make use of that art. For how could the speech of anyone who wishes to follow many writers in a single compositional
method not be irregular, unbalanced, self-contradictory and inconsistent, inharmonious, incoherent, so long as it embraces the gentleness of this one, the ardor of that, the embellishment of one
and the negligence of another (which indeed is sometimes, like a
woman's face unadorned with cosmetics, more attractive than ornate writing) and six hundred other various and different types
and properties of composition?[21] It seems to me that the ancient
poets, although they would say that he was now water, now fire,
now a beast, never imagined that Proteus might display more
than one form under the same aspect.[22] This was not only because
they didn't believe it possible, but also because they didn't see how

propterea quod, quo pacto[22] diversae facie res inter seque variae apte coniungerentur, non videbant.

18 Sed iam de tuis literis hactenus, vel potius de ea tuarum literarum parte, ad quam quidem respondere me operae pretium duxi. Nam ad omnes neque multum necesse fuit et haec ipsa satis multa esse possunt, praesertim tibi, qui non modo ea quae scripta sunt, qualia sunt, recte perspicies, sed illa etiam, quae scribi in hanc sententiam possunt, ex iis quae leges, per te ipse facile considerabis.

19 Venio igitur ad illam partem sermonis nostri in qua ea mea sententia fuit, ut dicerem eos mihi vehementer probari, qui prosa oratione scripturi Ciceronem sibi unum ad imitandum proponerent, heroicis carminibus Virgilium. In quam omnino sententiam, non sane ut primum eiusmodi res tractare animo cepimus, statim adducti sumus, sed post multas cogitationes ac per quosdam quasi gradus ad eam accessimus, ut non temere illa inventa finem progrediendi fecisse atque in ea quievisse videamur. Nam initio quidem illud mihi saepe veniebat in mentem, ut in philosophiae opinionibus atque sententiis, sic in scriptorum generibus et stilo, nullis nos legibus subiici, nemini addici atque astringi oportere, sed quod in quoque probaretur, id sequi. Quae profecto sententia tuae fuisse sententiae similis atque cognata videtur. De qua quidem me tentantem conantemque eo in genere toto multa illae tandem rationes depulerunt, quas superius te ut etiam de tua deducerent, si possent, collegi.

20 Itaque ea sententia deiectus ad illud me contuli, ut ducerem aequius[23] esse et profecto conducibilius novam intactamque ab aliis rationem ac plane suam quemque conficere scribendi, idque putarem omnes homines, nisi invidi atque malevoli essent, laudaturos. Quod cum placuisset, vellem autem, quantum in eo possem, experiri, omnis nostra cogitatio, diligentia, studium, omnis denique noster labor irritus atque nullus fuit. Nihil enim inveniebam, quod

things that were different and varied in appearance might be properly connected with each other.

But enough about your letter or, rather, that part of your letter to   18
which I thought it worth my while to reply. It wasn't necessary to
take up every point, and the many points that I have made will be
enough, especially for you, who not only will see clearly the quality
of the arguments made, but will readily take into account on your
own what could have been said on this subject by inferring it from
what you've read.

Thus I come to that part of our discussion in which I gave my   19
strong approval to those who, intending to write prose, resolve to
imitate Cicero alone and who intend to imitate Virgil if they are
going to write heroic verse.[23] I did not arrive at that general view
all at once when I first began to study the subject, but only after
much thought and step by step. So it doesn't seem to me that I've
made rash findings the goal of my procedure and kept to them
complacently. Indeed, at first it often occurred to me that in the
case of literary genres and styles, as in that of philosophical opinions and convictions, we should not be subject to any laws and we
shouldn't be enslaved or confined by anyone, but that we should
follow whatever had won favor in each case. This position, actually, seems to have been similar and akin to yours. Indeed, the
arguments that I presented above in order to draw you too, if possible, away from your opinion finally drove me from mine as I
tested and tried out many ideas of that kind.

Once I had departed from that view, I came to believe that it   20
was more reasonable and profitable for everyone to devise each
his very own, novel and untried method of composition. And I
thought that all men, unless they were envious and malevolent,
would praise that idea. But although I had been pleased with this
theory and wanted to test it as much as I could, all my cogitation,
diligence, effort — in short, all my labor — was futile and worthless.

non vel ab aliquo veterum scriptorum stilo haustum videri facile
posset, vel omnino si id effugeram, tamen cum ad illorum scripta
conferebatur, mihi non summopere displiceret. Quippe quod venustatem sermonis, proprietatem, maiestatem eorum saeculorum
non redolebat, nullum antiquitatis vestigium, nullam notam refe-
rebat. Ad hanc frustrationem laboris nostri[24] illa cogitatio accessit,
quod animadvertebam eos qui se neminem imitari profitebantur,
partim scribendo parum admodum profecisse, partim etiam suis
cum libris atque scriptis plane invisos et despectos iacere. Quamobrem ea etiam sententia damnata, aliam inire rationem statuimus,
quae quidem eiusmodi fuit.

21   Volo autem singulos tibi animi mei motus consiliorumque va-
rietates perscribere, ut si aliqua ex parte prodesse tibi error meus
possit, ea ne celere. Nam quoniam ita natura comparatum videbam, ut quotiens magnum aliquid atque arduum moliri homines
cuperent, eius si facinoris exemplum haberent aliorum, qui idem
aliquando essent conati, ea re multum illis curae ad id, quod aggredi statuissent, multum laboris, multum etiam ambiguitatis, multum denique difficultatis demeretur: cogitare cepi iis in studiis,
quibus semper dediti fuimus, optandum esse, ut quem quisque
imitari posset, qui scribere aliquid cuperet, ne deesset. Itaque sive
ut in itinere conficiendo cum ducem[25] nacti sumus, securiore
animo viam ingredimur, sic in reliquis rebus alacriores ad illa sumus, quorum doctores et magistros habemus, sive etiam ad omnem excellentem laudis et gloriae cupiditatem nulla re magis quam
aliorum aemulatione incitamur. Mihi quoque idem faciendum pu-
tavi, cum poeticis in studiis tum in oratoria disciplina, quod per-
multos fecisse intellegebam, ut in utraque earum artium et ducem
quem sequerer et gloria illustrem quem aemularer eligerem, mi-
hique ipse quasi signum proponerem ad quod quidem conatus
omnes nostri cogitationesque dirigerentur.

22   Id cum deliberavissem, magna me haesitatio tenuit: deberemne
eos qui mediocritatem non excederent, an illos potius qui essent

For whatever I invented was either obviously derived from the style of an ancient writer or, if I had succeeded in avoiding that, still gave me no pleasure when I compared it with their work. For it failed to give off the fragrance produced by the charm, propriety and grandeur of ancient diction. It bore no vestige or mark of antiquity. Adding to my frustration was the following thought. I realized that, of those who professed to imitate no one, some had made very little progress with their writing, while others lay unseen and despised along with their books and treatises. That is how I came to condemn this view as well and decided to start in on another method, which was of the following kind.

But I want to give you a detailed description of my thought 21 processes and the various strategies I used; I won't conceal my errors if they can be of any profit to you. I saw that, according to nature's design, whenever men desired to accomplish something great and difficult, if they could follow the example of others who had at some time attempted the same feat, it alleviated much of their anxiety, their labor, even much of their uncertainty and difficulty about what they had decided to achieve. I therefore began to think that it would be desirable in the literary pursuits to which I had always been dedicated to have someone whom everyone who desires to write could imitate. As we travel more confidently when we find a guide,[24] so we show more readiness to engage in other matters when we have teachers and masters; and nothing excites in us every fine desire for praise and glory more than the emulation of others. I therefore thought that both in my poetical pursuits and in the discipline of rhetoric I too should do what I knew many others had done, so I chose in both arts both a guide to follow and a famous hero to emulate; and I gave myself a kind of standard or flag toward which I could direct all my efforts and thoughts.

After I had decided on that course, I hesitated as to whether I 22 should start with writers of moderate ability or the ones who were

omnium eminentissimi statim initio aggredi, quos omni studio colerem, ad quorumque similitudinem me quam diligentissime compararem? Nam si animum ad summos adiecissem, illud verebar ne me vel rei difficultas ab incepto deterreret vel certe frangeret suscepti oneris magnitudo, cum me parum proficere optimorum scriptorum longeque praestantissimorum exemplis comparationeque cognoscerem. Sin autem mediocribus me tradidissem, equidem sperabam fore ut cum ab illis, quantum vellem, profecissem, et facilior mihi esset et plane tutior ad eos transitus, qui primi haberentur. Sed angebar animo quod, ut odore novum vas, sic quo primum rudimento stilus imbueretur, permagni interesse audiebam; mentem etiam et[26] cogitationem meam multo libentius in summis excellentibusque viris fixam erectamque detinebam. Vicit tamen sive timor sive imbecillitas plane nostra voluntatis propensionem qua trahebar. Itaque dedidi me iis magistris instituendum quorum scripta non tam laudarem quod bona, quam reciperem quod paratiora optimis commodioraque ad imitandum viderentur.

23   Eos igitur acerrimo studio summaque diligentia cum tam diu essem sectatus, quoad mihi videretur me eius quod concupieram magnam esse partem consecutum, ad illos me contuli[27] quos esse facile principes omnium hominum testimonio sentiebam, ut eos item sequerer animumque meum atque mentem ad ipsorum rationes hauriendas imbibendasque traducerem. Id cum sedulo etiam atque etiam experirer, mea me delusum spe sane atque deceptum cognovi. Non enim solum faciliorem mihi eorum imitationem aliorum scriptorum imitatione non esse factam, sed multo etiam difficiliorem, praeclususque ad eam aditus potius quam patefactos videbam. Nam quam mihi usui putabam fore insumptam in exprimendis mediocribus operam, ea sane impedimento fuit. Animus

the most eminent, writers to whom I might devote myself with all
my zeal and after whose likeness I might train myself with the
greatest possible care. If I had applied myself to the best, I was
afraid either that the difficulty of the task might deter me from the
outset or that the tremendous burden that I had assumed might
break me, since I knew that I had profited too little from the examples and comparison of the finest and most famous writers. But
if I should surrender myself to the mediocre, I had a real hope
that, after I had profited from them as much as I wanted, my transition to the writers whom people considered the best might be
both easier and more secure. But I was troubled because I heard
that the first rudiments one learns tinge a style the way smells do a
new pot, and that this made a great difference.[25] I was also far
more willing to keep my mind and thought attentive when fixed
on the best and most excellent men. Yet timidity or my obviously
feeble will conquered the inclination leading me in the latter direction. I therefore dedicated myself to the instruction of teachers
whose writings I did not so much praise because they were good
as accept because they seemed more accessible and convenient to
imitate than did the best.[26]

After I had followed them for a while with great keenness and
care to the point where it seemed to me that I had achieved a great
part of what I had desired, I turned to those whom I thought, relying on the universal testimony of mankind, to be unquestionably
the best, so that I might likewise follow them and apply my mind
and spirit to drawing upon and imbibing their methods. After as-
siduously testing this approach again and again, I realized that I
had been deluded and deceived in my expectations. I saw that imitating other writers had not made it easier, but more difficult to
imitate the best. In fact they obstructed rather than cleared the
way to imitating the best. The effort that I had spent in copying
mediocre writers and which I thought would be useful to me was,
in fact, an impediment. After I had industriously trained and ac-

23

enim iam noster diligenti exercitatione illorum scribendi rationibus eruditus atque assuetus eundem morem diu retinuit, a quo,
quoniam aberat is quem de optimis hauriri oportebat, contra
quam existimaveram fiebat, ut scilicet multo minus ad eos expri-
mendos essem idoneus quam si me numquam mediocribus tradidissem. Quare multis me meis laboribus id unum esse assecutum
cognovi, ut imitari summos incipere mihi certe ne tum quidem li-
ceret, propterea quod ea didiceram animumque meum iis quasi
maculis infeceram, quibus residentibus perfectae rationis ulla in eo
depingi recte facies imagoque non posset.

24   Deleri vero ea, quae quis diuturno studio in animum induxit
suum, non tam saepe facile est quam oportet. Sed nihil est profecto tam perdifficile[28] tamque durum, quod non labore nostro
posse vinci superarique videatur, praesertim si in eo quantum facere et consequi possumus, contendamus. Itaque summa a nobis
adhibita diligentia. E memoria tandem nostra deletis penitus iis,
quae alte tunc imitatione non optimorum insederant, in ea rationibus omne meum studium ad illos contuli, optimos atque summos,
quos dico. In quo quantum profecerim si me roges, sane nihil tibi
respondebo, praeter hoc unum, mei me consilii non poenitere,
praesertim cum eorum scripta lego qui aut nullum aut omnes aut
non tantum optimos effingere praestareque voluerunt. Sed non de-
bebis tu quidem ab hac capescenda scribendi ratione absterreri,
etiam si minus tibi id, quod aliis persuadere cupimus, videmur
esse ipsi consequuti. Non enim, quantum potuimus, in eo impen-
dimus vel temporis vel laboris, quippe qui etiam vernaculo sermone quaedam conscripsimus cum prosa oratione tum metro
plane ac versu. Ad quae quidem conscribenda eo maiore studio in-
cubuimus quod ita depravata multa atque perversa iam a plurimis
ea in lingua tradebantur, obsoleto prope recto illo usu atque proprio scribendi, brevi ut videretur, nisi quis eam sustentavisset, eo

customed my mind to their methods of writing, it long retained the same character. Since this character was far from what I should have been drawing from the best writers, the opposite of what I had expected happened, namely, I was much less capable of copying the best than if I had never devoted myself to the mediocre. Hence I realized that my many labors had achieved just this one result, so that not even then could I begin imitating the best writers, because I had learned these other stylistic traits and had tainted my mind with them as if with stains. So long as what I had first learned remained in my mind, no shape and image of the perfect method could be correctly depicted in it.

It often is not so easy as it ought to be to efface what a man has instilled in his mind by long study. But really, nothing is so very difficult and so hard that it seems we cannot conquer and overcome it by our efforts,[27] especially if we try as hard as we can. I therefore applied myself with the greatest diligence. After I had completely erased from my memory those stylistic traits, which by then had become deeply seated from imitating inferior writers, I turned all my efforts on the greatest and best, those of whom I speak. If you should ask me how much I have achieved here, I shall of course say nothing except this: I am not sorry for my decision, especially when I read the writings of people who have not wanted to copy and outdo any single author, or those who want to copy and outdo all authors or inferior authors. But you should not be deterred from undertaking this method of composition even if I seem to you not to have achieved myself what I want to persuade others to try. For I have not spent as much time or labor therein as I could have, since I have also written certain vernacular works in both prose and verse.[28] I brooded over these writings with that much more effort because a great many were already producing in that language many works that were so depraved and perverse — correct and proper compositional method having nearly disappeared — that it seemed that very soon, unless

24

prolapsura, ut diutissime sine honore, sine splendore, sine ullo cultu dignitateque iaceret. Quare non oportebit te exemplum a nostris scriptis capere, ut quantum nos latino sermone optimis imitandis aemulandisque profecimus, tantundem putes alios nec eo amplius iisdem artibus posse proficere, sed id potius cogitare, cum nos certe aliquid ea simus via consecuti (si modo id aliquid est, quod a nobis confectum est) qui quidem [tamen]²⁹ alias etiam scribendi vias ingressi sumus, illos qui nihil agere, nihil conari aliud statuent praeter id unum, in eo plane esse quaecumque volent consecuturos.

25   Habes omnem rationem consilii mei, quoque pacto in eam tandem sententiam, quae tibi quoque vellem probari posset, venerim, quam perplexis cogitationibus, quibus maeandris, vides. In qua porro adhuc eo libentius conquiesco, quod aliis prius tentatis omnibus diligenter orationum³⁰ viis ea me tamquam portus ex longo errore diu iactatum excepit. Hanc qui et initio ingredi poterunt et ingressi numquam se ab ea deflecti sinent—quemadmodum illi qui in cursu nihil offendunt, celerius curriculum conficiunt, quam qui lapsi aliquotiens sunt, sic ipsi ad metam citius sine ulla offensione pervenient—quamcumque iis metam suum sive ingenium sive industria sive omnino utrumque statuerit. Quod profecto etiam sub fortuna positum atque casu interdum videtur, ita multa in vita saepe accidunt, quae avocent ab instituto³¹ animum aliorsumque quam oportet ducant. Sed illud tenere omnes debebunt et, quantum in quoque est, niti atque perficere, qui aut oratoriae aut poetices studiis delectabuntur, ut cum Ciceronem tum Virgilium semel complexi numquam dimittant, numquam ullis aliorum scriptorum illecebris ab eorum imitatione aemulationeque revocentur. Qui si non ita omnibus artis atque ingenii luminibus abundarent, si non universis scribendi virtutibus praediti cumulatique

someone offered it support, it would collapse and lie for a long time without honor, without splendor, without any devotion and respect.[29] You shouldn't then take my writings as an example and conclude that others can accomplish only so much and no more in the same arts as I have accomplished in Latin by imitating and emulating the best writers. You should rather think that, while I have certainly achieved something by following that path (assuming I have achieved something) even though I have gone down other roads of composition as well, whoever decides to concentrate on this one approach to composition will surely achieve whatever he desires therein.

You have a full account of my reasoning. You see how perplexed 25 were my thoughts, by what meanderings I at last came to the view that I wish you too could approve of. I now rest even more content with this theory because, after diligently trying all other routes to eloquence, this one brought me safely to port after long wandering on stormy seas. Those who will be able to enter this course from the start and, having entered it, will never permit themselves to be turned from it, will achieve whatever goal their own talent or industry or both has determined for them; just as runners who avoid stumbling will finish the race sooner than the ones who repeatedly slip, so those engaged in literary imitation will reach their goal more swiftly themselves if they avoid stumbling. To be sure, this sometimes seems to depend on fortune and chance. So many things happen in life that summon one's soul from its designated pathway and lead it in the wrong direction. But those who will take delight in the study of oratory or poetry will be obliged to stick to this path and try to complete it to the best of their ability, so that having once embraced Cicero and Virgil, they will not let go, they will not be distracted from imitating and rivalling them by the enticements offered by other writers. If these two authors did not so abound in every brilliant skill and talent, if they were

conspicerentur, essent autem ipsi ceteris una tantum virtute proba-
tiores, tamen eos nos unos sequi tantummodo imitarique dicerem
oportere, propterea quod vicinius ad perfectam rationem illis duci-
bus, quam ullis aliis progredi et contendere³² possemus. Nunc vero
cum nulla omnino virtus, nullum scribendi lumen, nulla egregia
indoles, nulla laus in ullo sit, quae non in utrovis eorum inesse
longe etiam praestantior atque absolutior reperiatur, multo id nobis erit constantius, multo diligentius faciendum, ne si alios imitandos sumpserimus, vel pravi iudicii vel imbecilli animi notam su-
beamus, cum aut in eligendo non prudentes aut in aggrediendo
timidi fuisse videamur.

26   Nam de Virgilio quidem nemo ambigit omnes in uno illo omnium poetarum (de latinis loquor) inveniri³³ posse virtutes summa
singularique dignitate. Addunt etiam admirabiliores, multo singulas et praestabiliores, ut si natura ipsa, hominum rerumque omnium parens, ea loqui versibus voluisset quae ab ipso perscripta
sunt, nec melius affirment, nec omnino aliter fuisse locuturam. Ciceronem quidam aiunt verbosiorem esse interdum quam necesse
sit, praesertim cum³⁴ de rebus a sese gestis deque consulatu illo
suo mentionem facit.³⁵ Ceterum illum non modo omnium eloquentissimum fuisse, sed ab eo eloquentiam ipsam esse genitam
atque natam putant. Ego vero id neque vituperare audeo. Potest
enim illi concessisse saepe dignitas sua aut inimicorum improbitas
aut reipublicae status aliquis aut³⁶ alia omnino causa atque respec-
tus.³⁷ Quare quae aliquibus supervacua in legendo videntur, ea in
agendo necessaria fuisse a multis poterunt existimari.

27   Neque defendere magnopere laboro, id enim si peccatum est,
non stili culpa sed animi vitio contractum est, addo etiam, si vis,
iudicii quadam perversione. Dum quae ab ipso praetereunda silen-

not seen to be naturally endowed and loaded with every literary virtue, but warranted more esteem than others for only a single virtue, I would still say that we should follow and imitate them alone because we could advance and draw closer to the perfect method under their leadership than under that of any others. But as it is, since there is no virtue at all, no stylistic brilliance, no remarkable gift, no topic of praise in any writer that is not to be found in far more excellent and purer form in these two writers, we will have to follow them all the more steadily, all the more diligently lest, by undertaking to imitate other writers, we gain the reputation of having either bad judgment or a weak intellect, since we would seem to have been either imprudent in our choice or timid in our pursuit.

Regarding Virgil no one doubts that all the virtues of all the 26 poets (I mean Latin poets) can be found in this one poet expressed with the highest and unparalleled dignity.[30] People add too that each of these virtues are so admirable and excellent that if Nature herself, the parent of all humanity and of creation, should wish to express in verse the things he had written, she would not speak, they maintain, either better or differently in any way. Some say that Cicero was sometimes more verbose than necessary, especially when he mentions his own accomplishments and his own consulship.[31] Yet they also think that he was not only the most eloquent of all men, but that eloquence itself was begotten and born of him.[32] For my part I dare not criticize that idea. Allowances can be made for the requirements of his own dignity, the wickedness of his enemies, crises in the republic or other reasons and considerations. So the things that appear superfluous to some when written down, many others can regard as necessary to actual delivery.

I don't belabor his defense, for if this [alleged verbosity] is a 27 failing, it is not a stylistic fault but the result of a spiritual flaw, even of a kind of perverse judgment, if you will. While it seemed

tio fuerant, ea illi digna visa sunt quae recenserentur; stilus vero et scribendi ratio eandem illam egregiam praeclaramque semper indolem retinet, eundem orationis splendorem ac[38] maiestatem praefert. Quamobrem non tam quidem accusandus esse videtur (si modo accusandus est) quod ea saepe commemoret quae a se reticeri aequius fuit, quam laudandus quod ita semper loquatur, ut commemorari aptius[39] non queant. Quid si iidem etiam parum constantem fuisse illum dixerint aut omnino imbecilliorem quam vel ratio vel eius dignitas postulabat? Num erit nobis propterea ab imitatione repellendus? Mihi plane, si idem sentiam — quamquam quid ego male mehercule sentiam de tanto viro? — sed si ego quoque idem sensero, mihi eius fortasse vita non usquequaque probabitur; orationis autem et stili ratio nihil improbabitur, qui esse optimus in vita non optima potest.

28   Tametsi id quidem, etiam si orationis esse vitium iudicetur, non ego huius imitationis aut ita partis extendo praestanda ut vitia sint, nec solum ut in facie naevi, sed ulcera etiam et cicatrices sint exprimendae. Quod qui faciunt merito ab Horatio, eo quem tu locum affers, irridentur. Aut modum praefinio sic, ut si quis tam praestans ingenio est, tam industrius, tam etiam felix ut anteire magistrum possit, tamen id fieri negem debere, cumque is illum ceteris in rebus aequaverit, si prudentiam adhibere maiorem volet, non probem. Mihi quidem et Phidias et Polycletus probantur, quorum alter Eladum sculpendis, alter Ageladem fingendis imaginibus, quos habebant magistros, superaverunt. Et Apelles, qui quidem in picturae artificio Pamphilum praeceptorem suum longissimo intervallo post se reliquit. Itaque valde mihi illud exoptandum esse videtur ita animatum, ita institutum[40] esse quempiam, spes ut illum sit omnium hominum eloquentissimum futurum, quod etsi longe maius atque praeclarius est quam quod temere sperandum esse videatur, nulla tamen naturae lex, nulla praescriptio prohibet conspici umquam ne possit. Etenim quemadmodum

right to him to recount things that should have been passed over in silence, his style and method of composition always remain uniformly remarkable and brilliant, always offer the same rhetorical splendor and dignity. It therefore seems that he should not so much be reprimanded (if he should be at all) because he often says things which it would have been better to omit, as praised because he always speaks of those things with a precision that could not be bettered. What if the same critics say that he was also too inconsistent or weaker than either his method or dignity demanded?[33] Must we therefore refuse to imitate him? If I were to feel the same way—although why, by Hercules, should I think ill of so great a man?—but if I too must share their feelings, I shall perhaps not approve of his life in every respect.[34] Yet no disapproval should be expressed concerning the pattern of his eloquence and style, which can be most excellent in a life that is not so.

28 Yet even if one should judge this verbosity a rhetorical fault, neither do I believe that we should imitate any part of his speech in such a way that we must present its faults, as if not only moles on a face but even wounds and scars were to be copied. Horace is right, in the passage you allude to, to ridicule people who do this.[35] Nor do I prescribe limits so that, if a man is remarkably talented, industrious and fortunate and can surpass his teacher, I don't say that he shouldn't do it. I wouldn't disapprove if he wants to exhibit greater technical mastery when he has equaled his master in other respects. I approve of both Phidias and Polyclitus, the former of whom excelled his teacher Eladus in sculpting, the latter his teacher Agelades in painting. There is also Apelles who left his instructor Pamphilius far behind in the art of painting.[36] Thus it seems that I should very much long for one so well disposed, so well instructed that we may hope him to become the most eloquent of all men. Even if this is something greater and more glorious than what it seems we should rashly hope for, still there is no law of nature, no stipulation that prohibits him from winning dis-

Cicero inter Latinos extitit, nam de Graecis nihil loquor,[41] qui
unus omnes quicumque ante illum boni scribendi magistri fuerunt, excelleret, quod quidem magnum atque divinum fuit, sic
profecto alius existere aliquando poterit, a quo cum reliqui omnes
tum etiam ipse Cicero superetur. Id autem nullo modo accidere facilius potest quam si quem anteire maxime cupimus, eum maxime
imitemur. Absurdum est enim confidere nos aliam invenire viam
posse quae melior sit quam est illa via quam Cicero, non tam quidem invenit ipse, quam ab aliis inventam ampliorem et illustrio-
rem reddidit, praesertim, cum, quo tempore id fieri necesse est,
quantum ipsi plane possumus, nondum exploratum habeamus.
Quod si quem maxime imitati fuerimus etiam assequemur, tum
adhibenda cura erit ut illum anteire valeamus. Sed omne nostrum
studium, omnis labor, omnis nostra cogitatio in iis assequendis
quos imitamur maxime omnium est insumenda. Non est enim
tam arduum eos superare atque vincere quos assecutus sis quam
assequi quos imitere.

29   Quare hoc in genere toto, Pice, ea esse lex potest. Primum, ut
qui sit omnium optimus, eum nobis imitandum proponamus:
deinde sic imitemur ut assequi contendamus: nostra demum
contentio omnis id respiciat, ut quem assecuti fuerimus, etiam
praetereamus. Itaque duas illas in animis nostris egregias pluri-
marum maximarumque rerum confectrices, aemulationem atque
spem, habeamus. Sed aemulatio semper cum imitatione coniuncta
sit; spes vero ipsa nostra non tam quidem imitationem quam suc-
cessum imitationis subsequi rectissime potest. Ac Ciceronis quidem imitatio omnibus, qui pedestri oratione scribere aliquid volent, opportuna esse poterit, quacumque illi de re atque materia sit
scribendum; idem enim stilus aptari rebus innumerabilibus potest.
Nec audiendi sunt, qui existimant Plinianam *De natura rerum historiam* Ciceroniano scribendi modo atque via tam percommode[42] ex-
plicari non potuisse, ut ab ipso est more illo suo explicata, quod
oportuisset in infinitam magnitudinem opus excrevisse, si ad illas

tinction. In fact, just as Cicero became eminent among Latin speakers (I say nothing of the Greeks) and alone surpassed all the fine masters of rhetoric who came before him—certainly a great and divine feat—, so it is perfectly possible that another will some-day become eminent and surpass everyone else, including Cicero himself. The easiest way that can happen, however, is by imitating most the person we want most to excel. It is absurd to believe that we can invent a better way than the one Cicero invented. He did not invent it himself, to be sure, but he did render richer and more brilliant what others had discovered This is especially true since, at the point in our development when this has to be done, we have not yet tested how much we are really capable of. If we shall ever equal those whom we shall have most imitated, at that point we should try to surpass them.[37] But first we should apply all our effort, all our labor, all our thought to equaling our models. For it is not so difficult to overcome and defeat those whom you have equaled as it is to equal those whom you are imitating.[38]

So this, Pico, can be our rule in everything of this kind: first, that we set before ourselves for imitation the best of all models; then, that we imitate that person with the aim of equaling him; and finally, that all our efforts have in view outstripping the man we have equaled. Thus we should harbor in our minds those two distinguished accomplices in most great affairs—emulation and expectation. But we should always couple emulation with imita-tion. And our expectation can most correctly follow not so much imitation as its success. The imitation of Cicero will be perfectly suitable for all those who wish to write in prose, whatever the sub-ject or material they must address, for the same style can be adapted to countless subjects. Nor should we pay attention to those who believe that Pliny [the Elder] could not have expounded his *Natural History* as conveniently in Cicero's mode or way of writ-ing as he did in his own manner. That work, they claim, would necessarily have grown to unbounded length if Cicero had added

29

multiplices innumerabilesque res de quibus erat scribendum exuberantiam Cicero suam ornatumque sermonis adiunxisset. Neque enim in omnibus eius scriptis, cum idem sit stilus, eadem tamen amplitudo inesse, idem verborum apparatus conspicitur. Sed quaedam uberiora sunt et tamquam succiplena, quaedam exilia et suo tantum robore nitentia, ut esse quasi sine cortice videantur. Neque si crescere eorum librorum magnitudo debuisset, non propterea fuissent ipsi nobis multo etiam gratiores, cum quanto plus ab eius calamo atramenti, tanto plus ab ingenio atque artificio dignitatis et pulchritudinis hausissent.

30   De Virgilio vero non idem possumus dicere, ut idoneus sit, quem, qui carminibus delectantur, imitari omnes queant. Neque enim qui aut elegos aut lyricos conficiunt versus, quique vel comoediarum vel tragoediarum[43] scribendarum studio detinentur, horum ullos Virgiliana carminum structura, numerus, ratio ipsa multum iuvabit. Sed imitentur ii quidem eos quos habent principes singulis in scriptorum generibus singulos atque illis assequendis superandisque sese dedant. Quod profecto nos aliquando fecimus, ut in elegis pangendis, qui optimus eo in genere poematis nobis visus est, eum imitaremur. Heroicis autem conscribendis carminibus qui se dederit, huic certe erit Virgilius ediscendus, ebibendus et quam maxime fieri poterit exprimendus, quemadmodum coram tibi dixeram, mihi videri.

31   Atque hanc quidem cum Virgilii, tum Ciceronis, tum aliorum excellentium in suo cuiusque genere scriptorum expressionem non ita intellegi volo, ut praeter stilum et scribendi rationem (uti autem me iisdem saepius verbis non paenitebit), nihil omnino a quoquam sumendum existimem. Nam et licuit id quidem certe omnibus et semper licebit. Quis enim opus legitimum conficere potest ullum qui nihil mutuetur, nihil a quoquam sumat, quod scriptis inserat atque interspergat suis? Quis non aut sententias aut similitudines comparationesque aut alias scribendi figuras atque lumina? Quis non aut locorum aut temporum descriptiones aut or-

his own luxurious and ornate speech to the manifold and innumerable matters that Pliny had to write about.[39] Although the style is the same in all Cicero's writings, neither the amplitude nor the verbal resources are conspicuously uniform in them. Certain works are richer and juicier; others thinner, relying only on their own robust strength, so they seem, as it were, stripped of their shell. If the length of Pliny's books had had to grow, they would have charmed us all the more for it. The more ink they would have drawn from Cicero's pen, the more dignity and beauty they would have derived from his talent and craftsmanship.

We cannot say the same thing about Virgil, that he is a suitable   30
model and that everyone who enjoys poetry should imitate him. For no one who composes either elegiac or lyric verse or is occupied in writing tragedy or comedy will profit much from Virgil's poetical structure, meter or general method. They should rather imitate whomever they consider the leading representatives of each literary genre and should devote themselves to equaling and surpassing them. I have done this myself at times. In composing elegies, for example, I imitated the poet who seemed to me the best in that genre.[40] But it seems to me that whoever dedicates himself to writing heroic verse will surely have to study, imbibe and copy Virgil as much as possible, as I explained to you in person.

Yet when I talk about copying Virgil, Cicero and the best writer   31
of every literary genre, I don't mean that, apart from style and method of composition (I shall not regret using the same words too often), you should borrow nothing at all from anyone.[41] For that of course always has been and will be permitted to all. Who can produce any decent work without borrowing, without appropriating something from someone to sow and sprinkle about in his own writings? Who does not borrow either maxims or similes and comparisons or other figures and ornaments of composition? Or descriptions of either places or times or some arrangement or se-

dinem aliquem ac seriem? Quis non etiam aut belli aut pacis aut
tempestatum aut errorum aut consiliorum aut amorum aut aliarum omnino rerum exemplum aliquod ab iis capiat quos multum
perlegerit, quos diu in manibus habuerit, cum Latinis, tum Graecis, tum certe etiam vernaculis, ut sunt nonnulli excellentes in ea
lingua viri? Itaque liceat quicumque id facere vult, ut semper licuit, sumantque ab aliis qui scribunt quod videbitur. Sed parce id
et pudenter faciant, non sane quia sumere etiam recte multa ne-
queamus—possumus enim et multi magni atque clari viri idem fecerunt—sed propterea quod praeclarius est illa omnia invenire nos
et quasi parere quam ab aliis inventa mutuari. Maxime vero earum
rerum ratio tum probatur[44] laudabilisque est, si id perficimus ut
quae mutuati sumus ipsi, ea splendidiora illustrioraque nostris in
scriptis quam in eius a quo sumimus conspiciantur, ut non minor
in exornando laus quam in[45] inveniendo fuisse videatur. Neque
enim mihi placet Atilius, qui Sophoclis *Electram* optime scriptam
male transtulisse dicitur. Sed noster Maro, qui ab Hesiodi *Georgi-
corum* libris multa sumens atque in suos transferens, ea omnia reddidit meliora. Quamquam quidem eius generis ita multa Virgilia-
nos omnes libros referserunt, ut appareat non tam illud[46] quod ex
se promeret desideravisse quam quod anteiret ex industria quaesi-
visse, multoque plus in victoria gloriae quam in inventione po-
suisse videatur.

32   Qua te quidem de re omni eo monitum volui quod sunt quidam qui non solum ea quae ad stilum scriptionemque pertinent,
sed illa[47] etiam quae dico quaeque de genere alio sunt cum sumun-
tur, uno imitationis nomine[48] includant.[49] Qui quidem mihi Ciceronem eo, quo supra commemoravi loco, legisse parum videntur,
ubi ille, quid imitatio sit, definit. Nam si ea profecto *imitatio est qua
impellimur ut aliquorum similes in dicendo*[50] *esse valeamus*, in imitatione

quence? Or examples either of war or peace, storms, wanderings, deliberations, love affairs or all sorts of other things? Who does not appropriate something from the authors in which he is deeply read, the authors he has long held in his hands, be they Latin, Greek, and even vernacular authors—as there are some excellent writers in that language? Whoever wants to do this therefore should have the right to do so, as people always have had.[42] Let them borrow what they like from other writers. But they should do so sparingly and modestly. Not of course because we cannot properly borrow many things—for we can, and many great and famous men have done just that—but because it is more distinguished to invent and contrive all these things ourselves than to borrow the inventions of others. Our method in these matters will be most acceptable and praiseworthy if we make what we have borrowed more splendid and brilliant in our writings than they are in the author's from whom we take them, so that there seems to be no less praise in the embellishment than in the invention. I don't approve the case of Atilius, who is said to have badly translated Sophocles' *Electra*, which was superbly written.[43] But our Virgil, who borrowed a good deal from Hesiod's *Georgics* and transferred it to his own work of that name, improved everything that he borrowed.[44] Indeed, so many passages of this type are crammed into all of Virgil's works that he seems to have desired not so much to produce something of his own as to have intentionally sought out precedents, and he seems to have regarded victory [over his predecessors] as more glorious than invention.

With regard to this matter I wanted to warn you that certain people include under the one term "imitation" not only techniques pertaining to style and composition, but even those that I am now talking about and borrowings from another genre. I think these people have not read carefully the passage of Cicero I mentioned above where he defines imitation.[45] For, if "it is imitation that enables us to succeed in making our speech like others'," yet imita-

32

autem non stili modo sed etiam materiae, ordinis, sententiarum aliarumque plane rerum extra stilum positarum ratio includitur, quid est cur non ego Aeneae, Ascanii, Didonis, Latini, Turni, Laviniae[51] tantum mutatis nominibus Virgilii Aeneida mihi totam sumam aut etiam ne mutatis quidem? Sic enim illi fuero similior![52]

33 Quare si nolunt ii parum haerentia videri dicere, aliud sumere, aliud esse existiment imitari, et cum heroicorum Catulli versuum rationem imitatum fuisse Virgilium dixerint, si modo id volent dicere, tum si eum affirmabunt cum ab illo tum a ceteris vel Latinis vel certe Graecis non poetis modo, sed etiam oratoribus ac philosophis multa sumpsisse, verissime pronuntiabunt. Ac mihi quidem ipse interdum videris, cum tuas literas lego, ita sensisse ut utrum quis aliquem imitetur, an ab illo sumat quod in sua scripta transferat, differre nihil duxeris. Quod si est, equidem laetor, unius tantummodo verbi interpretatione mutata, rerum non minimarum neque sane spernendarum inter nos magna ex parte controversiam posse finiri, cum hoc certe modo, prope idem quod tu, omnes esse bonos imitandos facile dixero.[53]

34 Quid enim mihi esse aut propter nostram benivolentiam iucundius aut propter aliorum existimationem de tua doctrina laudabilius potest quam nulla me in re abs te magnopere dissentire, homine multarum maximarumque rerum disciplinis erudito, summo ingenio, summa integritate praedito, et in secunda fortuna temperato, in adversa erecto atque in omni vita magno ac probato viro? Cuius tam multi leguntur iam habenturque in manibus egregie perscripti libri, ut me non solum opinione hominum facile vincere, sed etiam obruere scriptis possis.

35 Sin vero aliter se res habet, tamen gaudeo nullas inter nos opinionum sententiarumque diversitates et contentiones[54] esse tantas

tion includes not only techniques of stylistic imitation, but also involves material, arrangement, maxims and other matters distinct from style, why don't I just appropriate all of Virgil's *Aeneid*, only changing the names of Aeneas, Ascanius, Dido, Latinus, Turnus and Lavinia, or even not changing them at all? I'll be even more like him that way!

If people want to avoid inconsistency, they should be aware   33
that borrowing and imitation are two different things.[46] And when they say that Virgil "imitated" Catullus' method of heroic versification — if that is what they want to say — then if they claim that he "borrowed" heavily both from him and from other authors as well, Greek as well as Latin, and not only from poets but even from orators and philosophers, what they say will be quite true. When I read your letter, you too sometimes seem to me to have felt that there is no difference between imitating someone and borrowing something for our own writings. If this is the case, I for my part am glad that, by changing the interpretation of only one word, we can in large part end the controversy between us over what is by no means a small or contemptible issue. For, understood in this way, I shall be saying pretty much the same thing as you, that all good authors are to be "imitated."

And what could give me greater pleasure than not disagreeing   34
much with a man towards whom I feel good will? What could be more laudable than not disagreeing with a man highly esteemed by others for his learning, a man learned in many important disciplines, a man of the highest abilities, the greatest integrity, who is temperate in good fortune, steadfast in adversity and great and esteemed in every part of life? So many of your outstandingly composed books are now being read and circulated that you could not only defeat me easily in public opinion, but even bury me under your writings.

But if the matter stands otherwise, I am still glad that no   35
differences and disputes over opinions and beliefs can be so great

posse tamque graves, quas profecto vel mea summa in te observantia vel[55] tuus erga me amor non levissime ferat. Praesertim cum de amore librum conscribas, de quo, qui ceteros doces, non vereor ne illud non didiceris, amandam esse imprimis veritatem. Idque qui faciat, in eo neminem laedere, aut etiam qui se facere existimat, nam id quidem in multis credi quam sciri facilius potest.

36   Quamquam non ego is sum qui me falli non putem posse, praesertim cum Aristoteleos tam multis in locis libros atque universam prope antiquorum philosophiam abs te reprehendi videam. Fieri enim potest ut quemadmodum ego recte me sentire existimo, qui tibi videor a veritate abesse longissime, ita tu recte sentias, cum mihi tamen videatur secus. Neque illud mihi assumo, ut his literis te atque ceteros, qui aliter sentiunt, ad meam opinionem atque sensum[56] traducam. Quid enim esset ineptius, quam cui aut Maro aut Cicero divina illa suorum scriptorum tot atque tantorum maiestate imitandos esse se non persuaserunt, id ei putare me una mea epistola persuasurum? Est tamen humani animi et, ut ego arbitror, non contemnendi, qua ipse verisimilitudine dubiis in rebus cognitioneque dignissimis ducatur, quam plurimos velle certos facere, ut aut reprehensione aliorum se corrigere aut comprobatione confirmare possit. Id me unum voluisse ut existimes, te etiam atque etiam rogo.

Vale. Romae Kalendis Ianuariis MDXIII.[57]

FINIS[58]

or so serious that either my great respect for you or your affection for me may not bear it as the lightest of burdens. Especially since you are writing a book on love,[47] and I have no doubt that you have learned about that subject what you teach others — that we should especially love the truth. Whoever does so injures no one thereby. Indeed whoever even thinks that he loves the truth injures no one, it being easier in the case of many people to believe than to know that they love truth.

I am not the type of man who thinks he cannot be mistaken, 36 especially when I see that you criticize so many passages in Aristotelian books, and almost all of ancient philosophy.[48] It is possible that, just as I think that I am right, though I seem to you very far from the truth, so too you may be right, though it seems otherwise to me. For my part I do not assume that this letter will win you and others who think differently over to my opinion and way of thinking. What could be more foolish than to think that with a single letter I am going to persuade someone that he should imitate Virgil and Cicero, when they have both failed to persuade him with the divine grandeur of their numerous great writings? Still, it is a characteristic of the human mind, and one I think by no means to be despised, to wish to inform as many people as possible of where probability in doubtful matters and where understanding in the most noble one lead a man, so he can either correct himself by means of the criticism of others or confirm his views by their approval. I beg you again and again to believe that this has been my only desire.

Rome, January 1, 1513.[49]

THE END

1   Ioannes Franciscus Picus Mirandulae Petro salutem.

Non eram nescius, Bembe, si quae de imitatione conceperam, ea ad te perscripsissem, fore ut in irritatos crabrones incurrerem; verum hoc me consolabar quod eorum aculeos plurimum habere dulcedinis et quidem suavissimae non ignorabam, ut qui sedem haberent in alvearibus dulcissimarum apum, quae tantum Arpinatis mellis ipso in ictu relinquere solerent, ut sine Paeoniis herbis, sine ulla vulneris obligatione, ipsa per sese sanitas accurreret. Qua in re me nihil sane fefellit opinio, tantum enim suavis acrimoniae prae se ferunt illi ipsi aculei, tantumque me tua simul et pupugit et oblectavit oratio, ut iterum pungi cupiam, quo possim iterum oblectari. Sed quamquam tu es in scribendo multo accuratissimus, locus autem ad me impugnandum amplissimus praeberi tibi videretur, quae tua tamen est modestia quibusdam illum quasi punctis angustum reddidisti. Nam et paucula quaepiam carpis et multa praeteris silentio. Multum vero de tuo imitationis instituto et naviter et docte perscribis. Ego vero ad omnia ea respondebo, et nonnulla etiam, si quando sese obtulerit occasio, quae priori epistola mea contra imitationem minime attuleram, non gravabor afferre, quo minus me paeniteat adversus morosos omnino, ne dicam scrupulosissimos, imitatores disseruisse.

2   Principio pugnare haec mea in epistola aut non cohaerere sibi videris existimasse, imitandos esse bonos omnis et imitatores vituperandos; putasti fortasse idem esse imitari simpliciter absoluteque et bonos omneis imitari. Quare, cum alterum laudarim, damnarim alterum, haud recte a me factum censere[1] queant probati re-

Gianfrancesco Pico to Pietro Bembo

Gianfrancesco Pico della Mirandola sends greetings to Pietro.   1

I was not unaware, Bembo, that I might stir up a hornets' nest[1]
if I wrote at length to you what I thought about imitation. But I
was consoled by the thought that hornets' stingers also bear in
them great sweetness, and indeed are utterly delightful, because
they live in the hives of the sweetest bees, which usually leave
so much Arpinian honey[2] in their sting that without Paeonian
herbs,[3] without any bandaging of the wound, it heals of its own
accord. My expectation in this matter has not at all deceived me.
Your stingers bear so much sweet pungency and so much has your
speech at once both stung and delighted me that I wish to be
stung again, to be once again delighted. Yet, although you are exceedingly careful in your letter and would seem to have given yourself ample space to assail me, your modesty has led you to narrow
your discussion down to certain "points", as it were.[4] For you
pluck out some small, random issues and pass over many in silence. But you do write, with energy and learning, a good deal on
your own principles of imitation. I shall respond to all that, and
also, if the opportunity offers itself, I shall not begrudge considering a few topics that I did not address in my earlier letter against
imitation. I don't want to regret having argued against fussy, not to
say extremely punctilious imitators.[5]

In the first place, you seem to have believed that the following   2
positions in my letter are contradictory or inconsistent: that we
should imitate all good writers and criticize imitators. You perhaps
thought that imitating all good writers means imitating them simply and absolutely.[6] So when I praised the former but condemned

rum aestimatores. Sed nulla est rerum, nulla est pugna verborum, neque enim illa eadem sed diversa sunt et ab alterutris longe semota, quandoquidem, cum 'omnes bonos' dixi, et unum etiam quempiam proprie atque signanter exclusi, quem, quisquis demum ille fuerit, qui duxerit omnino imitandum, et irridetur ab Horatio et a Platone condemnatur. Cur igitur eos laudaverim quos contempsit antiquitas? At qui Maronem aemulatorem dixi, qua parte aemulatio praestat imitationi, tantum abest ut eum inter imitatores collocaverim.

3   Neque opus fuit, Bembe, ut affirmarem imitari non oportere, quando non usquequaque nec unum quempiam, quod tute ipse arbitrabare, sed bonos omneis dixi nobis proponendos, ut imitaremur eis videlicet in rebus in quis maxime illos excelluisse putabamus. Nihilo tamen minus genium invertendum non esse penitus admonebam, sed dirigendum esse filum orationis ad cognatam animi propensionem ideamque dicendi. Laudavi sane eos qui[2] ab uno quoque excerpant sibi id, in quo similes merito, ut evadant, conari debeant; damnavi qui uniuscuiuspiam scriptoris naevos, cicatrices, vitia, excrementa effingere procurant, quae ita in corporis oratione quantumvis eximia cernuntur ac in humanis persaepe corporibus.

4   Potes igitur, Bembe, percipere me et dialecticae regulae illius non esse oblitum, repugnare sibi ipsi inter disputandum fas non esse, et frustra me ad Pauli Cortesii epistolam abs te fuisse relegatum, non propterea solum quod alia est inter te et me quam inter illum et Politianum fuit controversia, sed quoniam, quae Paulus conatus est, assecutum non magis illum vel aliud agens subiudicavi quam Politianum Tullianam scribendi rationem indeptum fuisse. Qua etiam in re tibi non assentior, quandoquidem potuisse illum existimo quemcumque voluisset scriptorem effingere eiusque rei aliquando praebuit indicia. Sed maluit ab eruditis haberi se homi-

the latter, the accepted experts in the field could hardly think me
right to do so. But there is no substantive contradiction here nor
one of language. These positions are not the same, but different
and quite distinct from one another. When I said "all good writers," I also especially and expressly omitted any one author whom
someone, whoever he might be, thought necessary to imitate exclusively. Horace derides and Plato condemns such an imitator.[7]
Why then should I have praised those whom antiquity despised?
Far from classifying him as an imitator, I called Virgil an emulator,
understanding emulation to be something superior to imitation.[8]

Nor did I need to assert, Bembo, that one ought not to imitate,   3
since what I said was that we should not imitate any one writer in
every respect, as you yourself used to think, but that we should
model ourselves on all good writers, imitating them in whatever
matters we thought they had most excelled. Nonetheless, I was
not advising anyone to turn his genius upside down but to order
his rhetorical style according to his spiritual propensity and the
idea of speech related to it.[9] Of course I praised those who excerpt
from anyone what merits their imitation. I condemned those who
are careful to reproduce any given writer's moles, scars, defects and
excrement, which draw attention to themselves in the body of a
speech as much as they do in human bodies.[10]

You can thus see, Bembo, that I have not forgotten that rule   4
of dialectic that one should never contradict oneself in a disputa-
tion, and you have referred me in vain to the letter of Paolo
Cortesi. For not only is the controversy between you and me
different from the one between Paolo and Poliziano, but it's my
impression that Paolo did not achieve what he attempted any
more than Poliziano attained the Tullian method of composition.
Even in this matter I do not agree with you, seeing as he could
have copied, I think, whatever writer he had wished, and has occasionally offered evidence to that effect.[11] But he preferred that the
learned consider him a man rather than an ape or one of the ser-

nem quam aut servum pecus aut simiam. Ac similitudo illa parentum quam nati referant, parum iuvit Cortesium, quamquam iuve-
nem ingeniosum et bene de literis merentem; extrinsecus illa
tantummodo cernitur; nec omnes naevos repraesentat nec capillo-
rum aut unguium quae multi affectant contemnenda praesegmina.
Suntque multi qui dissimiles parentibus habentur, egregio tamen
colore muniti et faciem et membra prae se ferenda, si non similia,
at notae minime deterioris; iudicanturque saepenumero non dege-
neres, sed longe praestantiores — ut mittam, quod haec filiorum
erga parentes imitatio natura constat, non arte, ut potior sit illa
simiae comparatio quam nati, cum hic affectatis gesticulationibus
patris vultum aut corporis reliqui habitum referre nequaquam possit; illa quoquomodo vel de longinquo hominum.

5   Quorum e numero, cum nequeas omni ex parte pulcherrimum
quod effingas corpus invenire, miror te pulcherrimum quod imite-
ris orationis corpus uno in scriptore prorsus invenisse, quod fieri
non posse tuo ex Cicerone rescire facile potuisti. Adde quod sub-
lunaria isthaec, ut etiam tibi antea plane testabar, non sunt omni
ex parte beata, cum distribuat Natura parens non uni tantum sed
multis sua munera, et suas unicuique rei propriasque virtutes elar-
giatur. Ex quo fit ut pulcherrimum illud quod quaeris orationis artificium ipsa in natura inque animo potissimum tibi, unde eius
proxima origo in verba et literas derivata[3] sit, indagandum, non
autem una uniuscuiuspiam authoris in pagina, in omnibus potius,
aut in plurimis omnium, quando uti in universo hoc quod oculis
cernimus, animantium omnium habitaculo, variae sunt rerum effi-
ciendarum sparsae virtutes, non coactae unam in oram, ita nec
uno in authore quasi angulo quopiam humanae reipublicae integra
et perfecta est norma loquendi constituta.

vile herd. And that similarity to one's parents that children show hardly helped Cortesi, although he was a talented youth who deserved well of literature. That likeness is only externally evident; it does not reproduce all the moles or hair or nail clippings which many think we should spurn. There are also many who are considered dissimilar from their parents who nevertheless possess a fine appearance, bearing a face and limbs that, if unlike their parents', are not at all of inferior stamp. In fact we often consider them not degenerate, but far superior. I let it pass that a son's imitation of his parents lies in nature, not in skill, so that the comparison with the ape is more apt than that with a son, in that the latter could not use affected gestures to bring to mind his father's face or the appearance of the rest of his body, while an ape can recall the appearance of a man after a fashion or from a distance.

Since you can nowhere discover an absolutely beautiful human body to depict, I am amazed that you have found an absolutely beautiful body of discourse to imitate in a single writer — something which you could have easily found out is an impossibility from your Cicero.[12] Add to this that sublunary things, as I clearly showed you before, are not in all ways blessed, although our Mother Nature distributes her gifts not just to one but to many and lavishes on each single thing her own distinctive virtues.[13] Hence you should investigate that most beautiful art of rhetoric that you seek most especially in Nature herself and in the soul, the proximate source from which it is derived in words and literature. This should not be done, however, on a single page of any single author, but rather in all or most of them. Just as in this universe that we see with our eyes, the home of all living beings, the various performative talents are scattered about rather than being gathered onto a single zone, so too the whole and perfect rule of speech has not been fixed in one author, as if in some corner of the human republic.

5

6   Cuius quidem rei priori in epistola multis te admonitum volui.
Sed quoniam satis ea non fuisse deprehendi, quoniam iterum du-
bitas et quid haec ipsa sit perfecta in animo species ideave dicendi
curiose sciscitaris, haud equidem dubitabo ea de re plura disserere,
et quamquam te ad Ciceronem relegare possum, nihilo tamen minus et quae ipse sentiat et quae ipse putem, ut omnis tandem a te
scrupulus extrudi possit et tuas hac de re dissolutas argumentationes agnoscere queas, susque deque narrare protinus aggrediar.
Quid (ait Cicero) *maius, quam cum tanta sit inter oratores bonos dissimilitudo, iudicare quae sit optima species et quasi figura dicendi?* A bono ad
optimum diiudicandum loquendi difficultas innascitur. Dices fortasse, Bembe, 'quaesivit illud ipsum Cicero; deinde invenit et,
quale nam esset, expressit.' At illum ipsum audi haec verba pro-
mentem. *Atque ego in summo oratore fingendo talem informabo, qualis
fortasse nemo fuit; non enim quaero quis fuerit, sed quid sit illud quo nihil
possit esse praestantius.* Fingit igitur Cicero qualem nec vidit nec
novit. At certe vidit in animo, quod enim fingitur ad alicuius imaginis exemplar, si nulla extat extrinsecus imago, ad eam ipsam imaginem quam mente gerit, quisquis ille fictor fuerit, id ipsum fabri-
cari necesse est.

7   Arrige aures, Bembe, et Ciceronis, non meis hauri verbis, quid
ipsa de idea orationis decernendum sit. *Ego*, inquit, *sic statuo, nihil
esse in ullo genere tam pulchrum, quo non pulchrius id sit unde illud ut ex
ore aliquo quasi et imago exprimatur. Quod neque oculis neque auribus
neque ullo sensu percipi potest; cogitatione tantum et mente complectimur.*
Idem, postea de Phidiae artificiosis imaginibus cum disseruisset,
non ex animali exemplo aut sculptis simulachris eas duxisse illum
affirmavit, sed *in ipsius* inquit

I intended in my earlier letter to suggest this to you in numer- 6
ous ways. But since I find that these remarks were insufficient,
since you still hesitate and ask particularly what is this notion or
idea of speech that is perfected in the soul, I shall for my part not
hesitate to say more on the subject. And although I can refer you
to Cicero, I nonetheless shall proceed to narrate indifferently both
what he himself thinks and what I believe, so that you may finally
be rid of every reservation and be able to see your arguments
about this business refuted. "Since there is such a great difference
among good orators," says Cicero, "what is a greater challenge than
judging which is the best type and figure, as it were, of speech?"[14]
It is inherently difficult to distinguish the best from merely good
speech. You will perhaps say, Bembo, "Cicero sought just that;
then found it and copied its qualities." Yet listen to the words of
Cicero himself: "In fashioning the best orator I shall construct
such a one as perhaps has never existed. For I am not asking who
he was, but what is that than which nothing more excellent could
exist."[15] Cicero therefore portrays an orator such as he neither saw
nor knew. But certainly he saw him in his soul. For that which is
fashioned after the likeness of some image, if no external image exists, must necessarily be made after the very image of that which
he bears in his mind, whoever the fashioner might be.

Pay attention, Bembo, and hear, not from my words, but from 7
Cicero's, what you should decide about the idea of oratory: "In my
judgment," he says, "there is nothing so beautiful in any genus that
may not be excelled in beauty by that from which it comes, like an
image that is copied from a face. That ideal source, which cannot
be perceived by eyes, ears or any sense, we grasp only in thought
and in mind."[16] Similarly, after discussing the skillfully made images of Phidias,[17] Cicero affirmed that the sculptor had produced
them not from a living model or from sculpted representations,
but "in his own mind," he said,

mente insidebat species pulchritudinis eximia quaedam, quam intuens in eaque defixus ad illius similitudinem artem manumque dirigebat. Ut igitur in formis et picturis est aliquid perfectum et excellens, cuius ad excogitatam speciem imitando referuntur ea, quae sub oculos ipsa non cadunt, sic perfectae eloquentiae speciem non videmus; effigiem auribus quaerimus. Has rerum formas appellat ideas ille non intellegendi solum, sed etiam dicendi gravissimus author Plato, easque gigni negat et ait semper esse ac ratione et intellegentia contineri; cetera nasci, fluere, occidere, labi, nec diutius esse uno eodem statu.

Qua de re magis miror te ab ipso quem colis Cicerone tantopere descivisse, qui affirmes te, non tua ex mentis penu, sed ex veterum libris traxisse et multo annorum spatio, multis laboribus ac longo usu exercitationeque et stili formam et dictandi simulachrum, nec ullum antea spectrum nec ullam prorsus imaginem bene dicendi tuo in animo conspexisse.

8 Verum enimvero, quando tu id fortasse nimia ex modestia et reris et scribis, ut quod tibi ipsi egregie loquendi munus acceptum referri debet, id antiquorum virtutibus quas aemulatus fueris tribuatur, ducam te per lineas quasdam sine maeandris ullis aut labyrinthis, quoad te ipsum et ad tuas animi dotes facilius pervenias; liceat enim mihi de te id, quod tibi de te ipsi non licet, et loqui et scribere. Tua illa, Bembe, commode apte Romaneque[4] dicendi virtus, nisi a te ipsa penderet, frustra Ciceronem legendo trivisses; quo pacto enim fieri queat non video, nisi nos ipsos ignoremus, ut Ciceronis cuipiam uni prae aliis scriptoribus placere possit oratio,

lay a certain uncommon notion of beauty. Intuiting this notion and fixing his attention on it he directed his skill and hand toward its likeness. So, as there is something perfect and excellent in sculptures and paintings, some contemplated form to which are related in imitation those things which do not themselves fall under the eyes, so too we do not see the Form of perfect eloquence; we seek its likeness with our ears. Plato, that gravest of authorities — not just on knowing but also on speaking — calls these forms of things "ideas," and denies that they come into being. He says that they always exist and are contained in our reason and intelligence. Other things are born, are in flux, die, corrupt and cease to exist in one and the same state.[18]

I am amazed that in this matter you have departed so far from that very Cicero whom you revere[19] — you who affirm that you have drawn the form of your style and model of your speech, not from your own mental storehouse, but from the books of the ancients over a great span of years with much labor, long practice and exercise — you who affirm that you have never seen any apparition or image of fine speech in your soul.

Indeed, since you perhaps think and write with too much modesty, so that the gift of distinguished eloquence that ought to be credited to you yourself is instead imputed to the virtues of the ancients whom you have emulated, let me lead you by certain threads without any meanderings or mazes to find yourself and your own spiritual gifts more easily. Permit me both to say and to write about you what you yourself cannot. If your ability, Bembo, to speak properly, fittingly and in a pure Roman manner did not depend on you yourself, you would have spent your time reading Cicero in vain. For unless we do not know ourselves, I don't see how it could be that Cicero's oratory, more than that of other writers, could please any given person who has not borne in his mind

8

qui eius ipsius orationis vel perfectam vel inchoatam imaginem
mente non gesserit, quando ea ipsa quispiam et ducitur et quaerit
et iudicat; simile enim simili (ut erat Democriti, nec sine ratione,
proverbium) divinitus copulatur.

9   Sed quid loquar de Tulliana oratione? Illa ipsa in universum,
qua de re tantopere loquitur Cicero, species ideave dicendi insidet
animo. Quae nisi insedisset, quo pacto fuisset tanto studio a multis atque ab ipso etiam auctore quaesita? Quod enim omnino
ignoratur, quaeri omnino non potest. Itaque si norat eam Cicero,
sane aut ex se aut aliunde illam novisse dixeris; si aliunde, unde-
nam quaeso? Ex aliorum libris? At fuisset inventa ex aliorum
animo, sed quonam pacto animus animum diversum potest in-
tueri, nisi verbis veluti signis atque indicibus et quibusdam quasi
speculis ad animalem reddendam imaginem natura fabricatis?
Quae quidem imago, quoniam diutius manere nequit, literarum
notis tamquam vinculis continetur; eam Platonici a primis illis
ideis fluere sanxerunt. Sed ubinam illae ideae et quo pacto inde
manarent animales imagines inter eos, non satis convenit; de-
generare quidem ipsas, cum deorsum exciperentur, plurimorum
consensu decretum est, adeo ut rationum potius cum illaberentur
in animos quam idearum appellatione dignas existimarent, pro
captu etiam et varia excipientium animorum conditione diversas,
quamquam suo in fonte nullam varietatem patiantur.

10   Atque hinc potes animadvertere minus recte sese habere quod
scripsisti, Xenophontem, Demosthenem, Platonem, Ciceronem,
alios *in ipso mundi ac rerum omnium auctore deo* recte scribendi speciem contemplatos. Cum enim inter sese diversissimi et sint et habeantur scriptores, aut exemplar diversitatis aut ipsos imitatores,
vel omnes vel plurimos, sive hebetudinis sive inertiae damnaveris.
Ad eam verius, quam propriis quisque in animis habebat ab ortu

either a perfect or inchoate image of his oratory. For it is by this very image that everyone is directed, searches and performs acts of judgment. Indeed, like is divinely related to like, as goes (and not without reason) the proverb of Democritus.[20]

What shall I say about Ciceronian speech? In general, this notion or idea of speech, about which Cicero says so much, resides in the soul.[21] If it had not, why would so many, including our authority himself, have sought it out so eagerly? For what is altogether unknown we cannot possibly seek. So if Cicero knew that idea, you will surely admit that he knew it either from himself or from another source; if from another, where ever do I seek it? From the books of other authors? I still would have found its source in their souls. Yet how can one soul intuit another without using words as signs, indicators and certain mirrors, as it were, fashioned by nature to produce an image in the soul? Since this image cannot endure for any length of time, it is retained by the characters of letters as if by bonds.[22] The Platonists have laid it down that it flows from the First Ideas. But there is no consensus as to where these ideas are and how psychic images flow between minds. Indeed, majority opinion decrees that the Forms degenerate when received below, so that they think it appropriate to call them "reasons" rather than "ideas" when they flow into souls.[23] They vary in proportion to [each soul's] capacity and the varying condition of the souls that receive them; while the Ideas undergo no variation in their source.

Hence you can see that you are not entirely correct in what you have written, that Xenophon, Demosthenes, Plato, Cicero and others have contemplated the notion of correct writing in God himself, the author of the world and all things. For since these writers are, and are considered to be, very different from one another, you will blame either the model of this diversity or the imitators themselves, whether all or most of them, either for dullness or laziness. They trained their thought more truly on the image

9

10

naturae insculptam et tamquam inustam imaginem respiciebant, quam et corporis temperamentum moderabatur, quod unusquisque obtinet ab alio diversum; illud tamen non ignorandum sublucere ipsa in mente perfectius quoddam simulachrum. Quo congenita ipsa et ex corporeis sensibus dissultans dicendi propensio et augeri possit et perfici atque ad excogitatam speciem imitando referri.

11 Qua ex re percipere facile poteris, cur non unum aliquem censuerim scriptorem omnium maximum atque summum, sed omnes bonos imitari oportere. Deest enim ille maximus, si perfecto illi quem gerimus animo ipsum committas. Dici enim non facile possit quantum is qui summus habebatur ipsa collatione decrescat. Ex omnibus autem facilius multo perfectio ipsa conflabitur, si quidem propriam unusquisque bonorum et peculiarem orationis virtutem sortitus non iniuria existimatur, sicut animum etiam et corpus, a quo illa ipsa pendet oratio. Quae sane ab exemplo petenda est, perfecto illo quidem, non uno aliquo chartis commendato. Magis autem ab omnibus bonis ea quam saepe diximus et nunc, ut eam ipsam inculcemus.

12 Videtur opus ratione, qua sparsae scilicet sunt virtutes ipsae et disseminatae, adeo ut unusquisque illorum proprium insigne gerat, quod non sit ei commune cum ceteris. *Tenenda autem sunt sua cuique non vitiosa, sed tamen propria;* ita enim censet Cicero. Atque id ipsum paulo post repetens, *expendere,* inquit, *oportebit quod quisque habeat sui, eaque moderari nec velle experiri quam se aliena deceant. Id enim maxime quemque decet quod est cuiusque suum maxime.* Sunt ne ista, Bembe, Tulliana verba singula quae subieci,

that each possessed engraved and burned, as it were, in his own soul from its natural origin. This image was moderated by the temperament of the body which is different in each person, yet we must not forget that a certain likeness shines in a more perfect way in the mind itself. Our congenital propensity to expression, torn to pieces by the [influence of] the bodily senses, may by means of this likeness be improved, perfected and directed in the process of imitation towards the form apprehended in thought.

You will now readily be able to see why I thought we should   11
imitate, not any one writer as the greatest and best, but every good one. For the greatest of writers is lacking when compared to the [perfect writer] we bear in our soul.[24] Indeed it would be difficult to say how much the writer who is considered the highest may suffer from that comparison. But we shall forge perfection much more easily from them all if each good writer who has been allotted his own particular virtue is fairly judged, just as he is judged on the soul and body he has been allotted and on which his eloquence depends. We should seek out this eloquence by example, to be sure, but by the perfect example, not by any single one put down on paper. It is rather from all good writers that we should look for the eloquence of which I have often spoken and now speak, in order to inculcate the thing itself.

It seems there is need for an account of how the abstract virtues   12
are sown and disseminated, so that each individual bears his own distinctive character which he does not share with others. "Each person must hold on to qualities that are not defective, but still peculiar to him," for this is what Cicero claims.[25] Repeating this notion a little later, he says that "we should weigh what each person possesses of his own, temper these qualities and not wish to try out how another man's would fit him. For what most belongs to any given person is most suited to him."[26] Are not these, Bembo, Cicero's very words that I have quoted, just like the others

sicuti et alia ex alio eius auctoris opere sumpta et sub oculos posita?

13   Ergo sequi debemus proprium animi instinctum et inditam innatamque propensionem, deinde variis aliorum virtutibus unum quiddam quasi corpus coagmentare. Sic pictor ille celebratus populum se dixit habuisse magistrum, sic ille alius quinque, non unam, virgines adhibuit ad simulachrum in Crotonis fano pingendum, quoniam uno in corpore non poterat[5] quae excellentem pulchritudinem omnino praesentarent reperiri. Praxiteles vero, cum una ex Phryne renudatam et ex mari surgentem Venerem effinxit, Cupidinem vero nullo ab animali exemplo praeterquam ex affectibus, quibus intus afficiebatur, expressit: satis dedit intellegi ex animo magis quam ex afformata quapiam et in materiam impressa imagine posse pulchritudinem effingi et manifestari, quando Cupidinem ipsum multo excellentissima pulchritudine praestitisse matri memoriae proditum est.

14   Ex animo itaque qui trahunt suo et qui ex multis aliorum in eloquendo virtutibus unum quasi corpus eloquentiae conficiunt, ii optime dicuntur imitari, non furari aut mendicare, quod ii praestant qui in concerpendis clausulis et hemistichiis veteris cuiuspiam auctoris consenescunt. Ii ipsi, si forte eveniat ut sine illo quem colunt peraegre proficiscantur aut casu quopiam impediantur, quo minus eius ipsius compotes sint, scribere illis nihilominus incumbat, haerent in vestigio nec hiscere verbum possunt. At si numquam loquantur nisi ex commentario aut numquam loquentur aut parcius omnino quam Lacones, deque aut nullis aut paucissimis rebus fiet oratio. Ergo vis orationis, quae conciliatrix est humanae societatis, semper erit ex commentario petenda? O vanitatem operosissimam, o servitutem incomparabilem hominum! instar avium caveis inclusarum, quae voces humanas et nullas, nisi

you have taken from another of his works and set before our eyes?[27]

We should therefore follow the instinct that is proper to and 13
the propensity that is inherent and innate in our soul, then join
together from the various virtues of others a sort of unique body.
This is why that celebrated painter said he considered the people his master,[28] why that other painter employed five maidens,
not one, to paint a portrait in the sanctuary at Croton, since
he could not find in any one body all the characteristics that could
represent the finest beauty.[29] Whereas Praxiteles used Phryne alone
to portray Venus nude and rising from the sea, he depicted Cupid
from no living model other than the passions that moved him
from within.[30] This example is sufficient to understand that beauty
can be portrayed and made manifest more from the soul than
from any image that has been formed and pressed into matter. For,
according to tradition, Cupid far surpassed his mother in the most
exquisite beauty.

So when people draw on their own soul and bring about some- 14
thing like a unique body of eloquence from the many rhetorical
virtues of others, we say that they are imitating in the finest possible way — not that they stealing or begging. Begging and stealing
are what people who grow old cutting up little clauses and hem-
stitches of some ancient author are best at.[31] If it should happen
that they set out from home alone without the one they worship
or become entangled in some situation where they do not have ac-
cess to him but are still obliged to write, they stop in their tracks;
they cannot utter a word. But if they never speak except from
their notebooks, or if they will never speak, or speak more sparingly than the Spartans, their oratory will deal with few matters or
none. Shall we always have to look for the power of rhetoric, the
conciliator of human society, in notebooks? What laborious van-
ity, what incomparable servitude men endure! They are like birds
shut up in cages, unable to utter a human sound or any sounds

quibus identidem ferulae etiam magisterio assueverint, reddere nequeunt.

15   Ac sane Marci Tullii de imitatione definitio quam attulisti nobis abunde suffragatur, tantum abest ut refragetur aut noceat. Nam 'aliquorum similes esse' oportere docuit qui imitarentur notas[6] alicuius, id autem est imitari virtutes, vitia relinquere; similis enim potest quispiam esse Ciceronis in facilitate et perspicuitate et maiestate, Caesaris in elegantia verborum et candore, Sallustii in brevitate et sententiarum gravitate, Columellae in ornamentis, Celsi in nitore, Plinii in lenitate. Idemque poterit elumbe illud et redundans et Asianum (si quod tamen est, at certe et antiqui et magni auctores ita sensere), in Cicerone damnatum effugere, eiusdem auctoris repetitiones nimias declinare, cavere a siccitate Cornelii, a nimiis Columellae floribus, a neglectu Caesaris, ab obsoletis et Catonianis Sallustii verbis abstinere. Neque enim tua illa recipio, imitatores cuiuspiam auctoris totam eius stili faciem exprimere oportere. Quod si naevi illam infuscarint, quid erit causae ut nequeant lucem pro tenebris reponere? Si etiam vulnera malas aut nasum deformarint, frontem aut oculos tantum nequeam imitari? Quasi aperta[7] Lacaenae et operta Thespiae non potuerit Apelles dumtaxat exprimere aut Lampete supercilia tantum aut aliqua solum ex iis quae apud Philoxenum laudavit Cyclops in Galatea. Poterit inquam id praestare is, qui ita erit animo affectus, ut quod est uniuscuiusque optimum et experiatur et agnoscat in sese, ut id tandem sequatur et ab eo quod illi est adversum penitus abhorreat.

16   Neque enim eum, qui huic obeundo muneri sit aptus, volo ut mentis emotae, ut obliviosus, ut tardus sit, sed perspicaci ingenio, memoria tenaci, solertia praeterea et industria non mediocri. Neque etiam volo, ut ex hoc et ex illo quicquam decerpat, ut ex modis loquendi dissimilibus ita orationem tamquam ex diversis

other than exactly the ones they have been schooled in by the fer-
ule of their master!

Surely Cicero's definition of imitation that you quoted, far from   15
challenging or doing damage to my position, fully supports it.[32]
For he taught that those who imitate the distinctive features of
some one author should "be like several authors," that is, they
should imitate their virtues but avoid their faults. For anyone
can be similar to Cicero in ease, clarity and grandeur; to Caesar
in elegance and simple language; to Sallust in brevity and gravity
of thought; to Columella in ornamentation; to Celsus in brilliance; to Pliny in smoothness. He will also be able to escape
that same lumbering, redundant and Asian quality (if it actually
exists, though great and ancient writers certainly thought so) that
was criticized in Cicero, avoid the latter's excessive repetitions, beware Tacitus' dryness, Columella's excessively florid prose, Caesar's
carelessness, abstain from the obsolete and Catonian language of
Sallust.[33] I do not agree with you that imitators of any writer
should express the entire face or appearance of his style. If moles
blemish it, why can't they replace the dark spots with light? If
scars deform the cheeks or nose, can't I imitate just the brow or
eyes? It's like saying that Apelles couldn't have copied just the ex-
posed features of the Spartan woman and the concealed ones of
the Thespian, or only the eyebrows of Lampetia, or only some of
the qualities that Philoxenus' Cyclops praised in Galatea?[34] The
imitator will be able to make manifest the best features, I say, if his
soul is in such a state that he can experience and recognize in himself what is the best in any single model, so that in the end he follows that, and is deeply repelled by anything inconsistent with it.

I don't want anyone capable of employing this gift to be dis-   16
tracted, forgetful or slow, but endowed with a keen talent, tena-
cious memory, skill and uncommon industry. Nor do I want him
to pluck features out here and there and stitch together his speech
from dissimilar styles like a patchwork quilt out of different pieces

pannis centonem consuat, sed ut conflentur omnia, exque iis ipsis tua propria phrasis, quae nulla sit eorum, praeclara illa tamen et digna laude coalescat, atque ita instar apum diversis ex floribus, non ipsos exprimes flores, sed dulcissimum illud aut Hymettium aut Hyblaeum mel coagmentatum.

17 Atque haec quidem satis (ut puto) futura sunt pro refutandis iis quibus nostra de multorum imitatione et idea animi propria reiciebas; respondi enim ad epicheiremata omnia, quamquam singulis, non eodem modo. Nunc quod neminem unum, quod tamen tu conducere existimas, imitari oporteat, et de tuo inter imitandum instituto verba faciam.

18 Imitari nos unum quempiam omnibus in rebus et modis scriptorem nec debere nec posse prioribus literis patefactum existimabam, atque ex iis quae hactenus disputavimus opinor abunde confirmari potuisse. Sed minute magis tractanda res est et exemplis etiam ut arbitror munienda. Si nullum tuum iudicium, Bembe, in scribendo sequare, sed auctoritati cuiuspiam authoris omnibus in rebus pareas, quid tandem ex ipsa tua imitatione conficies? 'Similis,' dices, 'fiam.' At quonam pacto? 'Imitabor,' inquies, 'omnia quoad similis evasero.' Sed si prorsus eadem non dixeris et eodem modo, eisdem verbis, figuris, liniamentis, numeris? Dissimilis et eris et iudicabere, atque hac ratione imitator non fueris, quoniam talis, nisi a proposito recedas, esse non potes, nisi similis evaseris; sin autem ea omnia praestiteris, similem tute ipsum fortasse factum arbitraberis; alii vel illum quem imitaris non te, qualem vis haberi, esse decernent, aut furem aut merum exscriptorem iudica-

of cloth.[35] All its elements should flow together, and your own diction should emerge, which is not at all like theirs, but coalesces in such a way as to be distinguished and praiseworthy in its own right. Like bees sipping from different types of flower, your diction will not express the flowers themselves but the sweetest mixture of Hymettian or Hyblaean honey.[36]

These arguments will certainly suffice, I think, to refute your critique of my statements about imitating many writers and the Idea that belongs to the soul. For I have responded to all your syllogisms,[37] though individually and not in the same way as you presented them. Now let me say a few words about why one shouldn't imitate just one person, something which you consider beneficial, and about your own practice while imitating.   17

I thought that I had made it clear in my previous letter that we neither should nor could imitate any one writer in all matters and ways, and the foregoing discussion, I think, might have confirmed this view abundantly. But I think the matter should be treated in more detail and fortified with examples as well. If you never follow your own literary judgment, Bembo, but always obey the authority of some author, what will you accomplish with your imitation in the end? You will say, "I shall become similar to him." But how? "I shall imitate all his qualities," you will say, "to the point where I end up being similar to him." But what if you don't say exactly the same things, in the same manner and with the same words, figures of speech, features and rhythms? You will be, and you will be considered to be, unlike him. In this way you will not be an imitator, since (unless you depart from your plan) you cannot be such unless you turn out to be like him. If, however, you manifest all his characteristics, you yourself will perhaps think that you have become similar to him, but others will decide that you are not the man you are imitating, the kind of man you wish to appear, and they will judge you to be either a thief or a mere copier. Or don't   18

bunt. An ignoras proditum memoriae criticum illum Aristopha-
nem, consensu docti illius coetus ad Philadelphi litterarium certamen congregati, eum damnasse furti, qui materiam ex sese non
fabricasset orationis, hoc est, non propria esset usus inventione?
Quid putas futurum fuisse si alicuius authoris caesa et membra
furto sustulisset? Tantum prisca illa aetas monebat studiosos literarum, ut homines tandem vellent se esse non simias. Quod sub-
secuta saecula custodisse illud sit indicio, quod et Terentius a furis
nomine maximopere abhorruit et Manlius gloriatus est sese *non
furtum, sed opus* editurum, ut qui neminem unum sequeretur, quasi
tacito doceret imitatores nimios a furibus nihil omnino differre.

19   Dices non esse necessarium uti nos aliorum inventione ut similes habeamur iis quos duximus imitandos, sed opus esse nostram,
qualiscumque ea fuerit, veterum nominibus, tropis, numeris, clausulis, periodis, tamquam proprium corpus panno peregrinisque
coloribus circumvestiri. Sed larvae et simulachra et evanidae
umbrae potius quam homines dicentur iis similes, quos cupiunt
repraesentare; deerit enim vividum robur et[8] spiritus. Atqui prioribus in literis ostendimus inventionem quae tamquam materia orationis et est et habetur, et dispositionem quae illi aptetur, et elocutionem quae utrisque conveniat, sequi oportere; si secus fiat risus,
non demiratio excitabitur, quemadmodum fieri quandoque assolet,
cum pictores quidam postremi ordinis, nec symmetriae ullius nec
colorum nec umbrarum memores, extrema quaepiam lineamenta
ducunt praeclaris pictoribus forte similia, actutumque autumant se
illos probe fuisse imitatos. Sed evenit ut suis quas pinxerint imaginibus postea nomen inscribant eius ipsius quem[9] repraesentare cu-
piebant animalis; alioqui quidnam essent moliti, haud quaquam

you know about the famous critic Aristophanes?[38] With the consent of the learned company that had gathered for a literary contest at Philadelphia, he condemned a man for theft who had not fashioned the material for his speech on his own, that is, had not relied on his own invention. What do you think would have happened if he had stolen the phrases and clauses of a single author? The ancient world recommended this course of action to students of literature so much that in the end they wanted to be themselves, not apes. Proof that subsequent ages maintained that belief is the fact that Terence greatly abhorred the name thief,[39] and Manilius boasted that he was going to publish a "work of art, not of theft," because he followed no one person,[40] teaching us tacitly, as it were, that excessive imitators are no different from thieves.

You will say that we do not need to use others' invention to be 19 considered similar to those whom we believe we should imitate, but that we need to clothe our own power of invention, of whatever sort it will be, with the words of the ancients, their tropes, rhythms, clauses, and periods, like dressing our own bodies with rags and foreign colors. But people who resemble those they wish to imitate are called scarecrows, phantoms or vanishing shades, rather than men, for they lack the strength and spirit of living beings. In my previous letter, I showed that invention, which is, and is considered to be, the matter of oratory, should accord with an arrangement that fits it and a style suited to both the invention and the disposition.[41] If a person should do otherwise, the reaction will be laughter, not admiration, as sometimes happens when certain second-rate painters, paying no attention to symmetry, color or chiaroscuro, believe that some mere outlines in their work are perhaps similar to those of eminent painters, and forthwith claim that they have properly imitated them. But it turns out later on that they write on the images they paint the name of the ensouled person they wanted to reproduce. Otherwise no one could recognize what they had laboriously contrived. But even if

internosceretur. Quod si paulo etiam eruditiores fuerint, ni tamen ex animo id ipsum prompserint simulachri quale auctor ille prompsit quem imitantur, neutiquam similes futuri sunt, etiam si omnem operam curam, omnem denique diligentiam posuerint in imitando. Est id ipsum saepenumero videre in curiosis imitatoribus, qui scribendo cum nequeant quem maxime vellent imitari, similes sese tamen haberi et cupiunt et dicunt, non minus et amantes et admirantes sua quam suos delphini filios. Ac memini olim me hospitio ad multos menses quendam excepisse virum doctum alioqui, nec malorum ut videbatur morum, sed tanta in effingendo Cicerone cura, ne insaniam dixerim, laborabat, ut semetipse, dum quod volebat omnino non posset, assequi paene cruciaret. Quapropter saepe quae composuerat dum recitaret, ut qui se filium esse non nosset, exclamabat identidem repetebatque: 'Audite simiam Ciceronis!'

20   Fit etiam quandoque ut vel unum tantum ex multis detur assequi, et id quod proprie maximeque imitandum esset pervertatur, quod olim a discipulo quodam Apellis factum me legisse memini. Nam cum magistrum imitaretur in Helena pingenda ac simulachrum gemmis, margaritis, auro, purpura refersisset, Helenae pulchritudinem sibi ipsi expressisse videbatur; non ita tamen visum Apelli, qui divit<i>ae cultu pulchritudinem imitatam admonuit. Hoc ne aliud quam manum et colores non convenisse cum animo, cui iudicandae pulchritudinis et arbitrium et potestas. An putas, Bembe, ullos nostri temporis Ciceroni fore in loquendo similes, nisi in intellegendo etiam similes fuerint? Sane Augustinus eos non probat qui linguam Ciceronis tantum, non autem pectus admirantur, ut qui probe noverit eruditam et ornatam linguam, nisi ab exculti pectoris imaginibus, prodire non[10] potuisse.

they are a little better trained, unless they bring forth from their
soul the very substance of the likeness, similar to the one that the
artist himself whom they are imitating brought forth, they will not
be at all similar to him, even if they put all their effort, care and
diligence into imitating him. This same phenomenon can often be
seen in the case of excessively labored imitators. Although in their
writing they cannot imitate the one that they would most like to,
they nevertheless both wish to be considered, and say that they
are, similar to him. They love and admire their own works no less
than dolphins do their sons.[42] I once received as a guest for many
months, I remember, a certain man who was otherwise learned
and not, as it seemed, of bad character. Yet he used to labor with
such care, not to say mania, at copying Cicero that as long as he
could not achieve what he wanted he was nearly tortured to death.
For this reason while he was reciting what he had composed, he
would often shout over and over, like someone who did not recognize himself as Cicero's son, "Listen to the ape of Cicero!"

It also sometimes happens that a man follows only one model, 20
and that which he should most of all imitate in his own way he
perverts, which, I remember reading, is what a certain student of
Apelles once did. When he imitated his master in painting Helen
and had crammed the portrait with gems, pearls, gold and royal
purple, he himself thought he had copied Helen's beauty. But
Apelles did not. He admonished him that he had imitated her
beauty by worshipping riches.[43] What he meant was that his student's workmanship and colors were not attuned to his soul,
which has the ability and authority to judge beauty. Do you think,
Bembo, that any men of our time will be similar to Cicero in
speech, unless they will also be like him in understanding? Augustine surely does not approve of people who admire only Cicero's
tongue and not his heart, for he knew very well that learned and
ornate language could develop only from the images in a cultivated
heart.[44]

21   Hoc, quid est aliud quam cum forma convenire materiam, et
elocutionem inventioni, atque dispositioni ad unguem iungi, et
tamquam (ita dixerim) ferruminari oportere? Sed finge quaeso
te materiam eandem aut non dissimilem; finge etiam potiorem no-
bilioremque invenisse: putabisne propterea posse te illam ipsam
Tulliana elocutione pertractare? Ubi enim eaedem erunt periodi,
caesa, membra, pedes, et numeri apud illum semper varii? Quae
quidem varietas indepraehensa est. Alii enim habentur in actioni-
bus, nam illa omnino est popularis oratio. Alii in libris philosophiae quos[11] doctis scribebat. Alii in epistolis atque iidem etiam
saepenumero diversi, ut diversi erant et animi affectus, et res de
quibus agebatur, et homines quibus sua sensa per literas significa-
bat. Periodi caesis membrisque constituuntur; haec vero nominum
verborumque compositione atque conflatu constant. Illa vero com-
positio atque commixtio tam est varia quam sunt in oratione clausulae, quas magis ad numerum nosse non potes,

   quam scire quot Ionii veniant ad littora fluctus.

Sola enim verbi cuiuspiam transpositione variantur. Nec pedes et
numeri stati sunt atque perpetui; eos ad aurium iudicium, quod
est quidem longe diversissimum, Cicero delegavit. Quare non semper ab exemplari, quasi a praetoris edicto aut a XII tabulis, pe-
tendi sunt, sed ex animi auriumque sententia. Neque enim audiendi, qui etiam a bonis iudiciis explosi, existimant sese Ciceronis
imitatores esse, modo duo nomina vel ad summum tria in calce periodi scrupulose etiam observarint, ut illud *esse videretur,* quoad numeros saepe repetierint, et tui et mei loca, quantum spectat ad elegantiam, diutissime pensitarint, quasi haec ipsa etiam quandoque

Doesn't this mean that the matter of one's speech should agree 21
with its form, that its style should be precisely linked to its invention and arrangement, as if they were cemented together, as one
might say?[45] But suppose that your material is the same as or
not dissimilar to [Cicero's]. Suppose that you have found even
better and finer material. Will you think on that account that you
can handle it with Tullian elocution? Will there be the same periods, phrases, clauses, feet and rhythms that in Cicero are always so
varied? In fact this variety is baffling and hard to grasp. Some
rhythms are proper to lawsuits, this being an entirely popular sort
of rhetoric; others are proper to the philosophical treatises he
wrote for the learned; others to letters, and here the same rhythms
are quite often different as his emotions, the matters under discussion and the men to whom he wrote his feelings differed among
themselves. Periods are comprised of phrases and clauses; but
these latter elements consist of a combination and blending of
nouns and verbs. That composing and combining, however, are as
varied as are the clausulae in a speech, which you can no more
enumerate

than know how many Ionian waves come to shore.[46]

They are varied by the mere transposition of any given word.
Nor are his feet and rhythms static and constant. For these,
Cicero trusts the ear's judgment, which is very diverse indeed.[47] So
one should not always take them from a model, like a praetorian
edict or the Twelve Tables,[48] but from the judgment of one's soul
and ear. Even men who warrant no audience, who have been
booed offstage by good judgment, consider themselves imitators of
Cicero, provided that they carefully observe at most two or three
words at the close of a period (like his famous "it would seem to
be the case"),[49] regularly repeat his rhythms and mull over passages of mine or yours, for the longest time, for whatever they
have to teach about elegance, as if Cicero did not vary these very

ille non variaverit, diversis et pedibus et numeris et lineamentis usus.

22   Atqui gratis etiam tibi pro vetere nostra amicitia concedo, ut istiusmodi sandalia, de quibus priore epistola fecimus mentionem, e Romanis ruinis tibi asciveris, ut in vestigiis Ciceronis inoffense possis ambulare. Do etiam ut tuis pedibus instar Sicyonei calcei eleganter aptentur. Ad reliqua corporis membra cum perveneris, quid fiet? Neque enim ex sandaliis homines vestiuntur; amictus alii asciscendi sunt. Sed quoniam eorum nomina verius quam rem tenemus, et figurae magna ex parte nobis compertae non sunt, periculum erit opinor ne paludamentum pro toga, ne lacernam pro abolla, ne tunicam etiam pro chlamyde capias, tanta est antiquarum vestium nostris temporibus ignoratio; puto etiam quandoque deligi inconsulto posse pro sago mastrucam et sarrabaram. Sed eo etiam procede, ut imagineris Apellem te aut Zeuxim, Phidiam etiam et Praxitelem et Lysippum et Pyrgotelem excitasse ab inferis, ut tibi non vestes, sed corpus Ciceronis repraesentent; ubi enim magni illi artifices tibi vel penicillo vel caelo vel arte fusoria imaginem eius ipsius sub oculos posuerint, suo ipsorum erunt officio perfuncti; pictus tamen ille vel marmoreus vel aereus Cicero fuerit, non carneus. Do etiam aliquid plus: carnem quae Ciceronis fuerat assequantur imitando. At animum, at spiritum quibus illa ipsa caro informabatur, num igitur verus ille solum habendus Cicero, qui scilicet formam orationis concipiebat animo, et vividum robur adiciebat et gratiam, mox huiuscemodi omnes promebat animi motus interprete lingua? Oportet itaque gerere animo conceptus Ciceronis, esse praeterea instructos rerum multarum et magnarum doctrina et experimentis, eos qui se existimant vivam linguam Ciceronis esse consecutos, ne, si Tulliano careant[12] spiritu, eos Cato nuncupet *mortuaria glossaria*. Dices fortasse te verba primum observaturum, inde numeros et lineamenta structu-

techniques from time to time by using different feet, rhythms and features.[50]

In view of our old friendship, I concede to you free of charge   22
that you've adopted from the ruins of Rome slippers of the kind I mentioned in my earlier letter, and thus can walk unimpaired in Cicero's steps.[51] I also grant that they fit your feet as elegantly as Sicyonian boots.[52] What will happen when you come to the other parts of your body? For people do not clothe themselves with sandals; other garments are required. But since we understand their names more truly than the actual thing, and for the most part we do not know what they looked like, you will run the risk, I think, of taking a military coat for a toga, a traveling cloak for a long coat, even a tunic for a mantle, so great is the ignorance of ancient garments in our times. I think we occasionally can even mistake a sheepskin and Persian trousers for a military cloak. But go on and imagine that you are Apelles or have raised Zeuxis, Phidias, Praxiteles, Lysippus and Pyrgoteles from the underworld to reproduce for you not the garments but the body of Cicero. For when these great artists have used brush, chisel or the art of metal-casting and have set the image of Cicero himself before your eyes, they will have performed their duty. Yet this Cicero will be painted or marble or bronze, not flesh. I'll even grant something more: that they equal Cicero's flesh through imitation. But shouldn't we think that the only true Cicero was his soul and spirit which informed that flesh — the Cicero who envisioned the form of oratory in his soul, added living strength and grace to it and then expressed all these spiritual motions through the medium of his tongue? So whoever supposes that they have acquired the living tongue of Cicero should bear in their mind Cicero's conceptions; they should have experience and knowledge, moreover, of a great many important affairs. Otherwise, if they lack the Tullian spirit, Cato may call them "Glossaries of the Dead."[53] You will perhaps say that you will first observe his words, then his

ramque omnem, nihilque prorsus afferre quod non sit etiam alla-
tum a Cicerone, nec aliis omnino loqui de rebus velle quam de iis
de quibus ipse disseruit. Hoc furari erit, Bembe, non imitari. Hoc
Aristophanes ille non ferret, tantum abest ut probaret, quando
etiam ut poena afficeretur censuit qui quae alii dixissent suis in
lucubrationibus ipse rettulerit, idque eius iudicium totius paene
Graeciae, quae tum maxime literis florere credebatur, consensu publico est approbatum.

23 Venio ad imitandi rationem, qua te ipsi tibi proposuisse dicis Ciceronem prosa oratione, versu Vergilium, et quam tibi dediscere et
abolere[13] ex animo phrasim perdifficile fuerit, quam ex fontibus
auctorum secundi ordinis imbiberas, ut quae impedimento esset
hauriendae celebratissimorum auctorum elocutioni. Nequaquam
enim tibi rem futuram cum iis, qui se neminem imitari profiterentur, quoniam scribendo parum admodum profecisse tibi viderentur, et cum suis libris atque scriptis plane invisos ac despectos iacere. Ego quidem, ni te viderem, Bembe, tam Ciceroni addictum
quam qui maxime, et in eius non solum verba (quod dici assolet)
iurare, sed apices etiam literarum et puncta, quibus interstinguitur
lectio, tamquam in arcanis custodire, conarer in id, uti docerem
fieri non posse ut sis omnino similis Ciceroni. Hoc enim aperit ratio naturae, quam ars imitatur, quae eadem omnino esse non potest ubi est naturae ipsius in temperamento diversitas. Hoc dictat
idea sive species ipsa dicendi, quae ita sese habet, ut numerus auctore Aristotele, qui vel additione vel detractione unitatis tam va-
riat, ut sine ulla authoritate quilibet etiam e medio possit videre id
ipsum esse $\pi\hat{\alpha}\nu$ $\dot{\alpha}\lambda\eta\theta\acute{\epsilon}\varsigma$. Quod si dixeris te ex imitatione, si non

rhythms, features and entire structure, that you will employ no expression that Cicero did not use, and that you do not want to discuss any subject at all that he did not discuss. This will be stealing, Bembo, not imitation. This is something Aristophanes would not stand for, far from approving of it, since he even thought that anyone who repeated in his own lucubrations what others had already said should be punished for it, and this sentence of his was approved by the public consensus of almost all Greece, and at a time when its literary reputation was at its height.

I come to your account of imitation, where you say that you took Cicero for your model in prose and Virgil in verse, and how difficult it was for you to unlearn and clear from your mind the diction that you had imbibed from the fonts of second-rate authors, to the point where it impeded you from drinking in the style of the most celebrated ones.[54] You add that you will have nothing to do with people who profess to imitate no one, because they seem to you to have accomplished too little in composition and lie despised and rejected along with their books and writings. If I did not see that you are as addicted as anyone to Cicero, and that you not only swear by his words, as the saying goes,[55] but even stand guard upon the diacritical marks over his letters and the punctuation marks that speckle his work as if they were sacred mysteries, I would try to teach you that you cannot be entirely like Cicero.[56] This is clear from the order of nature which art imitates. The order of nature cannot be exactly the same where there is a natural difference in temperament. This temperament is dictated by the idea or form itself of speech whose constitution, according to Aristotle, is numerical. Number varies with the addition or subtraction of a unit, so that anyone can see from everyday experience, without any authority, that in itself it is "completely evident."[57] But if you say that from imitating someone you become, if not similar to him, nevertheless close to him to some extent, how I shall my-

similem, propinquum tamen aliqua ex parte fieri, ipse quidem tibi ut gratulabor, quod imitando profeceris atque inter imitatores, quando ita voluisti, egregium tibi locum vendicaveris.

24   Ita tamen non assentiar solum Ciceronem, quamquam eximius ille solent et extra omnem aleam haberi[14] prosa oratione, sic numeris omnibus consummatum ut despectis ceteris is nobis omnino sit proponendus, in quem nostra studia et cogitationes dirigamus; seligenda potius ea in quibus eminet et asciscendi ceteri sunt qui, quamquam aliqua re inferiores, praestare tamen aliis in rebus existimentur. Quod non solum iis, quibus usi sumus, rationibus tueri possumus, sed exemplo veterum omnium boni nominis scriptorum, qui non illum unum, sed multos potius imitati sunt, et se ipsos in primis secuti — hoc est, propriam animi ideam propensionemque dicendi, qua de re priori in epistola longo quodam discursu fecimus mentionem. Quorum exemplum secuti sunt nostra tempestate plurimi, inter quos Hermolaus Barbarus civis tuus, Ioannes Picus patruus meus, Angelus Politianus, et qui iis aetate anteibat Theodorus Thessalonicensis. Magnos hosce viros fuisse nec tu negaveris, nec ullus, arbitror, qui inter viros bonos et de literis bene audientes locum obtinuerit. Eorumne aliquis, te quaeso, Bembe, Ciceronem est imitatus figura dicendi? De Hermolao id afferre non potes, qui sese totum Pliniis addixit, Theodori sectator, qui in transferendis Aristotele et Theophrasto, Plinii, Celsi, Columellae delectatus est charactere, eis auctoribus quos interpretabatur consentaneo. Verbis sane quibusdam Ciceronis utitur, at non phrasi. Alioqui satis ei non fuisset quantum chartarum aut in Piceno aut in ripis Baenaci decennio conficitur. Et si quando aut epistolas scribit aut in vertendis auctoribus Graecis et Latio inferendis prooemiatur, dici iure non potest Ciceronis assecula.

self congratulate you! Yes, you have made progress via imitation
and you have claimed for yourself an illustrious place among imitators, since that is what you wished for.

Still, I shall not agree with the view that, however excep-   24
tional, however usual it is to consider him a risk-free model for
prose, only Cicero is so accomplished in all rhythms that we
should despise everyone else and give him our exclusive attention
and consideration. We should, rather, select the features that he
excels in and admit other authors as well. There are those who,
though inferior in some way, are still considered to excel in other
areas. I can defend this position not only with my previous arguments, but also by the example of all ancient writers of good re-
pute, who preferred to imitate not him alone but many men, and
who primarily followed themselves — that is, their own mental
idea and propensity of speech which I mentioned in the long discussion of this matter in my earlier letter.[58] Their example has
been followed in our time by many men, including your compatriot Ermolao Barbaro as well as my uncle Giovanni Pico, Angelo
Poliziano and Theodore of Salonika who lived in the previous period.[59] You will not deny that these are great men, nor would any
one, I think, who holds any status among good men and men with
some literary reputation.[60] I ask you, Bembo, has any of these men
imitated Cicero in the idiom of their speech? You cannot say that
of Ermolao, who dedicated himself entirely to the two Plinys. He
was a follower of Theodore who, in translating Aristotle and
Theophrastus, was delighted by the style of Pliny, Celsus and
Columella, a style that was suited to the authors he was translating.[61] To be sure, he uses certain words of Cicero, but not his diction. Otherwise the number of pages that are produced in ten
years either in Picenum or on the banks of the Benacus would not
have sufficed for him.[62] And if he occasionally either writes letters
or composes a preface when translating Greek authors into Latin,
he cannot rightly be called a follower or hanger-on of Cicero.

25   Patrui stilus (ut de incomparabili ingenio et doctrina sileam) Ciceroni magis accedit quam Plinio, sed proprium quiddam et peculiare prae se fert. Politianus varius in dicendo ut qui diversos quandoque voluerit effingere, crebrae tamen in eo acutaeque sententiae, multaque lectione et eruditione non vulgari sua refersit opera. Si hos, Bembe, nullum antiquitatis vestigium redolere putas, si 'invisos et despectos iacere,' quoniam vel omnes vel eorum aliqui 'se neminem imitari forte profiterentur,' tibi non subirascar quidem; monebo tamen ut dicas meliora, vivunt enim in memoria hominum victurique sunt, et forte magis, quo magis hominum studia processerint: neque enim reiicio Pindaricum illud:

    ἀμέραι δ᾽ ἐπίλοιποι
    μάρτυρες σοφώτατοι.

26   De me vero illud tantum afferam, bene mecum actum putaturum fuisse, si valuissem Ciceronem effingere tantisper dum posset dici: 'vide quam belle is egerit, qui in imitatoribus arcendis ipse egregius imitator esse videatur.' Magnopere tamen laetitia non exultassem; illam potius imitationem maximi facerem de qua Paulus loquitur apostolus. Nam, quamquam recte loqui praeclareque disserere Dei donum esse non ambigo, quatenus elegans dicendi munus in bonis ducitur, si rerum tamen honestarum et quae ad felicitatem conducant pondus non subsit, erunt ne aliud verba Ciceronis quam *inanes sine mente soni, nugaeque canorae?* Propterea censui me meis in scriptis, ut in omni vita, res magis quam verba praestare oportere, maioremque omnino vim impendere in dirigendis ad normam verae religionis animi affectibus, quam in oratione ad Ciceronis amussim lineanda et illo 'esse videretur' fine terminanda.

My uncle's style (to say nothing of his incomparable talent and   25
learning) comes closer to Cicero than to Pliny, but also offers
something uniquely his own. Poliziano's diction varies, like someone who has at times wished to imitate different authors, but nevertheless his observations are frequent and acute, and his works
packed with his extensive reading and uncommon learning. If you
think, Bembo, that these men exhibit no fragrant traces of antiquity, that they lie "despised and rejected" because some or all of
them "professed to imitate no one,"[63] I shall certainly not be an-
noyed with you. Yet I will advise you to speak better of them,
since they live and will continue to live in the memory of men,
perhaps even more so as humanist studies advance. For I do not
deny Pindar's words:

> the days to come
>   are the wisest witnesses.[64]

As for me, I shall add only that I would consider myself a suc-   26
cess if I had the ability to copy Cicero just long enough so that it
could be said, "Look how well this man has done who in discour-
aging imitators seems himself to be a remarkable imitator."[65] But
this would still not make me ecstatic; I would value most of all the
sort of imitation that the Apostle Paul talks about.[66] For although
I have no doubt that correct speech and brilliant discourse are a
gift of God, since the gift of elegant speech is numbered among
goods, nonetheless, if there is no underlying solidity of honorable
activity, and activity concerned with our ultimate happiness, will
Cicero's words be anything but "empty sounds without meaning,
musical trifles"?[67] For this reason, I believe that in my writings, as
in all my life, I should occupy myself with reality more than with
words,[68] and spend more energy on governing the passions of my
soul by the standard[69] of true religion than on straightening out
my diction in accordance with the ruler of Cicero and ending my
sentences with that phrase, "as it would seem."

27   Atque hactenus de nostra controversia, quam augere potius viderer potuisse quam minuere, si quae a Graecis rhetoribus quibusdam et nonnullis Latinis afferuntur eventilassem. Sed nostra quam aliena ad praesens attulisse forte praestiterit. Tu autem amice potius quam eleganter scriptam epistolam contemplatus, cui nec iustum triduum impendi, boni consulas quaeso. Neque enim egi ut qui quartanam laudant aut qui scribunt encomia Thersitae et bombylos panegyricis prosequuntur. Scilicet putasne tempus mihi superesse ad exercendum ingenium, quod vix possum tueri ne tot molestiarum quibus premor molibus plane succumbat? Putasque praeterea me non ex animo locutum, sed ad ostentationem potius, ut qui nolim aliis convenire? Vera loquor aut, si decipior, falsa tamen me scribere non putasse existimes velim, et libertate potius ingenii ductum quam servitute. Illa enim ipsa libertate fretus, philosophorum, etiam qui maximi fuerunt nostra aetate, non probare doctrinam saepenumero soleo, ut qui religionis nostrae res tam ratas certasque habeam ut nihil certius existimem. Hominum vero sensibus propriaque industria nitentium doctrinas et placita tam probem quam sese mihi aut vera offerunt aut veri omnino similia.

Vale.

So much for our controversy, which I could have increased 27
rather than diminished, I think, if I had aired some ideas of certain Greek and Latin rhetoricians. But for the present, it will have
been better, perhaps, to have cited our own rather than others'
views. Once you have considered my letter, however, which I have
written in a friendly rather than elegant tone, and on which I have
not spent the regulation three days, please judge it favorably. For
my intention was not like those speakers who praise the quartan
fever[70] or write encomia of Thersites[71] and honor the silk-worm
cocoons with panegyrics.[72] Surely you don't think I have the time
to practice my skill, when I can barely keep from succumbing to
the overwhelming troubles that press me?[73] And you don't think,
moreover, that I haven't spoken from the heart but for show, like
someone who wanted to be disagreeable? I am speaking the truth,
or if I am deceived, I would still wish you to believe that I did not
intend to speak falsely, but that I was led more by the freedom of
my inborn talent than by slavishness. Because I rely on that very
freedom, I often disapprove of the teaching of philosophers, even
the greatest of our time.[74] I am the sort of person who considers
the substance of our religion so fixed and certain that I believe
nothing could be more certain. In fact, the teachings and tenets of
people who rely on their senses and their own industry I would
approve just so much as they present themselves to me either as
true or altogether similar to the truth.

Farewell.

THE END

1 Cynthius Ioannes Baptista Gyraldus Coelio Calcagnino suo
s. p. d.

Arsi pene semper, vir clarissime, incredibili quodam desiderio
cognoscendi in quo vis imitationis, sine qua neminem ulla in arte
proficere posse mihi persuadeo, locata foret. Non enim, mi Coeli,
ex illorum sum numero, qui tantum mihi tribuam et tantum[1] ingenio meo, perexili quidem, faveam, quod imitationem, quam Tullius ipse Romanae eloquentiae parens plurimi fecit, ut nunc Erasmus et ante ipsum Politianus impudenter despiciam. Quis enim
nescit, quod etiam Marcus Tullius Cicero in *Oratore* testatus est,
omnem dicendi rationem, imitatione summota, non modo sterilescere, sed prorsus evanescere? Et licet hac in re a doctissimis plerisque multa acceperim, tamen mihi hactenus (tanta est doctorum
virorum hac in re dissensio) minime innotuit ipsius vis imitationis.

2 Sunt enim qui inanem tantummodo verborum sonum imitatori
observandum proponant; non nulli vero leporem inspiciendum;
quidam facilitatem; complures ductum; plerique figuras et aculeos.
Nec desunt ii, qui sententias integras, nulla verborum facta muta-
tione, imitatorem citra vitium excerpere posse contendant. Quae
etsi ad imitationem non parum conferunt, tamen vix mihi apta videntur ad eum exacte exprimendum quem imitari velim; et eo mi-

Giambattista Giraldi Cinzio to Celio Calcagnini

Giambattista Giraldi Cinzio sends warm greetings to his Celio   1
Calcagnini

I have nearly always burned, noble sir, with an incredible desire to know wherein lies the essence of imitation. For I am per-
suaded that without this essence or power no one can succeed in
any art. I am certainly not one of those, Celio, who gives myself so
much credit and favors my own talent, meager as it is, to such an
extent that I impudently despise, as Erasmus does today and
Poliziano did before him, the practice of imitation that Cicero
himself, the parent of Roman eloquence, valued so highly. Indeed,
who does not know, as even Marcus Tullius Cicero has testified in
the *De Oratore*, that when imitation has been neglected, one's entire method of speaking not only becomes sterile but entirely dis-
appears?[1] Although I have learned much from many experts in the
field, I still haven't the least idea of the meaning or essence of imitation, so much do learned men disagree on the matter.

Some indeed claim that the imitator should pay attention only   2
to the empty sound of words; others, that he should look for
charm; certain others, ease; still others, a method of treatment;
and many others, that he should imitate figures of speech and
clever remarks. Nor is there any lack of people who contend that
an imitator may, without committing a fault, extract whole sentences without changing the words at all. Even if these techniques
make a significant contribution to imitation, they hardly seem
suited to the purpose of accurately reproducing the sort of man I
would want to imitate—the less so as I have found scarcely one or
two people who would propose that I imitate some one person in

nus, quo vix unum aut alterum inveni, qui sic aliquem imitandum mihi proposuerit, ut omnia ab eodem accipiam.

3   Nam quoniam vix fieri posse opinantur, ut unius industria omnia perficere potuerit, haec quae ad orationis candorem et stili gravitatem attinent, more apum hinc[2] inde perquirenda arbitrantur. Nam veluti apes in melle condiendo,[3] non ex uno tantum, sed ex omnibus floribus id sibi colligunt ex quo mel ipsum condant,[4] ita a Cicerone schemata, epicheremata, parabolas, sales; a Quintiliano leporem, gratiam, energiam; a Sallustio sanguinem, cutem, carnem; a Caesare nervos, chartilagines, ossa; a Plinio animam,[5] vim, spiritum; et brevi quaecumque orationem illustrem reddunt, a diversis exquirenda praecipiunt.

4   Ego vero in hanc sententiam eo minus descendo, quo ad oratorem instituendum haec mihi non secus attinere videntur, quam si ad unius hominis generationem quaedam humani seminis colluvies expeteretur. Vix enim fieri potest quin illius oratio, qui sic omnia a pluribus mendicat, exilis, arida, enervata, mutila, inculta, molesta, ab omni decoro, ab omni denique energia sit prorsus aliena, illisque ipsis obstrepens, qui eam composuerunt. Quaecumque enim lumen orationi addere deberent, si ad unius similitudinem invicem connecterentur, ea a diversis excepta et in unam veluti congeriem coacta, illi obscuritatem ac tenebras afferunt. Nam quis omnes hosce poterit imitari et in unam orationis faciem redigere, cum sint ipsi dissimillimi inter se, nec omnibus[6] unum sit dicendi genus?

5   Quapropter, licet Erasmus, nostra tempestate de literis[7] optime meritus, in *Ciceroniano* suo, in quo in literatos omnes lividule genuinum frangit,[8] ab unius Ciceronis imitatione (credo quia is ad eius phrasim minime accessit) eloquentiae cupidos, veluti canis in vestibulo latrans,[9] plurimum deterreat, in superioremque senten-

such a way as to adopt all aspects of my style from the same person.

Since people think it hardly possible that the industry of a sin- 3
gle man could bring to perfection all aspects of style, they believe
that whatever qualities achieve rhetorical brilliance and stylistic
gravity should be sought out hither and yon the way bees do.[2] In
fact, just as bees, in giving zest to their honey, gather the material
for it not from one but all flowers, these men teach that we should
take figures of speech, syllogisms, parables and wit from Cicero;
charm, grace and energy from Quintilian; blood, skin and flesh
from Sallust; sinews, cartilage and bone from Caesar; vivacity,
force, and spirit from Pliny; in short whatever makes an oration
brilliant should be sought from different authors.[3]

What makes me tend to dissociate myself from this view is that 4
these techniques seem intended to train an orator as one might re-
sort to a mixed-up mess of human seed to produce a single man.[4]
For it is almost inevitable that, if a person goes begging for all his
qualities from several authors,[5] his diction will be meager, dry, life-
less, choppy, unkempt, tiresome — in short, devoid of all decorum
and all energy.[6] Such diction is jarring even to those who compose
it. For whatever qualities should add a luminous clarity to diction
when connected to each other by their common resemblance to
one writer, in fact lead to obscurity and darkness when pulled out
of diverse authors and thrown into a single heap. Who will be able
to imitate all these writers and reduce them to a single eloquent
style when they themselves are so unlike each other and belong to
different literary genres?

Hence, Erasmus, the most honored literary figure of our time, 5
jealously grinds his teeth at all the literati in his own *Ciceronianus*
and vehemently discourages lovers of eloquence from imitating
Cicero alone (I think because his own style was so different), bark-
ing like a dog in an entranceway and siding with the above opinion

tiam manibus pedibusque[10] descendat, quod etiam Ioannes Franciscus Picus Mirandula, illustris acrique vir ingenio, duabus in epistolis ad Petrum Bembum, virum clarissimum et in utraque lingua eruditissimum, egit, tamen, cum existimem in omnibus rebus esse aliquod summum et optimum, ita etiam aliquem in eloquentia esse crediderim, qui in dicendo omnia munia obierit; ad huncque, veluti ad perfectam quandam orationis imaginem — quam quidem[11] cogitatione assequi possumus, viribus autem non possumus — omnes conatus esse referendos. Quod si is qui imitari voluerit, eo prorsus non pervenerit quo et desiderium et mentis aciem intenderat, tamen ipsi non inhonestum erit in secundis et tertiis consistere. Cum igitur Marcus Cicero omnium calculis eo eloquentiae pervenerit, ut ipso omnis eloquentia nihil maius fingere possit, in eius lectione mihi semper insistendum, quod Cortesio etiam Bemboque, sanioris (ut credo) iudicii quam priores, videtur,[12] ab incunabulis usque constitui — licet, vel ob aetatem iuniorem (valentiorum enim laterum haec sunt) vel quia neminem ducem hoc in stadii curriculo habuerim, parum me adhuc promovisse[13] cognoscam.

6 Idem enim in literis quod in castris et praeliis evenire arbitror. Nam ut quicumque strenuum sectantur imperatorem et in bellorum discriminibus versatum, ab eoque rei militaris peritiam addiscunt et ad tuendas civitates et ad hostium acies oppugnandas, longe peritiores atque acriores sunt iis qui se et minus illustribus et non satis expertis addixerunt, sic ii veram dicendi peritiam mihi callere posse videntur, qui ipsum eloquentiae parentem sectandum sibi proponunt, et ipsum ad amussim effingere conantur. Vix enim fieri potest, quod qui Ciceroni addictus fuerit exactam eloquentiam, maximam rerum copiam, et integram artis oratoriae peritiam abunde non calleat.

with all his strength.[7] That is what Gianfrancesco Pico della Mirandola, a brilliant man of keen talent, also says in two letters to Pietro Bembo, a nobleman learned in both languages.[8] Nevertheless, since I believe that there is a highest and best in all things, I am convinced that there is also someone who has discharged every duty of eloquence.[9] I believe all our efforts should be focused on this man, as though he were the perfect image of speech—an image we can certainly[10] attain in thought, if not in essence.[11] But if someone who wants to imitate fails to reach that towards which he has directed his desire and consciousness, it will still not be dishonorable for him to stop at the second- or third-rate authors.[12] Since by everyone's calculations Cicero has reached so high a level of rhetorical excellence that all eloquence can fashion nothing greater than him, I have been determined since earliest childhood always to concentrate on reading him. This course also seemed best to Cortesi and Bembo, who were men of sounder judgment, I think, than their predecessors. To be sure, I know that I have as yet made little progress, either because of my young age (for these studies require a stout frame) or because I had no one to follow in running this race.

For the same thing happens in literature, I think, as in military 6 camps and battles. Anyone who follows a vigorous commander well versed in the crises of battle, learning from him the military skills of protecting cities and attacking enemy lines, is far more skilled and sharper than the soldier who is assigned to less illustrious and inexperienced commanders. In the same way, it seems to me that the men who know true eloquence the best are the ones who take as their model the very parent of eloquence and try to copy him as exactly as possible. Indeed, it is hardly possible for a person who has devoted himself to Cicero not to develop a precise eloquence, an abundance of extremely valuable material,[13] and a complete and practical knowledge of the art of rhetoric.

7   Nam ut omittam illam immortalis ingenii beatissimam ubertatem perpetuamque illam orationis ac felicissimam facilitatem, quis
est ipso Cicerone vel ad docendum vel ad delectandum vel ad
commovendum acutior? Quis ad nectendos argumentorum nexus
promptior? Quis ad propositum firmandum acrior? Quis in astu-
tiis parandis versutior? Quis ad dolos evitandos callidior? Quis ad
inimicorum impetum sustinendum promptior? Quis in re augenda
vel minuenda vehementior? Quis ad animos vel ad iram vel ad
odium vel ad[14] dolorem incitandos vegetior? Quis ab iisdem per-
motionibus[15] ad amorem, ad lenitatem, ad misericordiam revocan-
dos aptior? Quis verborum copia locupletior? Quis sententiarum
pondere gravior? Quis figuris iucundior? Quis translationibus
magnificentior? Quis totius orationis serie magis elaboratus? Quis
in dicendo candidior? Quis in re peroranda felicior?[16] O unicam
atque felicem, immo beatam[17] M. Tullii eloquentiam! Grandilo-
quus Cicero, salibus et lepore concinnus, acer, elaboratus, varius,
acutus, gravis, accuratus, subtilis, lenis, in quamlibet dicendi formam paratus, nec minus in otio quam in negotio gratus! Insunt
Tullio arma, tela, faces, quibus et manum comminus conferre possis et eminus iaculari fulgereque quandoque et tonare et fulmina
vibrare, si libeat. Sunt item in ipso excessus amoeni, in quibus las-
sus desideas et expatieris et tibi indulgeas et ingenio lascivias si libeat. Quid multa? Nihil vel egregii vel rari summive in oratione
esse potest quod in Cicerone, veluti in speculo, non luceat. Quem
si e medio tollas, non lucem modo aut candorem, sed spiritum,
animam, vitam ipsam a dicendi facultate prorsus auferas necesse
est. Non erit ille igitur prorsus insanus, qui, inventis ac paratis
frugibus, glandibus vesci velit, quique rivos insectetur et fontem
cum limpidissimum tum uberem relinquat, aliundeque potius
quam ab ipso sole lumen habere[18] desideret?

To say nothing of the most blessed richness of his immortal talent and that constant and most felicitous rhetorical facility, who is more keen-witted than Cicero himself in instructing, delighting or exciting?[14] Who is readier at weaving arguments? Who is shrewder at establishing or confirming his proposition? Who is more adroit in producing strategems? Who is keener when it comes to escaping traps? Who is quicker to hold off the attack of enemies? Who is livelier in exaggerating or understating a matter? Who is more vigorous in exciting our spirits to anger, to hatred or to grief? Who is more apt at recalling those spirits from these same deep emotions to love, gentleness or pity? Who is richer in vocabulary? Who is weightier in his opinions? Who is more delightful in his figures of speech? Who is more magnificent in his metaphors? Who, more painstaking in the structure of his entire speech? Who is more brilliant in speech? Who is better at perorations? O unique and fruitful, indeed blessed[15] eloquence of Marcus Tullius! Grandiloquent Cicero, harmonious in charm and wit, keen, painstaking, varied, shrewd, grave, precise, subtle, smooth, ready for any form of speech, no less pleasing in leisure than in business! In Cicero there are arms, spears and torches with which you may fight hand to hand, hurl from afar, sometimes flash and thunder and, if you so desire, wield the thunderbolt.[16] There are likewise pleasant digressions where you may rest when weary, enlarge on the subject, indulge yourself and, if you like, let your talent run free. In short, there can be nothing remarkable, rare or eminent in speech that does not shine in Cicero as if in a mirror.[17] If you took him away, you would necessarily remove not only the light or radiance but the spirit, soul and life itself from the art of rhetoric. A man would be insane to prefer feasting on nuts when fruit has been found and set before him;[18] to follow streams and leave behind the cleanest and most abundant spring;[19] to seek light from any source other than the sun itself.[20]

8   Non tamen ego imitatorem a ceterorum authorum lectione ita
deterrebo ut ceteros omnes despiciendos, solum Ciceronem legen-
dum censeam (quis enim me temeritatis non prorsus damnet, si
hoc ausim affirmare?) velimque unius authoris angustiis omnia ingenia metiri, quasi in aliis nihil sit aut egregium aut admirabile
quod observari possit; absit a me temeritas haec! Sunt enim et
aliis suae virtutes. Quare ego illud vel ultro cuicumque[19] concesse-
rim, ut[20] cum firmati erit iudicii et extra periculi aleam positus —
quod tum potissimum erit, cum Ciceronis dictionem ac stilum
usque adeo imbiberit, ut quoscumque et mentis conceptus et ingenii conatus Ciceronis more possit vel eloqui vel literarum monumentis commendare[21] — tum demum et antiquos omnes et recentiores etiam (non enim seculis nostris usque adeo fata invida
fuerunt, ut inter nostrae aetatis homines quidam etiam non sint,
qui orationis gravitatem ac dicendi candorem ita invicem coniun-
xerunt, ut cum Cygno Arpinate quodammodo contendere posse
videantur et iam iacentem prostratamque Romanae eloquentiae
dignitatem sublevare) et legat et observet excerpatque ex his quicquid ad orationis ornatum attinere videatur, sive sententiae fuerint
sive verba; ex his enim duobus omnis oratio constat.

9   Quaecumque vero excerpta fuerint, ad unius Ciceronis imitationem convertenda censeo. Neque enim in Catonis duritie conse-
nescendum est, ita ut horridus prorsus evadat.[22] Neque rursus
lascivientium flosculi adeo legendi sunt, ut voluptati tantum et
luxuriae indulgere velle videatur. Quod profecto non eveniet, si et
mollium lasciviam et antiquorum duriciam ad unius Ciceronis
splendorem veluti ad examen et regulam quandam deduxerit.[23]
Hoc enim duce, quae duriora fuerint mitescent, et rursus langui-
diora nervos ac maturitatem quandam accipient orationis. Quod si
mollia nervos ac dura gratiam non admiserint, ab integro iudicio

I nevertheless shall not discourage the imitator from reading   8
other authors to the point where I lay it down that he should
read Cicero alone, despising all other authors (for if I dared advance such a view, who wouldn't condemn it as thoughtless?). Nor
would I have all talents measure themselves within the narrow
confines of a single author, as if there were nothing distinguished
or admirable to be aware of in other authors; let me stay far away
from that sort of rash thoughtlessness! Other authors too have
their own virtues.[21] So I would willingly allow anyone to read
them, once his judgment is formed and beyond risk of danger,
which will most preferably occur when he has imbibed Cicero's
style and diction to the point where he can express verbally or put
into literary form any conception or intellectual design at all in the
manner of Cicero.[22] At this point only may he read and take notes
and excerpt whatever thoughts or words he thinks might be useful
for adorning his speech — for all speech consists of thoughts and
words. He may do this both with all the ancient authors and even
with more recent ones, for the fates have not been so hostile to our
times that some of our contemporaries have not succeeded in mar-
rying gravity of speech with brilliance of expression, so that they
seem able to contend in a sense with the Arpinian swan and to
raise up the dignity of Roman eloquence that now lies prostrate.[23]

Whatever excerpts one makes, I think, should be turned into   9
an imitation of Cicero alone. One shouldn't grow old in Catonian
austerity so that one ends up being repulsive. Nor again should
one go picking the flowers of frivolity so that it seems one wants
only to indulge in pleasure and extravagance. This won't happen if
one reduces the playfulness of the soft and the hardness of the
aged to the splendor of Cicero alone, as to a kind of test and rule.
For with Cicero as a guide, what is too harsh will be softened, and
again what is too torpid will acquire sinews and a kind of ripeness
of speech. But if what is soft does not admit of strength and what
is austere of gracefulness, sound judgment will certainly cast them

prorsus abicientur. Ut enim inter homines quidam sunt naturae adeo hebetis, ut nulla cura vel bonis moribus imbui vel optimis artibus illustrari possint, ita etiam quaedam sunt adeo per se rudia, ut nullum prorsus admittant orationis ornatum, quamquam et[24] haec a Ciceronis assecula felicius tractabuntur quam ab aliorum nemine. Nam si ea quae Musices sunt et aliarum etiam artium, quantumlibet rudium, verborum ac orationis concinnitatem quandam accipiunt, si de his eloquens aliquis egerit, et felicius ab eo tractabuntur quam ab inventoribus artificibusque ipsis, cur idem non evenerit[25] in dicendi facultate, illi praesertim qui in Cicerone[26] diutius[27] versatus fuerit eiusque imbiberit dicendi modum?[28]

10   Quamobrem, Coeli optime, cum ea me semper tenuerit cupido, ut quantum humana opera fieri potest, Tullio quandoque simillimus efficiar (satis enim mihi lucrifecisse arbitror,[29] si huius vestigiis aliquando inhaerere mihi fas fuerit, quem numquam mirari desino), cumque ex tuis lectionibus mihi satis perspectum sit quantum Ciceronem ipsum admireris et quam libenter bonarum literarum sectatoribus operam tuam impertiaris quamque ingeniis faveas,[30] ad te, veluti ad totius eloquentiae lumen, pro tenebris meis fugandis audacter[31] me contuli, ut quid in Cicerone ad ipsum, quantum in me erit, effingendum, animadvertendum sit, ex te perspiciam. Nec rem hanc mihi infeliciter cessuram arbitror, si tu, in quo tot ac tanta sunt ornamenta dicendi, penum[32] hanc mihi patefeceris et thesauros hosce reservaveris. Nam cur non bene sperem te mihi duce? Quem alterum nostrae aetatis Ciceronem non immerito appellaverim? Nam cum nihil in te sit non admirabile, tum illud praecipue et ego et universus doctorum coetus admirari solemus, quod in ipso quotidiano sermone tanta affluas ubertate et facundia, tanta rerum copia, ut non modo ex ore tuo verba vel ipso

aside. For as some men have such weak natures that no amount of care can imbue them with character or make them distinguished for polite learning, so too there are certain things so crude that they do not admit of rhetorical embellishment — although even these things may be discussed more happily by the follower of Cicero than by the follower of any other author. So if material related to music and to the other arts too, however unpolished those arts might be, acquires a kind of verbal and stylistic harmony when treated by an eloquent person and are handled more felicitously by him than by the composers and artisans themselves, why won't this also occur in the faculty of speech — especially in the case of the man who is long versed in Cicero and has imbibed his way of speaking?

On this account, good Celio, since I have always desired to be-   10 come one day as much like Cicero as is humanly possible (indeed I'll consider that I've profited enough if it's allowed to me to follow now and then in the footsteps of this man who never ceases to amaze me), and since it is clear enough to me from your lectures how much you admire Cicero, how willingly you share your work with those who enjoy good literature and how you show favor to men of talent, I have come boldly to you, as to the light of all eloquence, to dispel my darkness, so that I might learn from you what in Cicero I should take note of in order to copy him, to the extent that I can. And I don't think the subject will end unhappily for me if you open this storehouse where there are so many and such great ornaments of speech and unlock this treasury for me. Why should I not have good expectations for myself with you as my guide? What other man could I with such justice call "the Cicero of our time"? While there is nothing that is not admirable about you, both I and the entire company of learned men particularly tend to admire how your ordinary conversation abounds with such richness and eloquence, such a wealth of information, that not only do words flow more sweetly from your lips than honey it-

melle dulciora manent, sed nihil tibi aut a natura denegatum aut a doctrina non delatum esse videatur.

11   Quare, Coeli optime, cum me in hoc iuvenilis aetatis tirocinio tibi instituendum tradiderim, per meam in te fidem, per tuam innatam erga literatos omnes humanitatem, per spes tuas perque tua vota, rogo ac obsecro ut desiderio meo facias satis. Nam si eloquentiae fores adeo mihi, ut spero, patefeceris, quod in illius penetralia mihi ingredi liceat, dabo operam ut te profectus mei numquam paeniteat. Et quicquid umquam dicendo proficiam (si modo aliquid umquam profecero), id omne Coelio Calcagnino acceptum ferri oportere non dissimulabo.

Vale. Ex Cynthiano meo ad VII kalendas Quintiles MDXXXII.

self, but nothing seems either to have been denied you by nature or not produced by your learning.

Hence, good Celio, since I have entrusted myself to you to be taught during my youthful period of apprenticeship, by my faith in you, by your inborn kindness toward all men of letters, by your hopes and vows, I beseech and entreat you to satisfy my desire. For if you open the gates of eloquence to me, as I hope, and I am permitted to enter its sacred precincts, I shall apply myself so diligently that you will never have cause to be displeased with my progress. And whatever progress I make as a speaker (assuming that I shall make progress), I shall not conceal that it is all to be credited to Celio Calcagnini.

Farewell. From my Cynthianum, June 23, 1532.

1   Coelius Calcagninus Cynthio Ioanni Baptistae Gyraldo s. p. d.

Quod ego nihil hactenus[1] tuis literis responderim, vir clarissime,[2] non est quod arbitrere, vel tua apud me studia parum habere ponderis, vel tuam excellentem litteraturam non tanti a me aestimari quanti merito ab aequo iudice aestimari debet. Sed ita nescio quo fato accidit, ut cum tuae ad me litterae perlatae sunt, essem tum occupationum mole prope[3] obrutus, tum ita viribus corporis destitutus (nam me insolita quaedam stomachi intemperies[4] dies aliquot male vexaverat), ut ego ipse mei compos non essem. Quare, amabo te, per communia Musarum commertia, facessat omnis de me sinistra cogitatio, persuasumque habeas me in studiosos omnes[5] albam esse lineam in albo lapide; doctos vero homines, in quorum censu[6] tu honorificum tibi tua virtute locum[7] vendicasti, non solum amare sed etiam admirari. An non ego sim mortalium omnium ingratissimus si pulcherrimis tuis litteris non faveam? Quibus tantum mihi tribuis, quantum neque, vel si immodice sim ambitiosus, agnoscam. Qua in re, et si ego[8] animadverto[9] te plus amori et bonitati tuae[10] dare quam iudicio, tamen non potest tua ista praeclara in me voluntas non mihi esse gratissima.

2   Ceterum[11] illud non dissimulabo me, quam primum litteras tuas[12] accepissem, constituisse ad propositam de imitatione disquisitionem non prius respondere quam avocationes expunxissem omnes et essem mihi ipsi per valetudinem restitutus, sed quoniam tu tuis litteris[13] urges ac propemodum cessanti[14] et[15] mihi faces subdis, non committam ut diutius officium meum desideres. Abiciam itaque omnem cunctationem et, quae mature digerere cogita-

Celio Calcagnini to Giambattista Giraldi Cinzio

Celio Calcagnini sends warm greetings to Giambattista Giraldi   1
Cinzio.

That I have not yet responded to your letter, noble sir, does not
mean what you may think: either that I set little value on your
studies with me or that I do not assess your excellent writing at as
high a rate as by rights a fair judge should. But by some mis-
chance it so happened that when your letter arrived I was nearly
buried under a mass of work and had lost so much physical
strength (an unusual stomach ailment had been troubling me for
some days)[1] that I was not in command of my faculties. So please,
by our common association with the Muses, let all unfavorable
thoughts about me depart, and be convinced that I am a white line
on a white stone[2] towards all men devoted to serious study; believe
that learned men, in whose company you have claimed a place of
honor by your virtue, not only esteem but also admire you. Would
I not be the most ungracious of all mortals if I did not delight in
your very beautiful letter? You give me so much credit therein that
I would not acknowledge it even if I were extravagantly ambitious.
If in this matter I notice that you rely more on affection and goodness than on judgment, I cannot but welcome your magnificent
good will toward me.

As for the rest, I shall confess that when I received your letter I   2
decided, with regard to your proposed inquiry into imitation, not
to respond before I had taken care of all distractions and been restored to good health; but since you are prodding me by letter and
practically lighting a fire under me in my idleness, I shall not become liable for making you need my friendly services any longer. I
shall therefore throw off all delay and, what I had intended to di-

veram, ea[16] tumultuario opere[17] in compendium redigam, ut intellegas me tuae voluntatis quam meae existimationis[18] rationem
habere maluisse.

Bene vale[19] et me ama tui amantissimum.

Idibus Quintilibus, MDXXXII.[20]

gest when the time was ripe I shall reduce in makeshift fashion to an abridgement, so you may understand that I have preferred to take more account of your good will than of my own reputation.

Farewell and hold me in your affection as your most affectionate friend.

15 July 1532.

Super imitatione commentatio[1]

1   Tuae litterae, vir clarissime, magnam mihi profecto spem attulerunt rem latinam et egregia studia facile posse aliquando reparari, postquam et vos naturae interpretes et abditarum artium professores studetis[2] pulcherrimas disciplinas cum eloquentia coniungere, quas proximo saeculo patres ac praeceptores nostri ita pugnare inter se existimabant, ut nulla conditione in foedus coire posse iudicarent. Eratque illa sententia, iam recepta atque approbata, philosophiam et oratoriam adversis frontibus pugnare, eosdemque philosophos et oratores nullo pacto posse reperiri. Sed eam sententiam perfacile ridebunt qui tuas litteras legerint, utpote[3] a summo philosopho profectas, in quibus tamen omnes dicendi veneres, omnes[4] eloquentiae suavitates[5] admiremur. Bene itaque ac feliciter res habet, postquam[6] et recte sapere et commode dicere conciliavimus, et iam linguae pectus, lingua pectori succinit.

2   Illud vero mihi iure admirari subit, unde tibi in mentem venerit requirere a me imitationis rationem, et quid illud sit quod nos potissimum imitari oporteat, cum tu ipse iam tantum dicendo profeceris, ut non modo tu te ipsum imitari possis, sed aliis quoque imitationis[7] exemplum praescribere. Sane si ego ad te, hominem tantae eruditionis tantique profectus, de imitatione scribere quicquam ausim, periculum est, ne quis me improbe facere clamitet,

Celio Calcagnini, On Imitation, to Giambattista Giraldi Cinzio

Treatise on Imitation

Your letter, noble sir, has brought me great hope indeed that Latin 1
culture and its distinguished studies can one day be easily re-
paired, now that you interpreters of the natural world and experts
in the secret arts[1] are showing zeal to marry the finest intellectual
disciplines with eloquence. In the previous age our fathers and
teachers thought these to be so much in conflict with each other
that they believed that no terms could be found to make a peace
treaty between them.[2] There was even the opinion, which is still
accepted and approved, that philosophy and oratory are diametrically opposed and that it is utterly impossible to find men who
are philosophers and orators alike. But people will be quick to
laugh at that opinion once they have read your letter, which,
though coming from a highly accomplished philosopher, nevertheless causes us to admire in it all the charms of fine speech and all
the attractiveness of eloquence. So the present situation is a happy
and sound one, now that we have reconciled true wisdom and apt
speech, and the tongue plays the accompaniment for the heart.

Yet I have reason to wonder where you got the idea to ask me 2
for a method of imitation and to answer the question what it is we
should most prefer to imitate, when you yourself have made so
much progress in fine speech that not only can you imitate, but
you can offer yourself to others as an example for imitation as
well. In fact, if I dared write anything about imitation to you, a
man of such great learning and success, I am afraid someone

qui Minervam doceam, in sylvas qui ligna feram; praesertim cum
ex tuarum litterarum testimonio intellegam te clarissimi cuiusque
conditoris super imitatione sententiam explorasse ac prope nihil
inexcussum reliquisse, ut iam mihi, vel si ingenio maxime polleam,
nihil fiat reliquum quod in medium afferre possim. Proinde, si a
ceteris ad satietatem inculcata ad aures revocem, actum agam; sin
abeuntes in diversum sententias quasi disceptator in[8] trutina ex-
pendam, neque rem facilem aggrediar in tanta opinionum varietate,[9] neque id sine multorum offensa efficere possim. Ne igitur ad
alterum aut alterum scopulum offendam, haec inita est a me ratio
atque hoc propositum est temperamentum, ut praetermissis aliorum sententiis quid ipse sentiam brevissime perstringam.

3   In confesso est imitationem omni[10] aetate fuisse pernecessa-
riam, cum enim ars nulla nullaque eruditio a[11] suis initiis absoluta
inveniatur, sed omnis per suos gradus producatur,[12] sane eum qui
cupit celeres progressus facere, oportet quae ab aliis inventa atque
observata sunt, ea sibi in exemplum proponere. Quod ni fiat, artes
omnes semper ad limen subsistant, neque ultra progrediantur, necesse est. Tantum enim semper promovebunt quantum unius hominis diligentia et cura adsequetur; quae vero ab aliis praemeditata
fuerint ac[13] praemunita, ea in oblivionem abire oportebit. Hac igitur ratione ars dicendi suis in rudimentis semper manebit, et qui
animum ad scribendum appulerit satis existimabit si, ex tribus
muneribus quibus fungi debet orator, unum modo assequatur,[14] et
quantum dicentis audientisque intersit, tantum possit in medium[15]
proferre; nam delectare et permovere aut parum aut sane[16] nihil
ad[17] se arbitrabitur pertinere.[18] Admirabiles ergo illas opes Demosthenis, uberrimos illos flores Isocratis, cumulatissimos illos
Ciceronis thesauros nullus agnoscet, sed, quasi tum primum oratoria in lucem prodeat, numquam ultra infantiam promovebit.

would charge me with improper conduct, teaching Minerva and bringing wood to the forest.[3] For from the testimony of your letter I understand that you have examined the views of all the most famous authorities on imitation and have scrutinized nearly everything. As a result, even if I were a person of supreme talent, there might remain nothing for me to offer to the public. If I reminded you what others have already driven home to the point of satiety, I would be undertaking something that had already been done. But if I weighed contradictory opinions in the balance like an arbitrator, I would be undertaking no easy task amidst such a variety of opinions, and I could not bring it off without offending many people. In order therefore to avoid both obstacles, I have begun this account and proposed this compromise: I shall leave aside the opinions of others and summarize very briefly my own views.

It is generally admitted that imitation has been highly necessary in every age. For since no art and no branch of learning is invented complete at the beginning, but each advances by its own steps, anyone intending to make swift progress must surely use the inventions and observations of others as his model. Unless he should do so, all arts would of necessity stop always at the threshold and make no further progress. For they will always advance only so far as the diligence and devotion of a single man reach, and what others have worked out and secured before will have to pass into oblivion. On this account the art of speaking will always remain in its rudimentary stages. Whoever applies himself to writing will think it enough if he should master only one of the three functions that the orator ought to perform and be able only to set out the differences between speaker and listener; he will think it is little or no business of his to delight or persuade.[4] No one will therefore appreciate the admirable riches of Demosthenes, the extremely fruitful flowers of Isocrates, the overflowing treasuries of Cicero. Like a new-born babe, oratory will never advance beyond

Hoc enim accidat necesse est, si ex rebus humanis imitationem ablegaveris.

4   Quam cum omnium qui recte iudicarint[19] consensus approbaverit, tum maxime in dicendo hoc nostro saeculo necessariam opinamur, quo non solum eloquentia desiit, sed vernaculus etiam ille, nostrorum maiorum[20] sermo, in desuetudinem abiit, cuius locum foedissima barbaries ex variarum gentium colluvione, quae superioribus saeculis Italiam invaserunt, coalita occupavit, ut iam proprias et consuetas patrum et avorum voces requiramus. Quid dicam quod huic vitio, quod par fuit omnibus machinis a nobis deturbari, ita patrocinamur, ut iam inventi sint qui illud rationibus foveant et certis regulis adiuvent, et si Dis placet, verae ac germanae latinitati praeferant? Quae res multa praeclare nata ingenia in transversum abduxit,[21] quippe quae inventis paratisque frugibus, glandibus tamen vesci malint.

5   Hoc est, hoc scilicet quod efficit, ut imitationis praesidio magis egeamus. Nam antequam maiestas imperii Romani pessum iret et splendor Latini nominis obsolesceret, cum cetera ad imitationem vocarentur, verba certe cum lacte nutricis hauriebamus. Neque in iis quaerendis multus labor relinquebatur,[22] sponte siquidem intra privatos penates occurrebant. Nunc autem in tam perdita tempora incidimus, ut in verbis perquirendis etiam frustra laboremus, nisi ad veteres ac[23] receptos conditores perfugiamus, quorum authoritate innitamur, quos imitemur, quorum exempla mutuemur. Nam protritae voces illae, quibus, non dico vulgus et tabernarum mancipes utuntur, sed ipsi proceres qui rerum in Italia potiuntur, tantum abest ut praesidii et[24] commodi quicquam ad eam rem nobis[25] afferre possint, ut multo maxime a via nos deducant ac[26] transversos agant. Decepti enim vicinitate et quasi vocum imagine, manifestos[27] etiam soloecismos barbarismosque incurrimus, adlecti

its infancy. This must be the result if you banish imitation from human affairs.

The consensus of all right-thinking persons has approved of 4 imitation, and we are of the opinion that imitation in speech is particularly necessary in our age. For not only has eloquence now disappeared in it, but even our ancestors' vernacular has fallen into disuse, replaced by the foulest barbarism, which has coagulated from the dregs of the various peoples that invaded Italy in previous centuries. That is why we now feel the loss of the proper and customary language of our fathers and forefathers. Need I say that we so protect this vice, which we should have used all our machines to knock down, that we now even find people who foster it with their theories, promote it with certain rules and, if it please the gods, prefer it to our true and genuine Latin?[5] This situation has sidetracked many nobly-born talents, for, "although fruit has been found and set out, they nonetheless prefer to feed on nuts."[6]

This is why we need the assistance of imitation all the more. 5 For, before the majestic power of Rome collapsed and the splendor of Latin fame faded away, while other matters required a process of imitation, we at least drank in words with our nurse's milk.[7] Nor was much labor lost to find them, since they arose naturally around the family hearth. Now, however, we have fallen on such ruinous times that we would even labor in vain to find words if we did not flee to the ancient and accepted authors, on whose authority we may depend, whom we may imitate and whose examples we may borrow. For the commonplace words that not only the vulgar and tavern-keepers use, but even the very noblemen who control Italian states, are so far from being able to lend us any assistance and usefulness in this matter that they actually steer us in the wrong direction and lead us astray. Beguiled by the closeness and resemblance of their voices to the ancients', we fall into even obvious solecisms and barbarisms.[8] We are ensnared especially by the mobs of notaries and bureaucrats who not only indiscriminately,

praesertim tabellionum et exceptorum frequentia, qui omnes has
sordes in tabulas formulasque suas, non dicam promiscue, sed ambitiose et cum plausu congerunt. Resque mira dictu evenit, ut
quanto quisque corruptius dixerit, eo inter suos populares maiore
laude provehatur, idemque ampliore quaestu dignus existimetur.

6   Quid vero ego in hoc censu tantum tabelliones et excepto-
res appello, cum iuris Romani et sanctissimae philosophiae aliarumque pulcherrimarum disciplinarum professores in hoc maxime
errore versentur?[28] Nam postquam artem dicendi a rerum cognitione excluserunt, idest (ut clarius dicam quod sentio), postquam
antiquos scriptores imitari desierunt, accidit illud quod fuit necesse, ut optimas et splendidissimas commentationes foedissime
inquinaverint. Non enim iam ex fontibus et conceptaculis, sed ex
impurissimis lacunis verba et totam dicendi rationem corrivant;
hi sunt apud quos sol et homo hominem 'causantur', et qui ar-
canos naturae effectus contemplantes admiratione 'afficiuntur',
quique quod in obligationibus praestare debent, illud se 'manuten-
turos' pollicentur.[29] Tametsi[30] suam causam tueri soleant ea ratione, quod plus pectori quam linguae tribuant quodque egregie
sentire quam perpolite loqui longe[31] praestet, numquam tamen illud effugient, quin iure vitio detur eos res praestantissimas ac
praecipuae[32] aestimationis in ordinem redigere ac neglectui habere.
Quod si, qui per desidiam feracem agrum sinebant sterilescere vel
equum ex publico acceptum incuriose habebant et strigosum esse
patiebantur, iis censoria nota inurebatur, quanto iustius eos[33] damnaveris qui admirabiles opes ingenii, qui philosophiam, tam quae
ad[34] mores et ad naturam quam quae ad inquirendam veritatem
spectat, rem inter omnes sanctissimam, qua nihil maius aut melius
a dis immortalibus hominum generi datum fatemur, despicatis-

but ambitiously and with applause and approval, collect all this filth in their drafts and accounts.[9] The result is something amazing: the more corruptly a person speaks, the more advancement and praise he receives from the public and the higher the salary he is thought to deserve.

Yet why do I name only notaries and scribes in this census, 6 when professors of Roman law and of theology and other extremely fine disciplines are also deeply involved in this error? For once they had excluded the art of rhetoric from the sciences, that is (to express my meaning more clearly), once they abandoned the imitation of the ancient writers, it was inevitable that they would end up befouling the best and most splendid studies. Indeed they now channel their words and entire rhetorical method not from springs and reservoirs but from the foulest ditches. These are the writers for whom the sun and man "cause" man,[10] who are "afflicted" with wonder when they contemplate the secret operations of nature, and who promise they are going to "manutent" what they are already obligated to do.[11] Although they like to protect their own cause by the argument that they value the inner person more than the tongue, and believe that having a fine understanding is far more excellent than speaking in a highly polished way, nevertheless, they will never escape the just criticism that they debase and neglect the finest and most valuable things. If anyone [in Roman times] permitted a fertile field to grow barren or dealt carelessly with a horse that he had received at public expense, letting it become too lean, he used to be branded for these things with the censor's mark.[12] How much more justly then will you condemn people who, by using a contemptible kind of speech, disfigure and spit upon the wonderful riches of talent, who spit on philosophy which treats alike ethics and nature as well as the search for truth[13] — philosophy, the most sacred pursuit of all, which we believe to be the greatest and best of all the things the immortal gods have given humankind? These people are no

simo orationis genere deformant atque conspurcant? Non secus ac
perditissimi illi ganeones, qui in Dionysii Syracusani convivio ex-
quisitissimas epulas inspuebant, ut soli ipsi sine aemulo eluaren-
tur[35] ac ceteros convivas rei foeditate ab iisdem absterrerent.

7   Et[36] sane proximae aetatis philosophis res magna parte ex voto
processit, nam plerique auspicato litteris initiati, perterriti porten-
toso orationis genere, cognitionem maximarum atque optimarum
rerum aversati sunt. Sed ego parcius hanc partem attingam, quod
illud genus hominum pridem multorum et clarissimorum stylo ex-
plosum atque proscissum est. Ego certe de iis nulla alia causa mentionem feci, nisi ut omnes intellegant ob id eos in hanc tam iustam
accusationem incidisse, vel quod nescierint vel quod grave duxerint
veteres imitari, suoque ingenio freti quod in ipsis fuit, circa abstru-
sas ac[37] profundas cogitationes se exercuerint. Quod vero aliunde
seligendum fuit, dicendi scilicet facultatem, prorsus abiecerint. Ex
quo factum est ut quae natura seiungi non poterant, orationis et
rationis consortia, quae ideo nobis data sunt, ut non modo nobis
sapere, sed recte etiam alios possemus admonere, dissilire ac dissi-
dere coeperint. Sed haec vetus expostulatio, cui facilius obtrectare
possimus quam mederi. Ex hac[38] tamen non difficulter fortasse
elici potest id, quod tu, Cynthi, a me per litteras efflagitabas: quid
sit illud scilicet potissimum quod in imitationem veniat. Recte
enim mihi videor respondere posse,[39] in eo plurimum esse imitationi locum in quo minimus est ingenio. Dicam hoc apertius, si
potero, ut intellegas me desiderio tuo, si modo facultas affuisset,
non defuturum[40] fuisse.

8   Ex iis quae in rationem[41] dicendi veniunt, quaedam insita sunt
in re nobis proposita, quaedam in nobis, quaedam neque in re

different from those depraved gluttons who spat on the most exquisite dishes at the feast of Dionysius of Syracuse so they could
gorge themselves without rival and keep the other feasters from
the same dishes out of disgust.[14]

And in fact the matter has turned out largely as the philoso-   7
phers of the previous age wished. For many men who had been
initiated into literature under good auspices were terrified by this
monstrous kind of speech and have rejected the greatest and best
sciences. But I shall touch on this topic rather sparingly, because
this type of man has long since been shouted down and lashed by
the pen of many famous writers. Indeed I have mentioned these
people only so everyone may understand that they have been justly
accused either because they didn't know how or because they
thought it burdensome to imitate the ancients, and, relying on the
talent that in them lay, occupied themselves with abstruse and
deep cogitations. But they discarded entirely what they should
have chosen from another source, that is, an ability to speak. The
result was that the partnership of rhetoric and reason, which could
not have been torn asunder by nature, which was given to us so
that we might have wisdom not only for ourselves, but also be able
rightly to advise others, began to burst apart and and go awry. But
this is an old complaint, which we can criticize more easily than
mend. Yet perhaps we can coax out of it without too much difficulty what you, Cinzio, asked of me in your letter: namely, what is
the most important element that comes into the process of imitation. I think I can respond correctly that there is the most room
for imitation where there is the least for natural ability. I shall state
this more clearly, if I can, so you may understand that I should not
have disappointed your wishes had my ability only been equal to
the task.

Of the elements that come into an account of speaking, some   8
aspects are inherent in the subject matter that is put before us,
others are in us, and some are neither in the matter nor in us, but

neque in nobis, sed peregre accersuntur. Quod si exemplo uti lubet quo res fiat illustrior, dicamus inventionem in re esse. Nam dicturus de caede Clodii, statim tibi proponis seriem ac rei ductum ad veritatem maxime accommodatum, et quid prius, quid posterius[42] factum sit, quid postquam ad manus ventum[43] est, quam potes perspicue, conaris enarrare. Non quod non possis ingenio quaedam praemollire aut exasperare, ut Cicero fecit Clodium insidiatorem ostendens eumque quantum potuit in invidiam vocans, contra Milonem ab omni eximens suspicione. Impudens tamen sit qui tam longe ab historia et a re ipsa gesta evariet, ut nota inficietur, et causam prodidisse suam in ipsis statim initiis coargui possit.

9   In nobis erit exordii apparatus, ut attentum, docilem, benevolum auditorem protinus reddamus. Id facile fieri poterit, si naturam atque ingenium hominum, apud quos dicimus, perspexerimus; aliam enim praefationem Cato, aliam Caesar approbaverit. Tum quomodo quis attentus, docilis ac benevolus effici possit, a nobis petimus. Eadem ratione natura nobis suppeditabit, quid prius, quid posterius, quid in medio orationis statuamus. Unde elucet admirabilis illa dispositionis coordinatio, qua, qui commode uti noverit, hunc Plato Dis coelestibus parem existimat. Ad eundem calculum venit ea pars quae argumentis colligit et probat, aut diluit ac refellit alienas argumentationes, in qua si quando comminus conferamus pedem, altercatio appellatur, quae una pars omnium maxime paratum atque procinctum ingenium postulat. Peroratio autem et amplificatio, novissimae quidem illae sed omnium potentissimae orationis partes, etsi a re ipsa multum trahunt,[44] ab oratoris tamen industria ac vehementia imprimis pendent, animo-

are brought in from without.[15] If you'd like an example to make this clearer, let's say that invention is in the subject matter. If you are going to speak about the murder of Clodius,[16] you immediately put before yourself the sequence and direction of events that is most suited to the truth; and you try to narrate as clearly as you can what happened earlier, what later and what has come to hand after the fact. Not that you couldn't soften or sharpen certain points using your natural talent, as Cicero does when he portrays Clodius as a subversive and excites hostility against him as best he can, while lifting all suspicion from Milo. A person would nonetheless be shameless to change the events so much from the historical facts that he denies the known facts and can be proven to have betrayed his own case from the very outset.

Now let's suppose that the preparation of an exordium — rendering the hearer immediately attentive, receptive and well-disposed — lies in us.[17] It can be done with ease if we have thoroughly considered the natural bent of the men to whom we are speaking; for Cato will approve of one preface, Caesar of another. Then we seek within ourselves how to make the listener attentive, receptive and well-disposed. In the same way, our nature will supply us with the ability to decide what to present earlier, what later and what in the middle of the speech. That is the source from which there shines forth an admirably coordinated sequence of ideas.[18] Anyone who knows how to manage this aptly Plato considers equal to the heavenly gods.[19] The same reckoning applies to the part of oratory that uses argument to summarize and prove one's own position, or to weaken and refute an opponent's arguments. In this part of oratory, if we ever fight at close quarters with an opponent, it is called "altercation," and this more than any other part of rhetoric demands a mind that is ready and girded for battle. And the peroration and amplification, the last but most powerful parts of the oration, even if they draw a good deal from the subject matter itself, nevertheless depend chiefly on the orator's effort and forcefulness

9

rumque[45] motus comitantur. Et hae quidem omnes, licet in nobis
sitae sint suaque in nobis habeant seminaria, a re tamen et a su-
biecta materia opes et temperamentum quoddam acquirunt,[46] et,
ut ita dicam, se ad argumenti proposti imaginem propemodum
effingunt. Sola est memoria quae ita in nobis tota delitescit, ut a
naturae beneficio magis quam ab ingenii facultate pendeat.

10   Ex iis quae neque in re neque in nobis posita sunt, sed tota peregre adveniunt,[47] ea pars est quae ad dictionem spectat, quae orationi suppellectilem et domesticum instrumentum subministrat et,
ut ita dicam, tectorium superinducit. Quam unam propriam oratori existimavit Cicero eamque ita admiratus est, ut eius expli-
candae gratia nobilem illum ad Brutum librum scripserit, cui titulum *Oratoris* fecit. Certe apud Graecos *rhetorice* non aliunde nomen
accepit. Facit enim phrasim, id est, eloquentiae corpus absoluit.
Et cum ceterae partes reliquis artificibus communes cum oratore
sint—nam et praefari et invenire et in membra digerere, tum refel-
lere et asseverare, et certo fine concludere quae scripta sunt, solent
omnis[48] qui nomen litteris dederunt—sed dicere pro dignitate et
verba invenire rei propositae accommodata, hoc vero proprium est
et praestantissimum magni illius eloquentiae institutoris[49] munus.
Hoc illud est quod nemo per se suisque viribus confisus vel diu-
turnitate temporis vel assiduitate studii vel ingenii felicitate umquam assequetur.[50] Hic regnat, hic rerum potitur imitatio. Quisquis vero hac parte imitari fastidit, potest ipse sibi placere fortasse,
mihi vero plane operam frustratur; eiusque profectus conclamatos
ac prorsus defletos puto.

11   Nam cum in oratione praecipua virtus sit perspicuitas, qui potest ille plane ac Latine loqui qui nescierit se propriis verbis id

and are associated with psychic motions. Although all these parts
of the oration are implanted in us and have their seedbed in us,
they nonetheless acquire resources and a certain proportion from
the subject matter, and almost model themselves, so to speak, on
the image of the argument that has been set out. Memory alone
lies so totally hidden in us that it depends more on the gift of nature than on one's intellectual abilities.[20]

Among the elements situated neither in the subject matter nor   10
in us, but which come entirely from without, is the element corre-
sponding to delivery, which supplies the speech its furniture and
domestic equipment and puts the roof in place, so to speak. Cicero
considered this element alone to be proper to the orator, and admired it so much that to explain it he wrote for Brutus that noble
book entitled *The Orator*. That and no other was certainly the
source of the name "rhetoric" in Greece. For the art of rhetoric
creates diction, that is to say, the very fabric of eloquence.[21] Now,
the other parts of oratory are common to other artists and to the
orator alike. For all those who have devoted their reputations to
written form are accustomed to introduce, to find and to arrange
their material into sections, and to refute, maintain and bring their
writings to an appropriately rounded conclusion. Yet to speak with
dignity and to invent expressions appropriate to the subject matter
under discussion — this is really the proper and most excellent task
of the great teacher of true eloquence. This is the task that no one
will ever achieve by relying on his own powers, either through the
passage of time, assiduous study or the good fortune of natural
talent. It is here that imitation reigns, here that it makes itself
master. Indeed, whoever disdains imitation in this part of oratory
may perhaps please himself, but to my mind he is obviously wast-
ing his time, and his efforts to improve, I think, give rise to wails
and lamentation.

Since clarity is a special virtue in oratory, how can a person   11
speak plainly and in good Latin if he does not know how he can

posse assequi? Propria autem verba appellarim quae in loco nata
sunt ad rem ipsam significandam, qualia sunt quae a Varrone pri-
migenia nuncupantur. Eius generis sunt[51] quae magnus ille dialec-
ticus in Cratylo apud Platonem invenit; quae summus philoso-
phus, non ille quidem naturaliter facta (sic enim eadem essent
apud omnes gentes), sed hausta ex proprietate naturae existimavit.

12   Quod si exornandae orationi quis studeat, quomodo id melius
facere potest quam si translatis commode vocibus frequenter uta-
tur? Translatae autem voces sunt quae, ex loco in quo natae sunt,
in alienum migrarunt, quae quasi stellae orationi interseruntur.
Omnia autem verba aut seorsum aut in contextu considerantur.
Seorsum, ut pura sint, usitata et rem significantia. Cum enim oratio instituta sit in auditoris maxime gratiam, quam indigna laude
sit, si obscura fuerit et apud homines consummatae praesertim
lectionis, egeat interprete? In contextu autem, orationis verba
concinna sint,[52] apte inter se cohaerentia, quae in ingressu orationis et in exitu maxime voluptati aurium inserviant. Illud vero cum
prudentia coniunctum est, ut qui dixerit, intellegat ac secernat in
quo genere versetur oratio. Nam eloquens ille quem se persaepe
quaesisse, numquam autem invenisse Antonius profitebatur, co-
gnoscet a se humilia subtiliter, magna graviter, mediocria temperate esse tractanda. At haec tam diversa nemo effecerit nisi qui
suscepto argumento obsecundaverit et ad genus dicendi verba tem-
peraverit; ex iis innumera schemata, ex iis antitheta, ex iis epicheremata et cetera in dicendo lumina effulgent.

13   Quid dicam de numeris? Quibus quasi ammentis contorta oratio fulgurat, tonat et in animos hominum tyrannidem exercet,

achieve this using the proper words? I should call words "proper" that have naturally occurred in a situation to signify the thing itself.[22] Words of this type are what Varro called "primitives."[23] Of this kind are the names which that great dialectician discovered in Plato's *Cratylus*.[24] Yet not even that excellent philosopher believed that such words were created naturally (they would thus be the same for all peoples), but that they were derived from natural properties.

But if someone wants to embellish his speech, how better to do   12 this than to use apt metaphors often? Metaphors are expressions that are applied to a situation different from that where they originally occurred.[25] They are sown into a speech like stars.[26] All words are considered either separately or in context: separately, to ensure that they are simple, in current use and signify their object. Since oratory has been established primarily to win the favor of the audience, how unworthy of praise would it be if speech were obscure and required an interpreter, even before an audience consisting of highly cultivated people? Considered in context, however, the words of a speech should be neatly arranged and should fit together aptly, so that they provide aural pleasure, above all at the beginning and end of a speech. It should be put together with prudence in such a way that the speaker understands and distinguishes the correct genre of speech. For that eloquent speaker whom Marcus Antonius claimed always to have sought but never to have found[27] will recognize that he must handle humble affairs with subtlety, great affairs with gravity, and affairs of the middling sort with moderation. However, no one will produce such diverse effects unless he moves in concert with the argument that he has undertaken and tempers his words to his type of speech. It is from these words that there radiates out the countless rhetorical figures, antitheses, syllogisms and other luminous effects of style.

What should I say of rhythms? When hurled with the power   13 of rhythm, a speech flashes and thunders, it tyrannizes the souls

utpote quos pro arbitrio in omnem faciem tum odii, tum misericordiae, tum indignationis commutat. In numerosa oratione Aristoteles paeana quartum omnibus praefert; Cicero, Brutus atque alii longe diversa sentiunt. Dichorius Asiaticis oratoribus familiaris est, et propemodum in deliciis habetur et, si vera fatemur, non est alius qui apertius auribus blandiatur. Quanta enim acclamatione Ciceronianum illud ex Rosciana[53] exceptum est?

> *Quid tam commune quam spiritus vivis? Terra mortuis? Mare fluctuantibus? Litus eiectis? Ita vivunt dum possunt, ut ducere animam de caelo non queant. Ita moriuntur ut eorum ossa terra non tangat. Ita iactantur fluctibus, ut numquam alluantur. Ita postremo eiciuntur, ut ne ad saxa quidem mortui conquiescant.*

Ego vero, ut dicam quod sentio, hunc aurium pruritum in iis omnibus pedibus animadverto, quos quattuor saltem syllabis metimur, et ‹qui› proximam a fine attollunt. Sit exemplo illud ex Corneliana: 'Neque me divitiae movent, quibus omnes Africanos et Laelios multi venalitii mercatoresque superarunt.' Ob id paeana tertium quarto multo libentius praetulerim. Hinc se germanos Ciceronis existimabant, qui hoc fine periodum clauserant: 'esse videatur.'

14   Atqui hunc verborum delectum, hunc apparatum nemo assequi potest, nisi qui se assiduae accurataeque lectioni dederit, qui in volvendis scriptoribus iisque praecipuis se diu exercuerit et quasi concoxerit, ut ad scribendum deinde subactam operam afferat: una[54] est enim imitatio, quae hac parte plurimum polleat: haec ob-

of men, changing them at will into every expression and permuta-
tion of hatred, then pity, then anger. In rhythmic speech, Aristotle
prefers the fourth paean to all other rhythms.[28] Cicero, Brutus and
others have very different opinions on the subject.[29] The Asiatic
orators are at home with the double trochee, considering it almost
as a delicacy, and to tell the truth, no other rhythm more obviously charms the ear. Consider how much praise was won by that
passage of Cicero from the *Pro Roscio*:

> What is so common as spirit to the living? Earth to the
> dead? Sea to the foundering? The shore to the shipwrecked?
> While they can, they live in such a way that they cannot
> draw their spirit down from heaven; they die in such a way
> that the earth does not touch their bones. Waves toss them
> about in such a way that they are never washed in them.
> And at the last they are shipwrecked in such a way that the
> dead do not grow quiet, not even when dashed against the
> rocks.[30]

To give you my opinion, I find fault with this tickling of the ears
in all those metrical feet of at least four syllables which stress the
penultimate syllable.[31] Take that passage from [Cicero's oration in
defense of] Cornelius, for example: "Nor do the riches move me
by which many dealers and merchants have surpassed all the
Africanuses and Laeliuses."[32] That is why I should much prefer
the third to the fourth paean. Hence, certain men considered
themselves Cicero's brothers because they had closed a period with
the ending, "it would seem so."[33]

But no one can develop this ability to choose or prepare his   14
words unless he applies himself to constant and careful reading,
trains himself for a long time studying the best writers, digesting
them,[34] if you will, so he may then apply his training and effort to
writing. There is one type of imitation that is highly effective in
this regard: it observes, excerpts and sets aside things which, when

servat, excerpit, seponit, quae, cum tempus postulaverit, quasi ex penu depromat. Haec olim erat oratori accommodata, cum adhuc in ipsis crepundiis Latinae linguae castitas ageret, cum in theatro, voce una parum commode enuntiata, universus populus actorem exsibilaret. Cur enim Cicero de bono oratore pronuntiaturus ad populum provocat? Cur Demosthenes una dictione corrupte, sed ea consulto prolata Αἰσχύνης μισθωτός, ὦ ἄνδρες, ἢ οὔ; acclamationem totius populi Atheniensis emeruit, μισθοτός, nisi quod protritae ac pervulgatae[55] erant dictiones, quibus docti, indocti promiscue utebantur?[56] Alioqui anicula una olitrix non annotasset affectatum atticismum in Theophrasto.

15   Ex quo nobis multo maxima illa difficultas adsurgit, de qua paulo ante diximus, dediscendi scilicet verba corruptissima quae alii Gothis, alii Langobardis, alii Mauris et Vandalis accepta ferunt; ego ex omnium faece hausta contenderim. Novissimus autem labor incumbet[57] ediscendi atque ebibendi scriptorum veterum beneficio, non dico quae optima sunt (nam in hoc veteres, salva adhuc populi victoris gentium maiestate, elaborabant) sed ea quae non sint pessima. Quae si non ornamentum orationi afferant, certe dignitatem non detrahant.

16   In collocatione autem verborum et numerosa oratione, illud non dissimulabo, non nullam quoque partem naturae deberi, quae acutis et gravibus omnem pronuntiationem modulata est. In imitatione tamen certum est partem longe maximam et ipsam quodammodo summam esse positam. Hinc est quod Platonem legentes heroicam quandam amplitudinem haurimus et afflatu prope divino incitamur. Qui vero frequentes sunt in lectione Isocratis, hi comptam et undique picturatam orationem effingunt, palestrae quam

the occasion demands it, it may produce as if from a storehouse.[35] This type of imitation was suited to the orator when the Latin language was still pure and in its infancy, when in the theater the whole audience would hiss an actor off the stage if he mispronounced a single syllable.[36] For why does Cicero, when he is about to give his views on the good orator, appeal to the people?[37] When Demosthenes pronounced a word incorrectly but deliberately in the statement, "Is 'Aeschunes' a hireling or not, fellow citizens?" why did he earn the shout from the entire Athenian people, "A hireling!" if not because these were everyday, common expressions that they all used, learned and unlearned alike.[38] Otherwise, a single old grocer woman would not have noted the affected Atticism in Theophrastus.[39]

Hence arises the greatest difficulty of all, which we discussed a 15 little earlier, that is, how to unlearn the utterly corrupt words that some say we learned from the Goths, others from the Lombards, and others from the Moors and Vandals, but in my opinion were derived from the dregs of all those peoples.[40] Contemporary efforts to learn thoroughly and imbibe — well, I won't say the *best* words (the ancients used to work at that when the majesty of an imperial people was still intact), but words that are not the worst — will rely upon the support of ancient writers. If such words fail to embellish one's speech, they at least do not detract from its dignity.

Now in the arrangement of words and rhythmic speech, I shall 16 not pretend that some part is not owed to nature too, which has regulated all diction using acute and grave accents. It nevertheless is certain that by far the greatest and, in a sense, the highest part of arrangement and rhythm belongs to imitation. Hence it is that from reading Plato we derive a certain heroic grandeur and are moved by an almost divine inspiration.[41] But close readers of Isocrates fashion a diction that is neat[42] and full of color, much more suited to the palaestra than to actual oratorical battle.[43]

iustae pugnae multo aptiorem. Qui apud Demosthenem versantur, hi bellicum quendam concentum animo concipiunt, ut paulo minus ad arma prosiliant et iam caedem et sanguinem spirent et vulnera afferre et accipere honestum putent.

17   At cum M. Ciceronem adimus, di boni, quis habitus oris, quae animorum imago non se nobis ingerit? Quantis ille hastas lacertis in orationibus iaculatur? Quos ille clamores, quos tumultus elicit, quoties indignatur? Quos ille luctus, quas deplorationes animis inspirat, cum misericordiae vela intendit? Quale illud: *O me miserum, O me infelicem! Revocare tu me in patriam, Milo, potuisti per hos; ego te in patria per eosdem retinere non potero?* et quae sequuntur, quae tantum secum ignis convehunt, ut totus auditorum animus exardescat. Quid in iis libris quos de philosophia conscripsit? Quam presse ingreditur, quam luculenter enarrat, quam fortiter redarguit, quam constanter asseverat! In iis autem libris, quibus rationem dicendi prosecutus est, rem plane admirabilem praestitit, ut cum libri illi minime sint eloquentiae capaces, is[58] tanta tamen eloquentia illos exornarit, ut non aliunde libentius eloquentiae rationem mutueris. Et quota haec portio innumerabilium laudum quas eminentissimus ille et plane incomparabilis orator promeruit, longe omni invidia maior! Quas praeter Ciceronem nemo facile enumeraverit.

18   Sed nos haec pauca ea tantum causa attigimus ut omnes intellegant ei qui profecturus est in dicendo, imitationem optimi cuiusque esse necessariam. Qua ablegata ac reiecta omnes conatus iacere ac non aliter esse destitutos oportet quam si navis oneraria pacato in mari remittentibus ventis, inhibentibus nautis fluctuet tantum, neque promoveat neque praestitutos portus sibi umquam polliceatur. Quod si nemo dubitat quin ad imitandum optimus quisque deligendus sit, neque id dubitabit Ciceronem sine contro-

Those versed in Demosthenes conceive a certain martial harmony in their soul, so that they all but rush to arms, now breathing carnage and blood, and think it honorable to inflict and receive wounds.

But when we come to Marcus Cicero, good gods, what habits 17
of expression, what psychic image does not rush upon us? How muscular he is hurling spears in his orations! The uproar, the tumults he starts! How quick he is to anger! O the grief, the mourning he inspires in our souls when he sets the sails of pity! For example, "How wretched, how unhappy I am! You, Milo, have been able to recall me to the fatherland through these men; shall I be unable to keep you here through the same?"[44] and following: the passage conveys so much fire that the whole soul of his listeners grows inflamed. What about how he writes in his philosophical works? How concisely he starts out! How lucid his narrations! How bold his refutations! How resolute his affirmations! And in his books on rhetorical theory he has offered something really remarkable. Although there is minimal room for eloquence there, he has nevertheless embellished these books with so much eloquence that you'd rather not borrow your rhetorical theory from anywhere else. And what a small portion is this of the countless praises that this most eminent and clearly incomparable orator has earned, a man great beyond the reach of envy! No one but Cicero has tallied up so many marks of praise, not by a long shot.

We have touched on these few points only so that everyone 18
may understand that imitation of all the best authors is a necessity for anyone who intends to make progress in speaking. If he banishes and rejects imitation, all his attempts must fail and be lost, like a cargo ship on a calm sea when the winds go slack and the oarsmen stop rowing; it merely tosses in the waves and neither advances nor ever promises to reach its intended ports.[45] But if everyone agrees that one should choose an author to imitate because he is the best, he will also agree that Cicero is indisputably prefer-

versia longe omnibus esse praeferendum. Nam ex ceteris una aut altera virtus peti potest; hic unus[59] omnia implet munia, solusque pomeria Romanae eloquentiae tantum protulit quantum imperatorum nemo victricibus armis imperium propagavit. Ut non iniuria Apollonius Molonis, cum Ciceronem Rhodi orantem audisset, ingemuerit vicem Graecorum, quibus, cum Romana virtus imperium abstulisset, id quod unum reliquum erat, eloquentiam scilicet, Cicero quasi spolium ex devictis ingeniis, in Romanam urbem referret.

19   Nec a me quisquam putet haec ideo dicta esse quod ceteros scriptores in ordinem redigam aut suo honore fraudatos velim. Absit enim a me hic furor! An ego Caesarem non suspiciam, qui ea scripsit animi magnitudine qua depugnavit? Certe ego, si mihi argumentum offeratur in quo ille versatus est, Caesarem quam Ciceronem imitari malim. Quid Livium, quid Salustium, utrunque diversa virtute eminentem? Quid Celsum in re medica? Quid Columellam in re agresti? Certe in historia naturae C. Plinium facile omnibus praetulerim, in cuius descriptione, nemo mirificas illas opes feliciore penicillo expressit; nemo dulcius, nemo aptius Aristotelem, Theophrastum, totamque illam doctissimam antiquitatem sub compendio repraesentavit. Certe me loca quaedam ex Cicerone excerpta et a Plinio repetita conferentem ingens admiratio pervasit, cum ea commodius ac subtilius a Plinio enarrata (meo quidem iudicio) offendissem; usque adeo multi interest, cui quis materiae describendae nomen dederit. Mirum est enim quantum in eo quisque promoveat, ad quod a natura factus videatur. Sed corrupta adeo ad nos Pliniana lectio pervenit ut, quod aiunt, Samnium adhuc quaeramus in Samnio.

able to every other author. For we can seek one virtue or another
from other writers; but this one man fulfills all the functions of
rhetoric and alone has advanced the boundaries of Roman eloquence as much as any of the emperors extended the empire by
their conquering arms. So Apollonius Molon, after he had heard
Cicero speaking at Rhodes, was right to groan on behalf of the
Greeks, from whom Cicero took eloquence — the only thing that
remained to them after Roman valor had taken their empire — and
brought it back to the city of Rome like booty from his victory in
a war of wits.[46]

This being said, no one should think that I therefore underesti-   19
mate the other writers or wish to cheat them of their proper hon-
ors. I hope I can avoid such madness as that! May I not embrace
Caesar, who wrote with the same magnanimity with which he
fought?[47] Certainly, if I should be faced with the sort of theme
that Caesar was expert in, I should prefer to imitate him rather
than Cicero. What of Livy or Sallust, both of whom are eminent, though they differ in their virtue? What of Celsus on medical topics? What of Columella on rural matters? On natural history, of course, I would far prefer Pliny to anyone else. For no one
describes the marvelous riches of nature with a more fruitful
quill; no one more pleasantly, none more fittingly reproduced Aristotle, Theophrastus and all the most learned ancients in abridged
form. In comparing certain passages that had been excerpted from
Cicero and repeated by Pliny, I was amazed to find that Pliny, in
my opinion of course, had narrated them more aptly and subtly.
His work thus matters a great deal to that art which someone has
named "describing the material."[48] It is remarkable how much each
person advances in what he seems to have been made for by nature. Yet Pliny's text has come down to us in such corrupt condition that we may still be looking for Samnium in Samnium, as
they say.[49]

20   Solent hoc loco[60] nonnulli percunctari nunquid ab eo, quem
nobis imitandum proposuerimus, liceat eadem prorsus verba nihil
immutata, nihil inversa in nostra scripta transferre. Anceps quaes-
tio et super qua neque verba neque rationes desideres, seu tu hanc
aut[61] illam partem[62] propugnandam seu oppugnandam suscepe-
ris. Quod si testimoniis uti malis, authoritas clarissimorum se
utrinque profert.[63] Mitto ceteros; sane Vergilius *Belli ferratos rupit
Saturnia postes* et *unus qui nobis cunctando restituit rem* aliaque loca innumera tum ab Ennio, tum ab aliis prisci saeculi scriptoribus bona
fide faeneratus deprehenditur. Sicut illud a Cicerone detorsit,
Proximus huic, longo sed proximus intervallo. Sed et ipse Cicero: *Timor
mihi omnem sapientiam expectoravit,*[64] et illud, *Arcem facere ex cloaca.*
Nonne et illud Terentianum a Livio Andronico acceptum est: *Tu
te*[65] *lepus es et pulpamentum quaeris?*

21   Contra alius dixerit imitationem nihil esse aliud nisi imaginem
ad quam stylum quis[66] orationemque conformet. Atqui in imagine
quaedam similia, dissimilia quaedam[67] sunt; nulla sunt eadem.
Nam si eadem, tum vero eveniet illud ridiculum quod Lucianus
argute illusit in *Iove Tragoedo,* ut tunc Demosthenem pulchre imitati videamur, cum Demosthenis orationem transcripserimus, et
manifesto in plagio deprehensi, quasi cornicula Aesopi, spectato-
ribus risum praebeamus, vel convicti adiudicatique creditoribus
nexum ineamus. Sane huc censuram direxit Aristophanes, cum
praefectus Bibliothecae Ptolemaei adiuratissimos scriptores pros-
cripsit, qui tanti aestimarunt aliena monumenta suis chartis inse-
ruisse, ut ea protinus sui mancipii facta esse[68] iudicarent.

22   Sunt etiam qui ab aliis accepta ideo mutanda non putent, quod
priores illi optima quaeque invaserint: quibus peiora substituere,
non modo turpe sit, sed etiam temeritati finitimum. Rursus alii

Some people investigating this topic ask whether we are permit- 20
ted to transfer the same expressions, unchanged in form or position, into our writings from the person whom we have proposed
to imitate. This is a question that admits of two answers, and you
wouldn't lack for either words or arguments if you undertook to
defend or attack on either side. But if you prefer to use testimo-
nies, the authority of the most famous men supports both camps.
I pass over other examples, but it's a fact that Virgil has been
caught borrowing in good faith, "Saturnia burst the iron gates of
war"[50] and "He alone restored the state to us by delaying"[51] and
countless other passages from Ennius[52] and other ancient writers.
Note, for example, how he here alters Cicero's phrase, "The man
closest to this one, but only by a long margin."[53] Cicero himself
says, "Fear has banished all my wisdom!"[54] and "To make a citadel
out of a sewer."[55] And wasn't Terence's saying, "You're a hare and
you're asking for game," taken from Livius Andronicus?[56]

On the other hand, someone might say that imitation is noth- 21
ing but an image on which someone models his style and oratory.
But some qualities in an image are similar, others dissimilar; none
is the same. If they are the same, the result will be that ridiculous situation that Lucian cleverly mocks in *Zeus the Tragic Actor*:[57]
that is, we look like we've done a lovely imitation of Demosthenes,
when we've only transcribed an oration of his. And though we
have been caught in an obvious plagiarism,[58] like Aesop's little
crows,[59] we give the spectators a good laugh; convicted and sen-
tenced, we get ourselves in debt with lenders. It was surely for
this reason that Aristophanes, when prefect of the Ptolemaic library, proscribed the most heavily indebted writers, who set so
much value on inserting other people's writings into their own
papers that they thought those writings had forthwith become
their chattels. [60]

There are also people who believe that we should not change 22
what we borrow from others because the earlier writers have taken

fortiter audendum et cum antiquis intrepide[69] digladiandum sua-
dent. Numquam enim nobis verba defutura vel propria vel trans-
lata vel ex contrario deducta. Exemplo sit, 'ea res mihi perpetuo
memoriae condita manebit'; 'eam rem nulla aetas mihi expunget
aut delebit ex memoria'; 'ea res nulla umquam oblivione obsoles-
cet.' In priore illa sententia fuit Cicero, cuius verba sub persona
Crassi enuntiata subiiciam, ut res melius intellegatur:

> In quotidianis autem cogitationibus equidem mihi adolescentulus pro-
> ponere solebam illam exercitationem maxime, qua C. Carbonem,
> nostrum illum inimicum, solitum esse uti sciebam, ut aut versibus
> propositis quam maxime gravibus aut oratione aliqua lecta ad eum
> finem, quem memoria possem comprehendere; eam rem ipsam quam
> legissem verbis aliis quam maxime possem lectis pronuntiarem. Sed
> post animadverti hoc, esse in hoc vitii, quod ea verba quae maxime
> cuiusque rei propria, quaeque essent ornatissima atque optima, occu-
> passet aut Ennius, si ad eius versus me exercerem, aut Gracchus si
> eius orationem mihi forte proposuissem. Ita si iisdem verbis uterer,
> nihil prodesse; si aliis, etiam obesse, cum[70] minus idoneis uti consues-
> cerem.

23   Adversus Ciceronem stat Quintilianus et gravissimo oratori, cui
alias reverenter semper assurgit, audacter repugnat. Eius quoque
verba non pigebit adscribere, ut quid[71] praeclara ingenia utrinque
attulerint agnoscatur:

over all the best material. It is thus not only unattractive but even
borders on rashness to substitute language that is worse. Still others persuade us to be daring and duel fearlessly with the ancients.
For we will never lack for words, whether we are looking for words
in their proper senses, metaphors, or words in inverted senses.
Take for example: "That event will remain perpetually stored in
my memory," "No length of time will strike or erase that affair
from my memory," and "No obscurity will ever overshadow that
affair."[61] Cicero held the first opinion above, and I shall quote
what he says under the persona of Crassus so you may better understand the matter.

> In my daily cogitations as a young man I used to practice the
> exercise that I knew Gaius Carbo, our enemy, used to fol-
> low: first I would read either the weightiest verses possible or
> some oration to the end which I might commit to memory;
> then I would articulate the matter that I had read, but in
> words as different as possible from the original ones. Later,
> however, I noticed an error in my method: the words that
> were most suited to each matter, that were best and most or-
> nate, had already been taken either by Ennius, if I was prac-
> ticing with his verses, or by Gracchus, if I happened to be
> working through one of his orations. Thus, if I were to use
> the same words, it would not profit me; if other ones, it
> might even damage me, since I was becoming accustomed to
> using inapt language.[62]

Quintilian stands against Cicero and has the audacity to fight 23
back against this most authoritative of orators, to whom he otherwise always defers respectfully. It will give us no displeasure to
quote him as well, in order to acknowledge what renowned talents
have said on both sides:

Neque ego παράφρασιν esse interpretationem tantum volo, sed
circa eosdem sensus certamen atque emulationem; ideoque ab illis
dissentio qui vertere orationes Latinas vetant, quia optimis occupatis,
quicquid aliter dixerimus, necesse sit esse deterius. Nam neque semper est desperandum aliquid illis quae dicta sunt melius posse reperiri, neque adeo ieiunam et pauperem natura fecit eloquentiam, ut
una de re bene dici, nisi semel non possit. Nisi forte histrionum
multa circa voces easdem variare gestus potest,[72] orandi minor vis est,
ut dicatur aliquid praeter quod in eadem materia nihil dicendum sit.
Sed esto neque melius quod invenimus sit nec par; est certe proximus
locus. An non ipsi nos bis ac saepius de eadem re dicimus, et quidem
continuas nonnumquam sententias? Nisi forte contendere nobiscum
possumus, cum aliis non possumus. Nam si uno genere duntaxat
bene dicetur, fas erit existimari praeclusam[73] nobis a prioribus viam
in dicendo. Nunc vero innumerabiles sunt modi, plurimaeque eodem
viae ducunt, sive brevitatis gratia sive copiae. Alia tralatis virtus,
alia propriis; hoc oratio recta, illud figura declinata commendat. Ipsa
denique utilissima est exercitationi difficultas. Quid quod authores
maximi sic diligentius cognoscuntur? Non enim scripta lectione se-
cura transcurrimus, sed tractamus singula et necessario introspicimus
et quantum virtutis habeant, vel hoc ipso cognoscimus, quod imitari
non possumus.

I do not want "paraphrase" to be simple interpretation but a contest and rivalry over the same meanings.[63] I therefore disagree with those who forbid adapting or paraphrasing Latin speeches, because, they say, since the best material has already been taken, whatever we say differently must be worse. For we should not remain forever hopeless of discovering something better than what has already been said. Nor did nature make eloquence so meager and poor that it is impossible to speak well on any matter except once. If an actor can make gestures that vary many aspects of his performance around the same lines,[64] is the power of oratory any weaker, so that once something is said one can say nothing more on the same matter beyond that? Let us assume that that is the case, and that there is nothing either better or equal for us to invent. There is certainly the next best thing. Do we not ourselves speak again and again about the same matter and, indeed, sometimes give a series of opinions about it? If perchance we cannot contend with ourselves, we cannot do so with others.[65] For if something is well said in only one form, one could conclude that our ancestors have barred us from the way of fine speech. There are today, however, countless means and several ways leading to the same end, whether thanks to brevity or to abundance. There is one virtue in metaphorical words, another in proper words. Direct speech recommends the latter, indirection the former. Finally, the difficulty of the exercise is itself very useful. Otherwise why is it that we study the greatest authors so much more diligently? Indeed, we do not rush through their writings in careless reading, but treat them one at time and necessarily examine closely how much virtue they have, or we recognize it by this very fact, that we cannot imitate them. [66]

24   Quod si mihi in re controversa liberum permittatur iudicium, illud videor sine cuiusquam iniuria posse dicere: quaedam esse tam proprie, tam apposite et ad rem explicandam accommodate dicta, ut vix commutari possint, nisi in deterius. Quale Caesarianum illud: *Altero commeatu omnes copias trans*[74] *flumen exposuit.* Et Plinius Caecilius cum lachrymas vectigales eorum appellavit, quorum haereditati pars detrahebatur: non potuit efficatius rem commonstrare. Cum Cicero *integrum* discipulum vocavit, satis indicavit hominem nullis adhuc imbutum rudimentis. Neque illud Ciceronis[75] quisquam melius dixerit, *aut opus sartum redimere, aut operam in diem locare.* Quod si haec usui veniant, nemini fraudi duxerim, iis sine ulla interpolatione uti. Quod si quis immutare tentaverit, me quidem iudice, non id faciet sine affectationis suspicione. Sed cum multo plura sint, quae variis modis dici atque exornari possint, et (ut ita dicam) eloquentiae capacia sint, is apud me longe potior fuerit qui pluribus luminibus orationem variaverit, et copiam in dicendo suam approbaverit. Quam rem video Senecam Ovidio vitio dedisse: sed vitium hoc tam amabile est et magnis ingeniis tam peculiare, ut non altero libentius velim bene institutos adolescentes laborare.

25   Illud erit in imitatione praecipuum, ut a pari, a simili et quasi ex eadem vicinia multa contrahas et quasi reponas *in promptuario, quae opportune deinde in rem tuam depromas;*[76] exemplo sit illud Cicero dixit, *turpe esse amicitiam ad calculos revocare.* Tu hanc dicendi imaginem mille modis effinges, multiformique persona indues; nam et 'beneficentiam nihil revocare ad calculos,' et 'probos in promerendo calculis non uti,' et 'ingratos vocandos esse ad calculos,' et

If I should be permitted free judgment in a controversial affair, 24
I think I can say without injury to anyone that certain things are
so properly, pertinently and aptly stated to explain a given subject
that they could hardly be changed except into something inferior.
Consider Caesar's statement, for example: "In the second crossing
he put all the troops across the river."[67] And Pliny the Younger,
when he described as public "taxes" the tears of those who were
being bled of part of their inheritance, could not have expressed
the situation more effectively.[68] When Cicero called a student "un-
spoiled," he disclosed just enough about a man who still lacked basic education.[69] Nor could anyone make the following Ciceronian
statement better: "either to buy the building in good repair or
arrange for future work."[70] If such expressions came into circulation, I would not think it fraud for anyone to adopt them in
their entirety. But if anyone should try to change them (in my
judgment of course), he will not do this without being suspected
of affectation. But since there are many more matters that can be
discussed and embellished in various ways and are susceptible of
eloquent treatment, as far as I am concerned, the man who varies
his speech with rhetorical devices and demonstrates his richness of
expression will be far more effective. I see that Seneca cites this
practice as a fault of Ovid.[71] Yet such a fault is so attractive and so
unique to men of great talent that I would not wish well-educated
youths to labor more willingly at anything else.

A paramount task in imitation will be for you to draw many 25
words from someone with whom you are well matched, a person
like you and, as it were, from the same neighborhood, and then
store them, if you will, "in your personal repository, so you may
then withdraw them into your own material at an opportune moment."[72] For example, Cicero said, "It is base to call friendship to
account."[73] You will shape this image of speech into a thousand
forms and dress it up in personalities of various kinds. For instance, "Kindness calls nothing to account," and "Good men do

'neminem esse qui cum bonitate summi numinis possit calculis de-
cidere,' et 'legem talionis tacito consensu antiquatam, quod pari-
bus calculis iniuriae pensari non possint,' commode pro loco et re
presente dixeris.

26   Quaerunt humanarum artium studiosi: quis fuerit celeber[77] et
ore omnium dictus 'canon Polycleti'? Ego eum[78] Doryphorum, illum viriliter puerum, fuisse arbitror, ex quo omnes omnium membrorum exemplum sumebant artifices, non ea quidem ratione, ut
tam excellentis imaginis membra convellerent, sed ut numeros eosdem tantum eandemque proportionem servarent; solus enim ille
artem fecisse artis opere iudicatur. Illud quoque testatum velim,
nullam esse partem in arte dicendi, quae diuturna lectione soler-
tique imitatione non multo fiat melior atque auctior, sive illa ex re
pendeat sive ex dicentis ingenio. Nam et exordia quae ex re petun-
tur, et inventio quae insita est in re, et coordinatio quae ingenii
functio est, cetera denique quae superius enumeravimus, si ad
imaginem optimi et probatissimi cuiusque referantur, infinitum est
quanto cultiora absolutioraque effici possint; sicut et reliqua naturae bona, si manu tractentur et mangonis artificio expoliantur,
supra fidem splendescunt atque illustrantur.

27   Me igitur iudice primus locus sit imitationi in delectu verborum, seu quae ad rem explicandam[79] seu quae ad exornationem
pertineant. In reliquis autem secundarius et postremus subsideat.
In actione incertum est plus natura an cura valeat. Certe suavitas
vocis et litterarum expressio, quam in Catulis laudavit antiquitas, quin et oris probitas, dignitas corporis et faciles membrorum

not use accounts when gaining merit," and "The ungrateful should
be called to account," and "There is no one whom the goodness of
the supreme divinity lets falls from his accounts," and "The ancient law of retaliation has been rejected by tacit consent, because
injuries cannot be paid for by equalizing accounts." In this way
you will speak aptly as the context and subject requires.

People interested in humanities ask, What was that famous 26
work commonly called the Canon of Polyclitus? I think it was that
manly boy, the Doryphorus, from which every artist borrowed the
model of each limb.[74] Their intention, of course, was not to tear
off the limbs of so excellent an image, but only to preserve the
same measurements and proportion. Indeed, Polyclitus alone is
held to have made art itself through that work of art.[75] I would
also cite this as evidence that there is no part of the art of rhetoric
which cannot be much improved by long reading and careful imitation, whether it depends on the subject matter or on the ability
of the speaker. For exordia, which are taken from the matter itself,
and invention, which is inherent in the subject matter, and arrangement, which is a function of one's natural talent and, finally,
all the other aspects of a speech that we mentioned above — if we
should apply to them the image of all the best and most authoritative writers, there is no limit to how much we can further refine
and perfect them. It is the same as with other natural goods: if
they are cared for and polished with a furbisher's[76] skill, they glim-
mer and shine beyond belief.

So in my judgment, the principle place for imitation comes 27
in the choice of words, whether they pertain to explaining or em-
bellishing the subject matter. In other aspects of speech, however,
imitation should remain in second place or lower. In delivery it is
uncertain whether nature or care is more effective. Certainly a
charming voice and good articulation, which the ancients praised
in Catulus,[77] but also an honest face, physical dignity and supple
motions of the limbs are things owed to nature. Nevertheless, not

flexus naturae debentur; nec tamen huic omnia. Alioqui Demosthenes non tantum operae dedisset Andronico hypocritae, non
Augustus Phonasco, non Cicero toties cum Roscio et Aesopo
contendisset, neque idem optasset aliquot locis suum sibi oratorem, non quidem palaestritam, sed neque omnino ἀπάλαιστον
contingere.

28   Atqui ne illud quidem omittendum puto, hanc ipsam imitationem, quam candidatis studiorum ita commendatam volumus ut
sine ea prope inanis sit omnis opera, tunc demum non solum inu-
tilem fore, sed iacturam etiam allaturam iis qui iam[80] suis viribus
uti possunt, et quod adagio tritum est, sine cortice natare. Alienis
enim semper vestigiis haerere et serperastris,[81] ut ait Varro, eum
uti, qui per aetatem stare possit atque ingredi, non modo turpe
est, sed periculosum etiam. Cum non facile eorum vires coalescant
qui alienis pedibus incedunt, alienis manibus pugnant, alienis oculis vident, aliena lingua loquuntur; sui denique obliti alieno spiritu
vivunt. Quippe hoc iis per me liceat qui nondum in suam tutelam
venerunt, quique per aetatem praemanso adhuc cibo aluntur, quorum adhuc membra fasciis effinguntur. At quorum adulta est aetas
et firmiores lacerti, ii iam prodeant ex umbra, iam prosiliant in
campum, iam cum ipso lanista contendant a quo olim solebant
dictata accipere, suasque cum eo vires expendant, nec cedant, sed
contra potius adsurgant periculum facturi, an ipsi[82] possint ordinem ducere et suo Marte de gradu adversarium deicere.

29   Nec sane hoc loco mihi absurdum videtur eius fabulae memi-
nisse, cuius authorem habeo Alexandrum ex Aphrodisiade,[83] phi-
losophum et in Academia et in Lycaeo praestantissimum. In lucem ediderat Venus Cupidinem. Mirabatur dea quod multos post

everything can be credited to nature. Otherwise, Demosthenes
would not have paid so much attention to the actor Andronicus,[78]
nor Augustus to his voice coach,[79] nor would Cicero have con-
tended so often with Roscius[80] and Aesopus,[81] nor again would he
have wished in several passages that his model orator grapple, not
like a wrestler indeed, but like a man not altogether foreign to the
palaestra.[82]

Yet I think that this, too, should not be left out: this very pro-   28
cess of imitation, which we wish young students to consider so important that without it all their effort is nearly worthless, will ultimately be not only useless but even harmful and injurious to those
who are ready to exercise their own powers and (to use a common
adage) swim without a preserver.[83] For to always follow in others'
footsteps and use knee-splints, as Varro says, is not only base but
even dangerous for anyone mature enough to stand on his own
and walk.[84] The powers of those who walk with another's feet,
fight with another's hands, see with another's eyes and speak with
another's tongue do not readily take root and grow strong. In the
end they forget themselves and live by another's spirit. By all
means, I say, let those remain dependent who have not yet come
of age, who are still being nurtured on pre-chewed food,[85] whose
limbs are still bound in swaddling-clothes. But let those who are
grown up and have more well-knit sinews now come out of the
shadows; let them now rush onto the field; let them now contend
with the gladiatorial trainer himself from whom they took lessons,
and let them measure their own powers by his; and let them not
yield, but rather rise up and, threatening danger, see if they themselves can become centurions and cast down their opponent from
his rank with their own martial valor.[86]

I do not think it absurd to recall a fable here, which was writ-   29
ten, I believe, by Alexander of Aphrodisias, an outstanding philosopher in both the Platonic and Aristotelian traditions.[87] Venus
had just given birth to Cupid. The goddess was amazed that for

menses a natali die, nihilo auctior fieret Cupido. Quae causa eius
moraretur incrementa neque intellegebat, neque quid facto opus
foret aut quomodo huic mederi posset incommodo prospiciebat.
Fatidicam igitur anum, Themin, adit, consulit, responsum accipit,
non ante illum iustos auctus habiturum quam Venus alterum
filium peperisset, in cuius aemulationem ille succresceret. Venus
responso Themidis accepto, it in Martis complexum, filium alterum parit, cui nomen Anterotis imponit, ceu tu Anticupidinis
dixeris. Tum vero, mirum dictu, quam repente, quam feliciter ado-
lescit ille! Certatim dixeris alterum in alterum contendere uter
pulchrius ac praestantius se porrigat. Mirantur di ceteri, tum vero
imprimis parentes, tam egregiam prolem exurgere.

30   Ex iis, puto, facile colligas nulla praeclara ingenia posse ingentes
profectus facere, nisi habeant Antagonisten,[84] ut Graeci dicunt,
qui cum decertent, qui cum colluctentur. Neque solum oportet ut
cum aequalibus viventibusque contendamus, sed cum iis etiam qui
olim scripserunt, quos 'mutos magistros' appellamus. Alioqui futuri semper infantes.[85]

many months after his birth the child grew no larger. She didn't understand why he wasn't growing, and didn't know what to do or how to remedy the problem. So she went to Themis, an old prophetess, consulted her and learned that he would not grow properly until Venus had given birth to a second son, in rivalry with whom Cupid would grow up. After hearing Themis' response, Venus took Mars into her bed and bore a second son, whom she named Anteros, or the Anticupid, as you might say. Then, marvelous to relate, how suddenly, how successfully he began to grow up! You would say that one was in a contest with the other to see who would show himself the more beautiful and outstanding. The other gods were amazed but his parents were especially surprised how he grew into such a remarkable child.

From this, I think, you may easily conclude that no brilliant talents can make great progress unless they have an antagonist, to use the Greek word, with whom they may compete, with whom they may wrestle.[88] We must contend not only with our equals and contemporaries, but also with those who wrote long ago, whom we call our "mute masters." Otherwise, we shall always be infants.

1 Lilius Gregorius Gyraldus Cynthio Ioanni Baptistae Gyraldo
s. p. d. [1]

Audieram quidem antea istic Ferrariae gentilem quendam
meum ad optimas artes, bonasque literas pleno gradu procedere;
famam hanc non nihil auxerat Fabius Antimachus, qui hic apud
nos medicum agit, iuvenis rarae et spectatae indolis. Nuper vero,
cum a Pico vocatus Manardus, non iam ut antea famam, sed cer-
tissimam quandam mihi tuae et eruditionis et elegantiae formam
impressit, ut eum ego erga te amorem ac benevolentiam concepe-
rim, ut miro ac incredibili tuarum literarum desiderio arderem.

2 Sed, bone deus, quanta nunc mihi facta est amoris et caritatis
accessio, cum cultam ad te Caelii de imitatione commentationem,
dignissimam illam quidem imitatione, mihi legendam transmisisti.
Caelii inquam illius, qui unus hoc ferme tempore Varronis et Plinii eruditionem, cum M. Tullii eloquentia coniunxisse visus est,
orbemque illum disciplinarum interiorumque ac reconditarum literarum clarissime patefecisse, quem iure quidem ego a primis an-
nis et colui semper et suspexi, et me non nihil ab eo fieri in coronis
gloriari soleo. Amorem ergo ac benevolentiam erga te meam cu-
mulatissime auxit Caeliana commentatio.

3 Sed quid dicam? Quod fieri vix posse credidissem, expectatio-
nem meam longe superavit tuarum epistolarum lectio, ex quibus
plane percepi eo te brevissime perventurum (nisi alia te forte studia impedierint) quo adhuc paucissimi pervenerunt, nedum sunt

Lilio Gregorio Giraldi to Giambattista Giraldi Cinzio

Lilio Gregorio Giraldi wishes Giovanni Battista Giraldi Cinzio   1
good health.

I had heard before that a certain kinsman of mine there in
Ferrara was advancing at full stride in humanistic studies. Fabio
Antimaco, who practices medicine here with us, enlarged somewhat on this report about a young man of rare and respected
gifts.[1] Recently, however, when Manardo[2] was summoned by Pico,[3]
he gave me a very distinct impression of your learning and elegance, not just a rumor, as before. Thus there was born in me such
love and goodwill towards you that I burned with a wondrous and
unbelievable desire to read your letters.

But, good God! how much more has my love and esteem now   2
grown since you sent on to me Celio's fine treatise on imitation,
dedicated to you, which itself is quite worthy of imitation! I mean
the Celio who seems practically the only person in our time to
have married the erudition of Varro and Pliny with the eloquence
of Cicero and to have revealed with the greatest clarity that sphere
of learning and esoteric literature that I have always had just reason to cultivate and admire from my earliest years. I am in the
habit of boasting that I have acquired something of an audience
thanks to it. Celio's commentary has therefore increased my love
and good will toward you abundantly.

Yet, how shall I put it? I would hardly have believed it possible,   3
but reading your letters far surpassed my expectations, and I saw
plainly from them that you would very shortly arrive (unless other
pursuits perhaps hinder you) where very few have hitherto advanced, much less dared to aspire. Continue at this pace, I beg

ausi aspirare. Perge quaeso hoc gradu, mi Gyralde carissime, hanc tu assidue incudem tunde, nec patiare ut barbarorum hominum studia te a tanto incepto deturbent et, ut adhuc praestitisse videris, tu tibi consta et quam coepisti simul et eloquentiae et sapientiae via grassare. Hic, me Gyralde, contineo, ne te, qui per te sapis abunde, docere videar, et sus Minervam, neve malignus aliquis aut invidus, ut sunt plerique omnes hac tempestate, putet me familiae necessitudini et nomini adulari blandirique magis quam ex animo dicere.

4   Ceterum quoniam ex tuis literis te cupere vehementer video, quid de imitatione Caeliana Picus ipse sentiat, meis ut tibi literis significem, longior sim, Gyralde, si cuncta velim hic tibi perscribere, quae statim ille, audita tua primum epistola, dein Caeliana commentatione dixerit, ut est homo omnium facundissimus, cum aliquid ipse suis verbis declarandum aggreditur. In summa, in sua se ait persistere sententia, quam longiusculis duabus ad Bembum nostrum epistolis pridem datis est executus, quas et te vidisse ex tuis literis facile colligo.

5   Porro, quoniam et meam quoque sententiam rogas, tametsi, ex quo Romana me tempestas sic fortunae fluctibus obruit ut nulla sit amplius emergendi spes reliqua, amissis non modo amicis et opibus, sed et corporis valetudine, totum me, ut non nihil a procellis sublever, lectionum varietati omnis generis auctorum addixi. Quae pro eorum oratione legentis stilum huc illuc in diversa rapiunt; nihilominus, ne non ex parte morem tibi geram, paucissimis accipe quod mihi nunc occurrit.

you, my dear Giraldi; strike this anvil with persistence.[4] Do not permit the pursuits of barbarous men to distract you from such a great beginning. And as you seem to have demonstrated so far, be true to yourself and continue in the path of combining eloquence with wisdom as you have begun. I here contain myself, Giraldi, lest I, like a pig teaching Minerva,[5] seem to be teaching you, who are wise enough on your own, or lest some malicious or jealous person, of which there is no paucity in our time, think that I am fawning and flattering for the sake of a family connection[6] and reputation rather than speaking from the heart.

I see from your letter that you would very much like me to   4
relate to you by letter what Pico himself thinks about Celio's approach to imitation. But it would be a rather long business, Giraldi, to write out for you here everything that he was quick to say after hearing first your letter, then Celio's treatise, for he is the most fluent of all speakers when he starts to discuss a subject in his own words. In a nutshell, he says he persists in the view that he developed in the two rather long letters that he sent some time ago to our friend Bembo. I gather from your letter that you too have seen them.

But now, since you ask for my opinion as well — even though   5
the Roman storm[7] has so overwhelmed me with floods of ill fortune that I no longer have any hope of not drowning in them, having lost not only my friends and my wealth but my physical health as well — in order to lift myself somewhat out of the stormy gale, I have dedicated myself entirely to a variety of readings of every sort of author. These readings pull the reader's pen[8] in different directions, now here, now there, in response to their variety of speech; nonetheless, in order to comply with your wishes at least in part, please accept these few words that now occur to me on the subject.

6   De imitatione generatim et in universum non satis recte quemquam hoc tempore praecipere posse crediderim. Nam (ut mihi
quidem videtur) bifariam imitatio ipsa est partienda, aut enim
candidato aut adulto praeponitur, hoc est (ut planius loquar), aut
rudi et vix initiato necdum satis offirmato, aut erudito et probe in
literis versato; neque enim cum tardis, et conclamatis est sane nobis laborandum. Ergo si rudes et candidatos, dociles tamen, ad
imitationem voces, multo optima mihi Bembi praeceptio videtur.
Idque etiam eo usque faciendum censeo antequam quicquam aliud
eruditionis et disciplinarum attingant, donec non tantum animus
imbutus ipse, sed eo etiam aures tritae ita occalluerint, ut ferre nequeant, imo etiam aspernentur, quicquid suae fuerit dissonum
imitationi. Iam vero si doctos et eruditos ad imitationem provo-
care velis, nostri Pici et Caeliana sententia idonea magis videtur,
ad eam praestandam. Nam utriusque ratio ab eodem fine non
valde declinare videtur, si modo utramque recte perpendas.

7   Tum illud quoque diligenti cautione curandum est, ne quid invita (quod aiunt) Minerva et repugnante natura hominem, ut ceteris in rebus, ita in imitatione aggredi praecipias. Quando diversae
ut facies, ita sunt species et imitationum ideae; sed suam quemque
iubeto naturam et (ut dicitur) genium sequi. Nam si me divinam
illam Platonis amplitudinem et Isocratis myrothecia imitatione
consequi iubeas, frustra id cupias; humi enim (ut vides) serpens,
vix ego queo flosculos colligere. Illud etiam non mediocri cavendum cura, ne dum imitatores esse cupimus, in vitium incurramus
quod Graeci ab inepta imitatione κακοζηλίαν vocant, vel quod
Lucianus cuidam Thucydiden[2] imitanti obicit.

I am inclined to think that in our time there is no one whose   6
teaching about imitation, by genres and in general, is entirely correct. For (as it seems to me) imitation ought to be divided into
two parts, depending on whether it is being presented to students
or to adults — that is, to speak more plainly, either to an untrained
beginner who is not yet fixed in his ways, or to an educated man
thoroughly familiar with literature. (I don't think we need waste
time on the slow-witted and hopeless cases.) Therefore, if you are
going to encourage imitation among ignorant beginners still capable of learning, Bembo's teaching seems to me the best by far. And
I think that they should continue in this way before touching
upon any other branch of learning and the disciplines, until not
only is their mind itself steeped in that form of imitation, but
their ears are also worn down by it and have become so calloused
over that they cannot bear, in fact will even despise, whatever is
discordant with their own method of imitation. But on the other
hand, if you would like to stimulate the learned and erudite to
practice imitation, the views of our friend Pico and of Celio seem
to be the ones more suited to set before them. For both their theories seem hardly to deviate from the same end, provided you weigh
their views correctly.

Also, you must always be careful, in imitation as in other cases,   7
not to instruct a man to undertake any matter when Minerva is
unwilling,[9] as they say, and nature resists. For the types and ideas
of imitation are as different as the countenances of mankind.
Rather, bid each man follow his own nature and genius, as it is
called.[10] For if you should bid me imitate the divine grandeur of
Plato and Isocrates' ointment box, your wish would be in vain;[11]
crawling on the ground[12] (as you see me doing), I find it difficult
to gather little flowers.[13] We should also devote no small care, for
as long as we want to be imitators, to avoiding the fault that the
Greeks call *kakozelia*,[14] which comes from inept imitation, the fault
that Lucian criticized in an imitator of Thucydides.[15]

8   Atque haec pauca tibi ea ratione duntaxat sint a me perscripta,
ne aspernari videar quam tantopere concupieram oblatam mihi be-
nevolentiae et necessitudinis nostrae complectendae occasionem.
Vale et me, si mutuo me[3] facere cupis, ama.

Mirandulae ad x kalendas Decembris MDXXXII.[4]

I have written you these few words merely so as not to look like 8
I've spurned the opportunity that I had so much desired and that
has been offered me of embracing your good will and our family
connection. Farewell. Please think as fondly of me as I of you.

From Mirandola. November 21, 1532.

De ratione conscribendi epistolas
De arte dicendi, etiam ecclesiastica

Philosophica M. Tulli: caput XIII

1 [. . .] Et reliqua sane quae ad Ciceronem imitandum spectant
aut ex iis percipi possunt qui prudenter hac de re scripserunt,
Quintiliano, Ioanne Francisco Pico, Vive, Longolio, Paulo Cortesio, Bembo, Bartholomaeo Ricio, Iulio Caesare Scaligero, qui
etiam contra *Ciceronianum* Erasmi scripsit, ne quid dicam de Bruto,
Salustio et aliis quibus, cum olim minus probaretur Ciceronis sty-
lus, ii nonnulla in eo notarunt quae ad hanc rem faciunt; aut ex in-
terpretibus iis, quos tamquam praestantiores non ita pridem acce-
pimus, in unum collectos ex Aldina officina Veneta, qui mox
subicientur.

2 Interim vero meminerint, quibus cura haec delata susceptave
est, ut id faciant quod his versibus monemur:

Rectis cum primum studiis intendere coepi,
Hoc perfectum habui, ut servarem quidve deceret,
Quid non. Nam sapere utroque hoc finitur, honesto
Et vero. Mox deinde igitur fit proxima cura,
Participare alios, tum quaeque ex ordine rerum,
Lecto, composito, puro sermone docere.

From the Cicero of Antonio Possevino, S. J.
On the Technique of Writing Letters.
On the Art of Speaking, including Ecclesiastical Speech

The Philosophical Speech of Cicero: Chapter 13

[. . .] We can learn about the rest of what pertains to the imitation   1
of Cicero from those who have written soundly on the subject:
Quintilian, Gianfrancesco Pico, Vives,[1] Longolio,[2] Paolo Cortesi,
Bembo, Bartolomeo Ricci[3] and Giulio Cesare Scaligero[4] (the last
of whom also wrote against Erasmus' *Ciceronianus*), not to mention
Brutus, Sallust and others in whom these [aforementioned] authors distinguished some relevant features, in that earlier period
when the authority of Cicero's style was less widely accepted. Or
we can learn about imitating Cicero from those commentators
whom we not so long ago accepted as the more distinguished,
those collected in a single work by the Venetian printshop of Aldo
Manuzio, and who will presently be appended below.[5]

Meanwhile, let those who have passed on or received this task   2
remember to do what the following verses advise us:

> When first I began to focus on right study,
> I considered it best to observe what is proper
> And what is not. For wisdom is bounded by honor
> And truth. Thus soon the next task arises,
> Sharing with others, then teaching each matter in turn
> In choice, well-ordered and pure speech.

3   Extant autem epistolae tres, una Petri Bembi, duae Ioannis
Francisci Pici, invicem scriptae de imitatione, quae attente le-
gendae sunt ab eo, qui cupit in hac tota re (quod ad linguam[1]
Latinam attinet) rectissime incedere. Inveniuntur illae inter opera
eiusdem Pici editae qui, ut erat peracri iudicio, omnibus autem
disciplinis excultus paene ad miraculum, ac vero cerneret Bembum
Ciceroni addictissimum, quaenam deberet esse sive in illo sive
potius in pluribus imitandis rectissima ratio, conatur exprimere.
Quam epistolam, cum Bembus non prorsus aequo animo excepis-
set, prudenter et eleganter suam tutatus sententiam, sic Pico de
eadem ipsa imitatione respondet, ut, cum pleraque docte moneat,
quale illud est, ut Ciceronis fusiorem saepe dictionem peccataque
animi vitio et iudicii quadam perversione contracta non sint imitanda;[2] impingat tamen in eiusmodi verba qualia sunt, "Mediusfidius," "Mehercule," "Animi nostri a diis immortalibus formati," "Si
quis deus," et cetera quae si revivisceret Bembus, haud dubito quin
statim e suis scriptis expungeret, nimirum[3] veritati et religioni minus quadrantia. Eidem igitur Bembo respondit iterum Picus doc-
tissima altera de imitatione epistola, quae, quoniam plena succi
est, eo autem consilio in hac *Bibliotheca* construenda ducimur, ut
non tantum auctorum nomina, quantum ipsas aliquas[4] res quae
maxime ad doctrinam cum pietate coniungendam faciunt, quasi
gemmis hinc inde collectis et proprio loco dispositis aptemus, id-
circo tertiam hanc epistolam Pici integram, ex qua duarum supe-
riorum sensus elici potest, adiungendam de Ciceronis operibus
tractationi, existimavimus.

There are extant three letters, one by Pietro Bembo and two by   3
Gianfrancesco Pico,[6] which they exchanged on the subject of imitation and which anyone who wants to go into this whole subject
(as it pertains to the Latin language) in the most correct way
should read carefully. They are found edited with the works of the
same Pico who, as a man of keen judgment and almost miracu-
lously cultivated in all fields of learning, discerned that Bembo was
utterly enslaved to Cicero. Pico tries to describe what the most
correct method of imitation should be, whether one is imitating
Cicero or a number of writers. After Bembo had received his letter
with anything but equanimity and defended his own opinion
soundly and elegantly, Pico responds on the same subject of imitation, and gives learned advice on a number of subjects, for example, that one should not imitate Cicero's often rather diffuse diction and the faults he contracted from a certain mental vice and
from a kind of distorted judgment. He lashes out against such expressions as "So help me god," "By Hercules," "Our souls formed
by the immortal gods," "If any god," et cetera which, if he were to
come back to life, Bembo would no doubt immediately delete from
his own writings, since they undoubtedly square too little with the
truth and religion.[7] Pico again responds to the same Bembo in another extremely learned letter on imitation. Since it's a rich letter,
and it is our plan in constructing this *Bibliotheca* to assemble not so
much the names of authors as those things that best serve to join
learning to piety, as though collecting jewels from hither and yon
and setting them in their proper place, for this reason I thought
that this entire third letter of Pico, from which one can glean the
sense of the two previous ones, should be added to my discussion
of Cicero's works.

Here follows Pico's second letter to Bembo: Ioannis Francisci Pici
Mirandulae Comitis Epistola de Imitatione ad Petrum Bembum.

Caput XIV (28ʳ-36ʳ) and, in the Paduan edition only, excerpts from Lilio's letter to Giraldi Cinzio: Ex epistola Lilii Gregorii Gyraldi ad Cynthium Gyraldum, Qua suam fert sententiam de Epistolis Petri Bembi, et Ioannis Francisci Pici de Imitatione. Caput XV (36ʳ-36ᵛ). The transcription from Lilio's letter begins with the phrase De imitatione generatim.

De arte conscribendi epistolas

De sermone distincte, ubi et de imitatione
et auctoribus qui aliquando legendi. Caput XV.

1 Ubi vero universe dixit de sermone, distinctius ad partes eius transit, phrasim, et verba. Phrasim vocat voces duas aut plures in sententia iunctas. Verba vero voces singulas. In illis elegantia et nitor requiritur. In his Latinitas et proprietas. Ea omnia vel ex auditu leviter, quia et rarus Latinus sermo est et pauci ea cura loquuntur qua scribunt, vel ex lectione, quae utilior ac tutior: sic tamen ut et adiungatur imitatio. Tu igitur mecum omnes legendos imitandosque tibi certo statue, non simul tamen aut omni aevo.

2 Discrimen aliquod temporum est, quod utiliter enotabo. Est puerilis quaedam et prima imitatio, est crescens, est adulta. In prima Cicero non praecipuus solum legatur, sed solus. Cui fini? Ut corpus scilicet illud et contextus orationis primum serio formetur uno quodam habitu et aequabili sermonis filo. Nescio an idem censerem si Calvus, Caelius, Brutus, Caesar et alii e classe oratorum extarent. Sed ut hodie res est, quis praeter Tullium periodos, membra, numeros, et continuatam illam orationis seriem nobis suggesserit? A qua, me quidem iudice, necessario initium facien-

From the Bibliotheca Selecta, Book 18
On the Art of Composing Letters

On speech specifically, where also is treated the subject of imitation and
the authors whom one should read from time to time. Chapter 15.

After [Justus Lipsius[1]] spoke generally on speech, he passed on   1
more specifically to its parts, the phrase and words. He calls the
phrase two or more utterances that are combined in sense. Words
he calls individual utterances. Elegance and splendor are required
in the former. Good Latin usage and propriety are needed in the
latter. All words either are learned poorly by listening, for Latin
conversation is uncommon and few people speak with the care
with which they write; or they are learned from reading, which is
more useful and safer, so long as imitation is added to the process.
So join me and verify for yourself that all authors should be read
and imitated, though not all at once or at every age.

I shall outline in a practical way a distinction among periods.   2
There is a kind of primary imitation for boys, there is adolescent
imitation and there is adult imitation. In the first phase[2] let the
student read Cicero not only as his principal author but as his
only author. Why? So that the framework and coherence of his
speech may be formed in earnest first with a certain single habit
and a uniform thread of speech.[3] I do not know that my opinion
would be the same if Calvus,[4] Caelius,[5] Brutus, Caesar and others
from the class of orators were extant. But as the matter stands today, who but Tully has provided us with periods, clauses, rhythms
and that seamless sequence of speech that is his? It is with this sequence (in my opinion, to be sure) that the young writer must
necessarily commence.[6] So let beginning students occupy them-

dum iuventuti. Cicero igitur primus primas teneat, et teneat solus. Sed quamdiu? Pro ingeniis tempus definiam: in molliore aliquo, annum; in duriore, alterum etiam annum. Et addo non inutiliter sub hanc ipsam curam, Manutii epistolas, Sadoleti, Bembi, Bunelli, atque in primis Longolii nostri, legi posse, non quia ipsi (libere dicam) valde probi, sed quia puerili quodam affectu Ciceronis illam orbitam anxio pede presserunt, ideoque per eorum vestigia tutior et facilior tibi cursus.

3   At in crescentem et iuvenilem imitationem alios admitto, sed successu tamen, nec ut saltu pergas, sed per quosdam velut gradus. Itaque meo consilio eos hic primum adeas qui a Cicerone minimum abeunt, et qui copia, suavitate, fluxu dictionis referant beatam illam facilemque naturam. Qualis Fabius inprimis et nonnihil Quintus Curtius, Velleius, Livius, Caesar, similiores futuri, nisi retinuisset et stitisset alia species argumenti. Hos igitur tunc lege, sed leviter. At cum omni studio quae selectae sunt sine labe phrases ex Plauto et Terentio. Hi ad epistolam (de orationibus enim aliter censeo) et familiarem scriptionem inprimis apti, quia revera epistola, quid aliud quam quotidiana dissertatio? Ut non errarit Artemo apud Demetrium, qui censet eodem modo dialogum et epistolam scribi. Et Plinius ab eadem causa epistolas matronae cuiusdam dilaudans, cum Plauto et Terentio, metro solutis, eas componit. Quin ipsum Plinium in secunda hac classe iure colloco, tersum, acutum, nitidum; sed non sine deliciis molliculum[1] interdum et parum virum. Cui comitem novum do, sed maiorem novis, Etruscum illum Angelum, qui (nisi quod affectatae interdum et

selves with Cicero first, and with him alone. But for how long? I would fix the time limit in accordance with their natural talent. In the case of the more malleable student, a year; in the case of the more difficult student, an additional year. And I add that under this program, the letters of Manuzio,[7] Sadoleto,[8] Bembo, Bunel[9] and especially our own Longolio[10] can be read to good effect, not because they are especially fine (to speak frankly), but because they have followed painstakingly in Cicero's path with a certain youthful passion, so your course is safer and easier because of their footprints.

I would allow other writers in the stage of adolescent and youthful imitation, but still gradually, so you don't advance by leaps and bounds but by particular steps. In my opinion, you may now approach those writers who least depart from Cicero and reflect his happy and fluent character in the richness, sweetness and fluidity of their diction. Especially Quintilian but also Quintus Curtius, Velleius Paterculus, Livy and Caesar, who would all resemble him more if another type of subject matter had not kept them back. Read these authors, then, but lightly. But with full attention read (expurgated) passages selected from Plautus and Terence. These authors are especially suited to the epistle and to private writing (I have a different opinion about speeches). For what else in fact is an epistle but everyday conversation? Thus Artemon[11] was not wrong, according to Demetrius,[12] to argue that the dialogue and the letter be written in the same way. It is for the same reason that Pliny, praising the letters of a certain matron, compares them, though in prose, with Plautus and Terence.[13] It is with good reason that I place Pliny himself in this second class, for he is terse, sharp and polished. Yet he is given to pleasure, sometimes tender and insufficiently virile. To him I give a new companion, but one greater than the moderns: the Tuscan Angelo,[14] who (except that he sometimes shows studied and af-

3

quaesitae in eo argutiae) cum illis ipsis priscis pari passu decurrere posse videatur epistolarem hunc campum.

4   Hoc velut tirocinii biennium sit, quo manus haec styli coercenda nonnihil intra puram togam. Cui iam deinceps in adulta imitatione libere permittam, exserat se et vagetur per scriptorum omne genus. Legat, videat et flores ex omni prato carpat ad eloquentiae hanc corollam. Sed in primis suadeam Sallustium, Senecam, Tacitum et id genus brevium subtiliumque scriptorum iam legi, quorum acuta quasi falce luxuries illa paulisper recidatur; fiatque oratio stricta, fortis et vere virilis.[2]

De excerptis: quo ordine ea instituenda et a quibus singula carpenda. Caput XVI.

5   Quid seligas et a quibus, partem fecit alteram, de qua, etsi exemplis dicere facilius potuisset quam scriptis, tamen breviter haec habuit. Lectionem ipsam non sufficere, ne repetitam quidem, immo nec in felicissima[3] memoria, sed opus esse excerptis quibusdam et notis rerum verborumque singularium quas imitemur. Quae excerpta memorialibus libellis, tamquam aerario, contineri vult, unde sermonis illae opes per tempus et ad usum promantur. Fieri autem libellos triplices: unum quem formularum; alterum ornamentorum; tertium dictionis. Duo illi ad sermonem universum magis pertinent, tertius ad distinctum.

6   In primo formulae duplices. Ad contextum istae: ordiendi, narrandi, continuandi, transeundi, abrumpendi, claudendi. Ad materiem istae: rogandi, gratias agendi, operam offerendi, laudandi, vi-

ected cleverness) seems able to race in this epistolary field stride
for stride with the ancients themselves.

This period of apprenticeship should last two years, during   4
which the student's writing hand should be confined somewhat
within a plain toga.[15] Thereafter I will let the student, in the adult
type of imitation, free himself and wander through every type
of writer. Let him read, observe and pluck flowers from every
meadow for his garland[16] of eloquence. But let me especially recommend that he now read Sallust, Seneca, Tacitus and that type
of brief and subtle writer, by whose sharp pruning knife his excesses may be cut back for a little while.[17] Let his oratory become
terse, strong and truly virile.

*On excerpts: in what order they are to be organized and from
which authors one should gather them. Chapter 16.[18]*

In the second part of his letter, [Lipsius] discussed what you   5
should excerpt and from whom. Even if he could have spoken
more easily on the subject using examples than by writing, nevertheless, in brief, he held the following view. Reading itself [he
said] does not suffice, not even repeated reading, and not even in
the case of the most gifted memory. Rather, he says, we need certain excerpts and notes on particular things and words that we
may imitate. He would have these excerpts be contained in memo-
randum-books, like treasuries from which those riches of speech
may be produced as time and experience dictate. Three kinds of
books should be kept, he says: one containing formulae, another
for embellishments and a third for diction. The first two pertain
more to speech in general, the third to speech in its distinct kinds.

In the first book there are two types of formulae. Those per-   6
taining to composition are: formulae of beginning, narrating, con-
necting, transition, interruption and closing. Those pertaining to
material are: formulae of solicitation, giving thanks, rendering ser-

tuperandi, asseverandi et quicquid istarum rerum communium est, quae in epistolam creberrime incurrunt.

7   Secundus ornamentorum, in quo distincte et per capita collocentur. Similitudines, allegoriae, imagines, acutiora dicta, sententiae et signa⁴ eiusmodi illustria lumina sermonis.

8   Tertius dictionis, quae bipertiri poterit phrasium et verborum. Phrases quidem insigniores aut nitidiores; verba quaecumque rara, nova aut novo sensu sive flexu usurpata. In phrasibus ut dispositio non cernitur, nisi quod seorsum poni possunt pro discrimine scriptorum—Tullii solae, Plauti et Terentii solae, historicorum solae—quod quisquam pro iudicio suo aut industria facito. In verbis ordo servetur alphabeti. Formularum liber e Cicerone maxime compleatur; adde Plinium, aut si quid aliunde transferri aut hauriri poterit opportune. Ornamentorum a Cicerone, Fabio, Plinio, historicis, Seneca, etiam a Graecis et inprimis Plutarcho. Phrasium exempla a Cicerone maxime et comicis petantur, nonnihil ab historicis atque etiam ab aliis, Varrone, Aulo Gellio,⁵ Suetonio, iurisconsultis, immo et interdum Apuleio.

9   Verborum uno verbo ab omnibus, nec inutiliter etiam a grammaticis et glossariis antiquis.

vice, praising, blaming, affirming and all those commonplace topics that often arise in the epistle.

The second book is for embellishments, arranged separately   7
and by headings. Similes, allegories, metaphors, pointed remarks,
maxims and figures are the brilliant highlights of that sort of
speech.

The third book treats of diction, which you can subdivide into   8
phrases and words. Phrases include those that are distinguished or
polished. Words include any rare or new words, or words that
have taken on a new sense or variation. Since in the case of
phrases order is not something that is looked for, except that they
can be listed separately under the heading of the different writers — that is, the phrases of Cicero by themselves, those of Plautus
and Terence by themselves, and those of the historians by themselves — let everyone do as his own judgment and industry suggest. In the case of words, you should keep to an alphabetical order. You should fill up your book of formulae mainly from Cicero.
Include Pliny[19] or anything else that you may suitably transfer
or draw from other sources. The book of ornaments should be
composed from Cicero, Quintilian, Pliny, the historians, Seneca, the Greeks too and especially Plutarch. You should obtain model phrases especially from Cicero and the comic writers,
something from the historians as well as others, including Varro,
Aulus Gellius, Suetonius, the jurists and occasionally even from
Apuleius.[20]

Your book of words, in a word, should be compiled from all au-   9
thors; even the ancient grammarians and commentators are not
useless.

De expressione et formatione styli per tria
genera imitationum. Caput XVII.

10   Tertium illud utilissimum sequitur, quid exprimas et quid vites. Frustra enim priora illa duo, si non istud, nec lectio aut selectio adiuverint, sine proba expressione. Ea, ut talis sit, per triplicem imitationem distincte fit, ut sciatur quid sequi deceat in unaquaque, quid vites. In puerili, duo haec proponendae. Primo, ut formulas inprimis et communia illa contextus totius imitetur. Secundo ut ductum, numeros, lineamenta et faciem Tullianae orationis. Et imitetur non industrie solum, sed paene affectate et cupide; sic, inquam, ut color quaesitus et fucus appareat, immo et furtum. Ut pueros nihil pudet, cum scribere discunt, per singulos literarum apices aliena manu duci, clausulas, membra et periodi cuiuspiam partem cum venia saepe inseret,[6] et centonem e Tullii purpura contexes, paulo post daturus suam: exercitii genus, quod olim in Germania huic rei Lipsius proposuit, fuit tale. Haec sequere. Quid fugies? Nihil, nisi ea quae grammatici vitant.

11   At in crescente, crescat mihi paullisper iudicium, et servari praecipiam haec tria. Primum, ut in furtis iam verecundior sis, non enim ultra decet. Secundum, ut in formulis exprimendis remissior; non enim ultra opus; sicut digiti in cythara aegri et cum[7] intentione initio ponuntur, iidem postea ad chordas et numeros sponte veniunt, sic mens istis paullum assuefacta. Tertium, ut phrases et verba meliora undique[8] assumas, et formes, ut sic di-

*On expression and the formation of style using the
three types of imitation. Chapter 17.*[21]

We next turn to that third, very useful issue: what you should imi- 10
tate and what you should avoid. The previous two subjects are in
vain without this third one: neither reading nor selection will help
without proper imitation. Since such is the case, you should use
the three distinct forms of imitation to know what properly to follow and what to avoid in each one. In the type for boys I would
make the following two recommendations. First, imitate especially
formulae and those features common to the whole structure or
plan; second, imitate the method, rhythms, features and appearance of Ciceronian oratory. You should also imitate not only industriously, but almost affectedly and avariciously — in such a way,
I say, that the desired rouge[22] and color appear, or to be more precise, the theft. As boys are not ashamed when learning to write to
be guided by another's hand through the individual shapes of the
letters,[23] you may be forgiven for often introducing clausulae,
clauses and a part of some period, weaving together a cento or
pastiche from the purple cloth of Cicero in order to produce your
own a little later. This was the sort of exercise that Lipsius once
proposed for this purpose in Germany. Follow these recommendations. What will you avoid? Nothing but what the grammarians
forbid.

In the adolescent sort of imitation, in my view, let the judgment 11
develop little by little, and I would make the following three recommendations. First, become more modest and restrained in your
thefts, for it is improper to go beyond a certain point. Second,
gradually give up your copying of formulae, since there is no further need of it; just as the fingers at first become sore from the
effort of playing the lute but later take naturally to its chords and
measures, the mind too becomes accustomed to formulae. Third,
appropriate better phrases and words from everywhere and shape

cam, cutem illam orationis tuae externam, atque haec sane praecipua hic cura. Quid vitandum? Vitium agnatum verborum delec-
tui, nimia asperitas aut antiquitas. Quod in comicis imitandis
praecipue mihi cave, et ne quid aut sordidum ab iis dictio tua tra-
hat aut obsoletum. Nam ut imperiti pictores in facie exprimenda,
rugam, naevum, verrucam facile imitantur; indolem negligunt et
ipsum vultum; sic saepe adolescentes rara aut extantia verba excer-
punt, ingenium omittunt et genium dictionis. Quae autem verba
sordida? Quae iacent, repunt,[9] e faece[10] vulgi et e triviis sumpta,
nec nisi iudicio discernenda.

12   Superest imitatio ultima, sive virilis, in qua hoc praecipio non
tam exteriorem illum ornatum spectari debere quam virtutes et
cultum internum, idest, figuras, imagines, acumina et ea, quae ap-
pellavi ornamenta. In quo una cautio, ut cum oratio perfici iam in-
cipiat et summa illi manus imponi, κακοζηλία vitetur et affecta-
tio—infelix sane vitium, et quod obrepit specie virtutis; ea est
nimium cultus studium et sine modo. Quod per te aegre videas
aut vites; felix cui doctor hic aliquis aut monitor amicus.

the outer skin, if you will, of your oratory; that is surely of special
concern at this stage. What should you avoid? The fault that is related to word-choice: excessive roughness and archaism. Beware of
this especially in imitating the comedians, and don't let your diction pull in from them anything that is sordid or obsolete. For as
inexperienced painters in depicting the face are quick to imitate
wrinkles, moles and warts,[24] yet neglect the face's natural character
and countenance, so too the young often excerpt rare or conspicu-
ous words but pass over the natural talent and genius of the diction. What count as sordid words? Words that are low and crawl
on the ground, words that are taken almost from the dregs of the
rabble and from streetcorners — these should not be used except
deliberately and with good judgment.

There remains the last sort of imitation, that of the full-grown   12
man, where I recommend that you attend not so much to external
embellishment — that is, to figures of speech, images, pointed remarks and what I have called embellishments — as to the virtues
[of speech] and internal refinement. At this stage you should take
a single precaution: when you are now ready to finish a speech and
put the last polish to it, avoid *kakozelia*[25] and affectation. This is an
unhappy fault, one that slithers its way in under the appearance of
virtue. This *[kakozelia]* consists in the excessive and immoderate
desire for refinement. You may learn this the hard way on your
own, or you may avoid it. Happy is he who finds here some
teacher or friendly advisor.

[*The following passages constitute Possevino's own expansion upon the
subject of imitation. They are to be found only in Antonio Possevino:
Bibliotheca Selecta (1603 and 1607),* De Arte Conscribendi Epistolas
XVIII *and are not in Lipsius.*]

De imitatione Ciceronis, et universe e praestantibus
huius saeculi viris. Caput XVIII.

13 At quando in hanc arenam imitationis Tullianae intulimus pedem,
praestat adhuc adtexere quae, excerpta e viris huius saeculi praestantibus, lucem toti negotio faciant, quamvis et eadem ista[e] non
tam scribendis epistolis quam universo generi dicendi ac de quacumque materia scribendi futura sint commoda. Sane vero Gregorius Lilius Giraldus, cum Franciscum Picum et Petrum Bembum
inter se contendere de hac ipsa imitatione vidisset, sententiam cor-
date tulit, quae eos quadamtenus inter se conciliaret. Eam, videlicet, ut — cum nemo eatenus generatim haud satis de imitatione
praecepisset — haec bifariam esset partienda; quae aut candidato
aut adulto proponeretur. Candidatum vocat rudem adhuc et vix
initiatum. Adultum autem eruditum et in literis probe versatum,
nam cum tardis et conclamatis censet non esse laborandum. Rudi-
bus itaque, docilibus tamen, ad imitandum Bembi praeceptionem
tamquam optimam proponit, eo usque, antequam aliud eruditionis aut disciplinarum attingant, donec (inquit) non tantum animus imbutus ipse, sed eo etiam aures tritae ita occalluerint, ut
ferre nequeant, immo etiam aspernentur, quicquid suae fuerit dissonum imitationi. Iam vero, si eruditos et doctos ad imitationem
provocemus, Francisci Pici et Caelii sententiam esse magis ido-
neam ad illam praestandam. Denique monet, nihil in imitatione
tentandum invita (quod aiunt) Minerva, sed suam ut quisque naturam et genium sequatur; cavendum autem ne inepta imitatione

*On imitating Cicero, general ideas from the
eminent men of this age. Chapter 18.*

Now that we have set foot in this arena of Tullian imitation, it will   13
help at this point to weave in some ideas which, taken from eminent men of this age, may shed light on the entire business, although these notions will be suited not so much to writing epistles
as to the general category of speech and of writing about whatever
you wish. It is with sound reason that, after he had seen [Gian]
Francesco Pico and Pietro Bembo arguing with each other about
this sort of imitation, Lilio Gregorio Giraldi shrewdly offered an
opinion which to some extent reconciled them with each other.[26]
His opinion, namely, was — since no one had as yet given a satis-
factory account of it by types — that imitation should be divided
into two parts: one recommended to the beginner and another
to the mature student. He calls the beginner anyone who is still
uneducated and has barely begun his studies. The mature student, he says, is educated and properly versed in letters, for he be-
lieves that you should not labor over the slow-witted and hopeless
cases. For those who are uneducated but teachable he recommends
Bembo's teaching as the best method of imitation, and says that
they should follow him before touching any other branch of learning and the disciplines until, he says, not only is their mind itself
steeped in that form of imitation, but even their ears are worn
down by it and have become so calloused over that they cannot
bear, in fact will even despise, whatever is discordant with their
own method of imitation. But if we should encourage the erudite
and learned to practice imitatation, he says that the opinion of
[Gian] Francesco Pico and Celio is more suitable to recommend
for that. Finally, he advises that no imitation should be attempted
when Minerva, as they say, is unwilling, but that each person
should follow his own nature and genius. Yet, he should beware

in vitium κακοζηλίας incurrat, vel quod Lucianus cuidam Thucydidem imitanti obicit.

E Francisco Pico, cum quo Caelius, Gulielmus
Budaeus et alii sensisse visi sunt. Caput XIX.

14 Porro Franciscus Picus optime et (ut ita dicam) nobilissime hoc de imitandi genere scripsit epistolas bene longas Petro Bembo, qui Leonis X. Pontifici Maximi fuit ab epistolis, ac demum Cardinalis.

lest his inept imitation lead to the error of *kakozelia,* the fault for which Lucian criticized a certain imitator of Thucydides.[27]

> *The ideas of [Gian] Francesco Pico with whom Celio, Guillaume*
> *Budé[28] and others seem to have agreed. Chapter 19.*

On this type of imitation [Gian] Francesco Pico has written a   14
quite long letter in a most excellent and (as it were) noble way to
Pietro Bembo, who was secretary to Pope Leo X and afterwards
became a cardinal.

[Here follows Possevino's paraphrase of Pico's second letter to Bembo.]

Note on the Text and Translation

Of the three literary debates included in this volume, the correspondence between Poliziano and Cortesi was the most widely republished; there were over thirty reprints from the late fifteenth through the mid-seventeenth centuries. Cortesi's letter was not published in editions of his own works but was included either in editions of Poliziano's works or in collections of works on imitation. Though most reprints of the Poliziano-Cortesi correspondence were to be found in printings of Poliziano's collected letters, the first edition was included in the 1498 Aldine of Poliziano's complete works, published four years after his death. This edition contained, among other works, 247 letters, arranged and in part edited, it is thought, by Poliziano himself.[1] The correspondence with Cortesi was placed in Book VIII of the twelve-book collection of Poliziano's letters. It is this 1498 edition which provides the base text for the edition of the letters found in this volume. Variants from the many other editions of Poliziano's collected letters (which by and large are insignificant and in any case cannot have been approved by the author) are not considered here.

The second quarrel, between Pico and Bembo, was reprinted somewhat less often than the Poliziano-Cortesi debate; there are twenty-one editions from the sixteenth through the early eighteenth centuries which contain one or more of the three texts. A striking feature of the reception of the Pico-Bembo quarrel, however, is that it was rarely republished in its complete form, which consists of two letters from Pico and one from Bembo. Of the twenty-one early printed versions of the quarrel, only four contain all three letters. All four of these were published in editions of Pico's works, twice in the editions of ca. 1515 and 1518, then later in the 1573 and 1601 imprints. All versions of the quarrel published in the works of Bembo, beginning in 1530, fail to include Pico's final response. Since Bembo's 1530 version was the basis of nearly all subsequent editions, many scholars writing before the Santangelo edition was published in 1954 appear to be unaware of its existence.

There has been considerable debate concerning which of the earliest versions of the quarrel constitutes the *editio princeps*. An undated volume of Pico's *Physici libri duo* (or, as it is sometimes incorrectly catalogued, the *Libri Phyci*), containing the complete quarrel, was initially mentioned by Bembo's editor, Anton Federigo Seghezzi, in 1729 (Bembo 1720, 4: 333). In a footnote, Seghezzi describes an edition which he did not attempt to date but which appears to be the oldest. Later in the eighteenth century, Girolamo Tiraboschi also found this same early edition and declared it to be the *editio princeps* of the quarrel, probably printed in Rome "shortly after 1513" (*Biblioteca Modenese*, [Modena, 1781–86], 4: 115). In the mid-nineteenth century, however, Jean Georges Théodore Graesse (in *Trésor de livres rares et précieux* [Dresden, 1859–69], 5: 285) declared the undated edition to have been published in Bologna by De Benedictis in 1523, no doubt because the printing appears similar to that used in other works by Pico published by that press in 1523. Graesse therefore concluded that the 1518 Basel edition constituted the *editio princeps* of the quarrel.

In part because he never personally found a copy of the earliest edition as it was described by Seghezzi and Tiraboschi, the most modern editor of the quarrel, Giorgio Santangelo (in *Le Epistole "De imitatione,"* 6–10), doubted its existence and chose to base his version on the 1518 Basel edition. But in a review of Santangelo's edition (see Bibliography), Raffaele Spongano disagreed with Santangelo and claimed to have examined a copy of the *Physici*, matching the description of both Seghezzi and Tiraboschi, in the Biblioteca Comunale in Bologna (shelfmark: 16.Q.IV bis 58).

Comparing this volume to the *De amore divino*, published in an identical style of print, which *did* include the place of publication, Spongano concluded that the two works derived from the same publisher, namely Jacobus Mazochius or Iacobo Mazzocchi in Rome, and that this edition was certainly printed before 1518. Spongano's arguments are convincing, and were reaffirmed shortly afterwards by Alberto Serra-Zanetti in 1959.[2] Working from this same Bolognese copy of the *Libri Physici*, Serra-Zanetti cautiously suggests that this edition is indeed anterior to the 1518 Basel version. Most bibliographers concur with Spongano and Serra-Zanetti and, thus this version (a copy of which can be found in the library of Princeton University), rather than the Basel edition, has been chosen as the base text here.

Significant differences can be found between the first version of his treatise and the one Bembo published under his own supervision in his *Opera* of 1530; hence variants from that text are presented here. The 1518 edition, which Santangelo used as his base text, shows only slight orthographic variants from the *princeps* and has not been completely recollated, though Santangelo's edition has of course been carefully consulted.

The third of the three debates consists of four texts: an initial letter by Giraldi Cinzio, Calcagnini's brief cover letter to his treatise, Calcagnini's treatise *On Imitation* itself, and the final letter by Lilio Gregorio sent to Giraldi Cinzio, commenting on the Cinzio-Calcagnini correspondence. It is clear that Giraldi Cinzio conceived of this debate as having four distinct moments, for each of the versions of the debate found in his works contains all four texts in succession. On the other hand, Calcagnini appeared not to see these texts as a unit at all and was apparently far more interested in his own formal treatise, first publishing it separately in an anthology of treatises on imitation in 1535. It appears again in his collected works, published posthumously in 1544. His brief letter to Cinzio, is, however, included in Book XIII of Calcagnini's *Epistolarum familiarum libri XVI*, part of this same 1544 edition of his collected works; but neither Cinzio's letter nor Lilio Gregorio's commentary were ever included in any version of the debate published under Calcagnini's name.

The Cinzio-Calcagnini-Lilio exchange has a complicated textual history, as somewhat different texts are found in the works of all three correspondents. The *editio princeps* of the complete Cinzio-Calcagnini-Lilio exchange is in the *De obitu* of Giraldi Cinzio, published in 1537, and this is used as the base text here; Giraldi republished all four parts of the exchange in another volume in 1540, with significant variants from his earlier version, and these are noted. The *editio princeps* of Calcagnini's treatise, however, was first published separately in 1535, in the *De imitatione eruditorum quorundam libelli*; it was printed again, in a slightly modified version, in Calcagnini's posthumous *Opera aliquot* of 1544. Finally, Lilio Giraldi's brief but important letter was also published separately in his own *Opera omnia* of 1580 and again in 1696, though these printings were clearly not done under his supervision. Nevertheless, because this exchange was reprinted with some differences in a limited number of early editions, the most important variants of the 1535, 1540, and 1544 texts have been included.

The last set of texts presented here, from the *Bibliotheca selecta* of Antonio Possevino, was initially published in 1593. The purpose of this encyclopedic work was to make available excerpts from what Possevino considered to be exemplary texts that students should be familiar with; in light of this, Possevino included, in his book entitled the *Cicero* (normally considered to be book eighteen of the *Bibliotheca*, but printed in the Roman text as an appendix with separate title page and pagination), a transcription of the entire third letter of the Pico-Bembo debate, a text that had received little attention heretofore. That same year, three other versions of the *Cicero* were printed independently of the remainder of the *Bibliotheca* in Padua, Cologne, and Lyon simultaneously. These editions do not differ dramatically, except for one curious fact that thus far seems to have gone unnoticed: the Paduan edition alone includes, as chapter fifteen, extensive excerpts from Lilio Gregorio's letter to Giraldi Cinzio. Though the Paduan edition has been cited as the *editio princeps* and thus has been used as the base text here,[3] it is exceedingly rare, as are the Lyonnais and Cologne editions, while the Roman version is more easily accessible.

Ten years later, in 1603, Possevino published an enlarged and revised edition of the *Bibliotheca selecta,* which was reprinted once, apparently without Possevino's approval, in 1607 and subsequently never reprinted. Here, Possevino begins his discussion of imitative practice by providing a paraphrase (often approaching an exact transcription) of the *Epistolica institutio* of Justus Lipsius, which had first appeared in 1591 and which enjoyed wide popularity during the course of the seventeenth-century, being reprinted throughout Northern Europe at least fifteen times between 1592 and 1702. It may well be the case that Possevino was not aware of Lipsius' text in its *editio princeps,* or at least not immediately after its publication, for he did not refer to this text at all in the 1593 version of his encyclopedic work. The remaining chapters of the 1603 *Bibliotheca selecta* provide a paraphrase, but not a transcription, of the letters by Pico and Lilio Giraldi.

Two base texts have been used for the discussions of the quarrel in the *Bibliotheca selecta* of Possevino. The first, briefer version, is contained in the part of the *Bibliotheca* known as the *Cicero,* published in 1593. The second, expanded version is that published in 1603 in Venice. Because this second version contains a paraphrase of the *Epistolica institutio* of Justus Lipsius, first published in Leiden in 1591, significant variants from Lipsius' text are given in the footnotes. The base text for the passages from Lipsius is the 1591 edition, which has been edited in a modern version by Young and Hester.[4]

In addition to the publications mentioned above, parts of the three debates were sometimes published in anthologies. One example is the 1535 anthology mentioned above, the *De imitatione eruditorum quorundam libelli quam eruditissimi,* which included the *editio princeps* of Calcagnini's *On Imitation.* This anonymous anthology is highly significant, attesting as it does to the popularity of the subject of imitation at this time. Moreover, its presentation traces a history of the subject, in that it includes only texts which refer to at least one of the others. Soon afterwards, in 1537, the text of the Poliziano-Cortesi debate was published within the *De elocutionis imitatione ac apparatu* of Jacobus Omphalius. In 1555, this treatise was reprinted in Paris with the text of the Pico-Bembo correspondence appearing in an appendix. The Omphalius collection was apparently quite popular and was republished three times in the next twenty years. Its final versions included the text of Bartolomeo Ricci's *De imitatione* as well. In this way, the *De elocutionis imitatione* established itself as a standard sixteenth-century anthology of texts on imitation.

A final anthology of imitation treatises, the exceedingly rare *Collectio praestantissimorum opusculorum de imitatione oratoria,*[5] was published in the German city of Jena in 1726, considerably after the time when the subject was most popular. This anthology begins with the *Ciceronianus* of Erasmus and includes a large number of other works on the topic, ranging from the *Cicero relegatus et Cicero revocatus* (1534) of Ortensio Landi to texts by Julius Pflug and Johann Sturm. It gives an incomplete version of the Poliziano-Cortesi correspondence (omitting several lines from the introductory paragraphs of each letter), and also gives only the first two letters of the Pico-Bembo debate.

Following the preferred practice of this I Tatti series, the orthography, capitalization and punctuation of all Latin texts have been modernized, and all abbreviations have been resolved. The distinction between consonantal and vocalic "u" has been indicated by "v" and "u" respectively. Obvious typographical errors have been corrected silently. Corrections to other errors in the base texts have been made on the basis of the other early editions where possible. Variants are referred to by the date of the editions in which they appear.[6] In Text 3, readings of a manuscript collated by Santangelo (Vatican City, Biblioteca Apostolica Vaticana Vat. lat. 2847, ff. 176r-179r) are occasionally cited using his siglum Vt.

As for the translations, it should be noted that no attempt has been made to modernize the debates by using gender-inclusive language, for all the authors included were male and were writing about male writers. Similarly, the translation, while striving for readability, does not attempt to oversimplify the syntax employed by the writers, as form is inseparable from content in the issues discussed by the several controversialists.

The volume as a whole represents a collaboration between editor and translator in all its facets. Most of the notes have been compiled by the editor, but the translator has also contributed to them here and there. Many notes were more easily compiled thanks to existing annotated editions of these and other texts, especially the Knott translation of the *Ciceronianus*, the French translation by Hersant of the Pico-Bembo and Poliziano-Cortesi debates, the Weinberg edition of the Cinzio-Calcagnini letters; and the Young and Hester edition of the Lipsius treatise.

NOTES

1. For further information about the textual tradition of Poliziano's letters see Angelo Poliziano, *Letters*, vol. 1, ed. Shane Butler (Cambridge, MA: Harvard University Press, 2006), in this I Tatti series.

2. Alberto Serra-Zanetti, *L'arte della stampa in Bologna nel primo ventennio del Cinquecento* (Bologna, 1959), 311 (notation 387).

3. Augustin de Backer and Carlos Sommervogel, *Bibliothèque de la Compagnie de Jésus*, 2nd ed. (Héverté-Louvain: Editions de la Bibliothèque, 1960), 6: col. 1080, n. 24 h.

4. Lipsius 1996 (see Abbreviations).

5. A copy of this imprint can be consulted in the rare books library of the University of Pennsylvania.

6. The earliest edition of the Pico-Bembo quarrel, the *Physici libri duo* referred to above, has been assigned the siglum "1515." The Princeton copy of this imprint has coeval manuscript corrections which are often correct and may have Pico's own authority behind them. The most important of these corrections have been included in the apparatus.

Notes to the Text

2. CORTESI TO POLIZIANO

1. possum *1498*

2. possum *1498*

3. PICO, ON IMITATION

1. exploratum nedum abunde perspectum atque compertum *added in Vt after* appararet

2. vero non putem] vero minime arbitror imitandum esse *Vt*

3. animus inclinat] res inclinatur *Vt*

4. *Emended:* Eamque *edd., Vt*

5. quod ad *1518*

6. *Omitted in 1518*

7. potuere *Vt*

8. haec *Vt:* hic *1515, 1518, 1530*

9. pusilla nimis *Vt, 1515:* pusillanimis *1518, 1530*

10. haec *Vt:* hic *1515 (but hand-corrected to* hec), *1518, 1530*

11. extimatione *1515*

12. haec *Vt:* hic *1515 (but hand-corrected to* hec), *1518, 1530*

13. *Emended:* titulus *edd.*

14. Quorum *1518*

15. quemque *Vt:* quemquam *1515, 1518, 1530*

16. qui quae *1518:* quique *1515 (but hand-corrected to* qui quae), *1530, Vt*

17. constat *Vt, 1515, 1530*

18. coagmenta nexis] coagmenta nec eis *1515, 1530:* coagmentaturque eis *Vt (and after correction by hand in 1515)*

19. confletur *1515, 1518, 1530*

20. qui *1515, 1530*

4. BEMBO TO PICO

1. Petrus Bembus Ioanni Francisco Pico s. p. d. *1530*

2. quam ne *1530*

3. profecto *omitted in 1530*

4. scriptionumque *1530*

5. docerentur *1530*

6. absolutissimam *1530*

7. rectissima *1515, 1530*

8. quemadmodum *1530*

9. omnis *1530*

10. sunt 1530

11. eis 1530

12. fuisse *omitted in* 1515

13. eorum 1530

14. qui 1515, 1530

15. item 1530

16. Totum 1530

17. haec 1530

18. alio 1515

19. erit 1530

20. item 1530

21. candorem 1530

22. modo 1530

23. ducerem. Aequius 1515

24. nostris 1515

25. duces 1530

26. ac 1530

27. converti 1530

28. difficile 1530

29. tamen *omitted in* 1530

30. rationum 1518, 1530

31. itinere *after* instituto 1530

32. pertendere 1530

33. invenire 1530

34. ab eo *after* cum 1530

35. mentionem facit] sermo inducitur 1530

36. at 1515

37. atque respectus *omitted in* 1530

38. et 1530

39. apertius 1518

40. instructum 1530

41. nam de Graecis nihil loquor *omitted in* 1530

42. commode 1530

43. vel tragoediarum vel comoediarum *transp.* 1530

44. probabitur 1515

45. in *omitted in* 1515, 1518

46. illum 1515, 1530

47. illam 1515

48. verbo 1530

49. includunt 1530

50. scribendo 1530

51. Latini, Turni, Laviniae *omitted in* 1515

52. aut etiam . . . similior *omitted in* 1530

53. cum hoc certe modo . . . facile dixero *omitted in* 1518

54. controversias 1530

55. vel . . . vel] et . . . et 1530

56. atque sensum *omitted in* 1530

57. Vale. Kalendis Ianuariis, MDXIII, Romae 1530

58. Finis *omitted in* 1530

5. PICO TO BEMBO

1. censeri 1515

2. qui *omitted in* 1515 (*but added by hand*)

3. derivata *after hand-correction in* 1515: derivatum *edd.*

4. Romanique 1515

5. poterant *1530*
6. *Corrected:* notae *edd.*
7. apta *before hand-correction in* 1515
8. *deleted by hand in 1515*
9. quod *1518*
10. non *omitted in 1515*
11. quibus *1515*

12. careat *1515*
13. abolere *after hand-correction in* 1515: aboleri *1518, 1530, before correction in 1515*
14. solent *added by hand in 1515: omitted by edd.*
15. FINIS *omitted in 1518, 1530.*

6. CINZIO TO CALCAGNINI

1. tantum *omitted in 1540*
2. hic *1537*
3. condendo *1540*
4. *corrected:* condiant *edd.*
5. acumen *1540*
6. omnium *1540*
7. his *1540*
8. in quo in literatos omnes, lividule, genuinum frangit *omitted in 1540*
9. credo quia . . . in vestibulo latrans *omitted in 1540*
10. manibus pedibusque *omitted in 1540*
11. forte *1540*
12. videtur *omitted in 1537*
13. profecisse *1540*
14. ad *omitted in 1540*
15. promotionibus *1537*
16. Quis in re peroranda felicior? *omitted in 1540*

17. immo beatam *omitted in 1540*
18. haurire *1540*
19. unicuique *1540*
20. quod *1540*
21. complecti *1540*
22. ita ut horridus prorsus evadat *omitted in 1540*
23. deduxerint *1540*
24. et *omitted in 1540*
25. eveniet *1540*
26. Cicerone] Ciceronis lectione *1540*
27. divitius *(sic) 1537*
28. eiusque imbiberit dicendi modum? *omitted in 1540*
29. arbitror *1540*
30. quamque ingeniis faveas *omitted in 1540*
31. fugandis summa cum fiducia *1540*
32. penu *1540*

7. CALCAGNINI TO CINZIO

1. hactenus nihil *transp. 1544*
2. doctissime *1544*
3. prope *omitted in 1544*
4. λυπεψία *1544*
5. studiorum lectatores *1544*
6. locum *1540*
7. locum *omitted in 1540*
8. ego *omitted in 1537, 1540*
9. animadvertam *1537*
10. tuae *omitted in 1544*
11. Ceterum *omitted in 1544*
12. cum primum tuas literas *1544*
13. his *1540*
14. ac propemodum cessanti *omitted in 1544*
15. et *omitted in 1537, 1540*
16. ea *omitted in 1537, 1540*
17. opere *omitted in 1544*
18. aestimationis *1540*
19. Bene vale] Vale *1540*
20. et me ama . . . MDXXXII *omitted in 1544*

8. CALCAGNINI, *ON IMITATION*

1. Ad Ioannem Baptistam Cynthium Gyraldum physicum Coelii Calcagnini super imitatione commentatio *1537*: De imitatione commentatio Caelii Calcagnini Ferrariensis ad Ioannem Baptistam Cynthium Gyraldum *1544*
2. studentes *1544*
3. utputa *1540, 1544*
4. omnia *1535*
5. scitamena *1535*
6. postquam *omitted in 1540, 1544*
7. imitationis *omitted in 1540, 1544*
8. in *omitted in 1544*
9. neque rem . . . varietate *omitted in 1535*
10. omnium *1535*
11. in *1540, 1544*
12. producantur *1535*
13. et *1540, 1544*
14. aucupetur *1535*
15. possit in medium] possit dicendo *1540, 1544*
16. certe *1540, 1544*
17. apud *1540*
18. arbitrabitur pertinere] putabit attinere *1540, 1544*
19. -arunt *1535, 1537*
20. maiorum nostrorum *transp. 1540, 1544*
21. abiicit *1540, 1544*
22. suppetebat *1535*
23. et *1540, 1544*
24. aut *1540, 1544*
25. nobis ad eam rem *transp. 1540, 1544*

26. et 1540, 1544
27. manifestarios 1535
28. versatur 1537
29. quique quod . . . pollicentur omitted in 1535
30. Qui tametsi 1535
31. longe omitted in 1535
32. magnaeque 1535
33. eos omitted in 1544
34. damnaveris . . . tam quae ad omitted in 1535
35. heluarentur 1535, 1544
36. etsi 1535
37. et 1535
38. hoc 1535
39. posse respondere transp. 1540, 1544
40. defuturum non transp. 1535
41. ratione 1535, 1537
42. posterus 1537
43. deventum 1535
44. trahant 1535, 1537, 1540
45. -que omitted in 1537, 1540, 1544
46. exquirunt 1535
47. peregre adveniunt] extrinsecus advocantur 1535
48. omnes 1535, 1540, 1544
49. institoris 1537
50. adsequatur 1535
51. sunt generis transp. 1535
52. sunt 1540
53. Rosiana 1537
54. Vera 1540, 1544
55. praevulgatae 1544
56. utebamur 1537

57. incumbit 1535
58. is omitted in 1535
59. una 1540
60. loco omitted in 1540, 1544
61. hanc aut omitted in 1535
62. partem omitted in 1535
63. proferet 1535, 1537
64. exportavit 1540
65. Tute 1540, 1544
66. quis stylum transp. 1535
67. quaedam dissimilia transp. 1535
68. esse omitted in 1535
69. fortiter 1535
70. quo 1535
71. quod 1535, 1537
72. possunt 1540, 1544
73. praeclusa 1537
74. terras 1535
75. Cicerone 1535
76. in promptuario . . . depromas omitted in 1537, 1540, 1544
77. ille after celeber 1535
78. eum omitted in 1535
79. examplificandam 1540, 1544
80. qui iam] quidam 1535
81. semper astris 1540
82. an ipsi] an ipsi quoque 1540, 1544: an et ipsi 1535
83. Alexandrum ex Aphrodisiade] Porphyrium 1535
84. -istem 1540, 1544
85. 1535 adds at end: Finis.

9. GIRALDI TO CINZIO

1. Lilii Gregorii Gyraldi ad
   Cynthium Gyraldum epistola
   1540: Lilii Gregorii Gyraldi ad
   Cynthium Gyraldum epistola
   de imitatione, bonae frugis
   refertissima *1580*
2. -didem *1540, 1580*

3. et me si mutuo me] etsi me si
   mutuo *1540:* etsi me mutuo
   1580
4. Mirandulae ad X Kalendas
   Decembris MDXXXII *omitted
   in 1540, 1580*

10. POSSEVINO, *CICERO*

1. lingua *Paduan edition*
2. imitanda *Roman edition: omitted
   in Paduan edition*
3. nimirum *Roman edition:*
   nimium *Paduan edition*

4. ipsae aliquae *Roman and
   Paduan editions*

11. POSSEVINO, *BIBLIOTHECA SELECTA*

1. *omitted in 1607*
2. utilis *1607*
3. nec infelicissima *1607:* nec
   felicissima *Lipsius*
4. et si qua *Lipsius*
5. Agellio *1603*

6. inseres *Lipsius*
7. *omitted in 1607*
8. *omitted in 1607*
9. repetunt *1603, 1607*
10. fere *1603*

Notes to the Translation

꽃S?종

ABBREVIATIONS

Alberti 1960–73 Leon Battista Alberti. *Opere volgari*. Edited by Cecil
Grayson. 3 vols. Bari: Laterza, 1960–1973.

Alberti 1964   Idem. "Alcune Intercenales inedite." Edited by Eugenio
Garin. *Rinascimento* 4 (1964): 125–258.

Alberti 1971   Idem. *De commodis litterarum atque incommodis*. Edited
and translated by Giovanni Farris. Milan:
Marzorati, 1971.

Alberti 1972   Idem. *On Painting and On Sculpture: The Latin Texts of De
Pictura and De Statua*. Edited and translated by Cecil
Grayson. London: Phaidon, 1972.

Alberti 1987   Idem. *Dinner Pieces: A Translation of the Intercenales*.
Translated by David Marsh. Binghamton: Medieval
and Renaissance Texts and Studies, 1987.

Alberti 2003   Idem. *Momus*. Translated by Sarah Knight. Edited by
Virginia Brown. Cambridge, MA: Harvard
University Press, 2003.

Barbaro   Ermolao Barbaro. *Epistolae, Orationes, et Carmina*.
Edited by Vittore Branca. 2 vols. Florence:
Bibliopolis, 1943.

Bembo 1954   Pietro Bembo. *Gli Asolani*. Translated by Rudolph B.
Gottfried. Bloomington, IN: Indiana University
Press, 1954. Reprinted Freeport, NY: Books for
Libraries, 1971.

Bembo 1966   Idem. *Prose della volgar lingua, Gli Asolani, Rime*. Edited
by Carlo Dionisotti. Turin: UTET, 1966.

Bembo 2005   Idem. *Lyric Poetry. Etna*. Translated by Mary P.
Chatfield and Betty Radice. Cambridge, MA:
Harvard University Press, 2005.

Berni 1864   Francesco Berni. *Dialogo contra i poeti*. In his *Opere*, 1–33. Ed. Eugenio Camerini. Milan: Daelli, 1864. Reprinted 1974.

Berni 1997   Idem. *Dialogo contra i poeti*. In *Renaissance Humanism at the Court of Clement VII: Francesco Berni's "Dialogue Against Poets" in Context*, 177–345. Edited and translated by Anne Reynolds. New York: Garland, 1997.

Bruni 1741   Leonardo Bruni. *Epistularum libri VIII*. Edited by Lorenzo Mehus. Florence: Paperinius, 1741. Reprinted with an introduction by James Hankins, Rome: Storia e letteratura, 2007.

Bruni 1987   *The Humanism of Leonardo Bruni: Selected Texts*. Translated by Gordon Griffiths, James Hankins, and David Thompson. Binghamton, NY: Center for Medieval and Early Renaissance Studies, 1987.

Bunel et al.   *Petri Bunelli Galli praeceptoris et Pauli Manutii Itali discipuli epistolae Ciceroniano stylo scriptae; aliorum gallorum pariter et italorum epistolae eodem stylo scriptae*. Geneva: Henri Estienne, 1581.

Calcagnini   Celio Calcagnini. *Opera Aliquot*. Basel: Froben and Episcopius, 1544. Contains Calcagnini's epistolary.

Cassirer et al.   *The Renaissance Philosophy of Man*. Edited by Ernst Cassirer, Paul Oskar Kristeller and John Herman Randall, Jr. Chicago: University of Chicago Press, 1948.

Cennini 1932   Cennino d'Andrea Cennini. *Il libro dell'arte*. Edited by Daniel V. Thompson, Jr. New Haven: Yale University Press, 1932.

Cennini 1933   Idem. *The Craftsman's Handbook*. Translated by Daniel V. Thompson, Jr. New York: Dover, 1933.

Cinzio 1864   Giambattista Giraldi Cinzio. *De' Romanzi, Delle Comedie e Delle tragedie*. Edited by Giulio Antimaco. 2 vols. Milan: Daelli, 1864. Reprinted Bologna: Forni, 1975.

Cinzio 1968   Idem. *On Romances*. Translated by Henry L. Snuggs.
               Lexington, KY: University of Kentucky Press, 1968.
Cinzio 1973   Idem. *Scritti critici*. Ed. Camillo Guerrieri-Crocetti.
               Milan: Marzorati, 1973.
Cortesi 1510   Paolo Cortesi. *De cardinalatu libri III.* [Castel
               Cortesiano, 1510.]
Cortesi 1972   Idem. "Proemium in Librum Primum Sententiarum."
               In *Eloquenza e teologia nel 'Proemium in Librum
               Primum Sententiarum' di Paolo Cortese*. Edited by
               Giovanni Farris. Savona: Sabatelli, 1972.
Cortesi 1973   Idem. *Liber Sententiarum*, "Proem." In *Renaissance
               Philosophy: New Translations*, 32–37. Translated by
               Leonard A. Kennedy. The Hague: Mouton, 1973.
Cortesi 1979   Idem. *De hominibus doctis*. Edited by Giacomo Ferraù.
               Messina: Il Vespro, 1979.
CWE   *Collected Works of Erasmus.* Toronto: University of
               Toronto Press, 1974–2006.
Democritus   *The Atomists Leucippus and Democritus: Fragments.* Edited
               and Translated by C. C. W. Taylor. Toronto:
               University of Toronto Press, 1999.
Dionysius 1969 S. F. Bonner. *The Literary Treatises of Dionysius of
               Halicarnassus. A Study in the Development of Critical
               Method.* Cambridge: Cambridge University Press,
               1939. Reprinted Amsterdam: Hakkert, 1969.
Dolet   Etienne Dolet. *L'Erasmianus sive Ciceronianus.* Edited by
               Emile V. Telle. Geneva: Droz, 1974.
Du Bellay   Joachim Du Bellay. *Deffence et illustration de la langue
               françoyse.* Edited by Henri Chamard. Paris: Didier,
               1948. Reprinted 1966.
Erasmus 1978   Desiderius Erasmus. *Literary and Educational Writings 2:
               Copia: Foundations of the Abundant Style (De duplici
               copia verborum ac rerum commentarii duo) and De
               ratione studii (On the Method of Study).* Edited by
               Craig R. Thompson. Translated by Betty I. Knott

and Brian McGregor. *CWE*, vol. 23. Toronto: University of Toronto Press, 1978.

Erasmus 1982   Idem. *Adages*. Translated by Margaret Mann Phillips. *CWE*, vols. 31–34 Toronto: University of Toronto Press, 1982.

Erasmus 1986   Idem. *The Ciceronian: A Dialogue on the Ideal Latin Style*. Translated by Betty I. Knott. *CWE*, vol. 28. Toronto: University of Toronto Press, 1986.

Ficino 2001–06 Marsilio Ficino. *Platonic Theology*. Edited and translated by Michael J. B. Allen and James Hankins. 6 vols. Cambridge, MA: Harvard University Press, 2001–2006.

Garin   *Prosatori Latini del Quattrocento*. Edited by Eugenio Garin. Milan: Ricciardi, 1952.

Giraldi 1551   Lilio Gregorio Giraldi. *Dialogi duo de poetis nostrorum temporum*. Florence: Lorenzo Torrentino, 1551.

Giraldi 1999   Idem. *Due dialoghi sui poeti dei nostri tempi*. Edited and translated by Claudia Pandolfi. Ferrara: Cadmo, 1999.

Guarino   Guarino Veronese. *Epistolario*. Edited by Remigio Sabbadini. 3 vols. Venice, 1915–19. Turin: Bottega d'Erasmo, 1967.

Kallendorf   *Humanistic Educational Treatises*. Edited and translated by Craig W. Kallendorf. Cambridge, MA: Harvard University Press, 2002.

Lipsius 1996   Justus Lipsius. *Principles of Letter Writing: A Bilingual Text of Justi Lipsii Epistolica Institutio*. Edited and translated by R. V. Young and M. Thomas Hester. Carbondale, IL: Southern Illinois University Press, 1996.

More   Thomas More. *Selections: English Poems; Life of Pico; The Last Things*. Edited by Anthony S. G. Edwards, Katherine Gardiner Rodgers, and Clarence H. Miller. New Haven: Yale University Press, 1997.

Muret   Marc Antoine Muret. *Opera Omnia.* Edited by David
               Ruhnken and Charles Henry Frotscher. Leipzig:
               Sergiana libraria, 1834–1841. Geneva: Slatkine, 1971.
Petrarca   Francesco Petrarca. *Le Familiari.* Edited by Vittorio
               Rossi. 4 vols. Florence: Sansoni, 1933–42. Reprinted
               1968.
Pico 1930   Gianfrancesco Pico della Mirandola. *On the Imagination.*
               Edited and translated by Harry Caplan. New
               Haven: Yale University Press, 1930. Westport, CN:
               Greenwood Press, 1971.
Pico 1963   Idem. *Ioannis Pici Mirandulae viri omni disciplinarum
               genere consumatissimi vita.* Edited and translated by
               Tommaso Sorbelli. Modena: Aedes Muratoriana,
               1963. Reprinted 1994.
Pico 1969   Giovanni and Gian Francesco Pico della Mirandola.
               Opera Omnia. 2 vols. Hildesheim: Georg Olms, 1969.
Pico 1986   Giovanni Pico della Mirandola. *De hominis dignitate,
               Lettera a Ermolao Barbaro. Seguito da: La filosofia di Pico
               della Mirandola di Giovanni Semprini.* Rome: Atanòr,
               1986.
Pico-Barbaro   Giovanni Pico della Mirandola and Ermolao Barbaro.
               "The Correspondence of G. Pico della Mirandola
               and Ermolao Barbaro Concerning the Relation of
               Philosophy and Rhetoric." Trans. Quirinus Breen.
               In his *Christianity and Humanism: Studies in the History
               of Ideas,* 11–38. Grand Rapids, MI: Eerdmans, 1968.
Poliziano 1970 Angelo Poliziano. *Opera Omnia.* Edited by Ida Maïer. 3
               vols. Turin: Bottega d'Erasmo, 1970.
Quondam   *Rinascimento e classicismo. Materiali per l'analisi del sistema
               culturale di antico regime.* Edited by Amedeo
               Quondam. Rome: Bulzoni, 1999.
Ricci 1549   Bartolomeo Ricci. *De Imitatione.* Venice: de Sabio, 1549.

Salutati   Coluccio Salutati. *Epistolario*. Edited by Francesco
                  Novati. 4 vols. Rome: Istituto Storico Italiano per il
                  Medio Evo, 1891–1905.

Scaliger   Julius Caesar Scaliger. *Orationes duae contra Erasmum.*
                  Edited and translated by Michel Magnien. Geneva:
                  Droz, 1999.

Scott   Izora Scott. *Controversies over the Imitation of Cicero.* New
                  York: Columbia University Teachers' College, 1910.
                  Davis, CA: Hermagoras, 1991.

Sylvius   Angelo Poliziano, *Illustrium virorum epistolae XII libris
                  distinctae cum succulentis Francisci Sylvii commentariis
                  . . . et cum Iodoci Badii addititia explanatione.* Paris:
                  Nicolaus de Pratis, 1520. Contains François du Bois'
                  commentary on the Poliziano-Cortesi
                  correspondence and additional comments of Josse
                  Bade.

Vasari 1896   Giorgio Vasari. *Lives of Seventy of the Most Eminent
                  Painters, Sculptors, and Architects.* Translated by E. H.
                  and E. W. Blashfield, and A. A. Hopkins. 4 vols.
                  New York: Scribners, 1896.

Vasari 1986   Idem. *Le Vite de' piú eccellenti architetti, pittori, et scultori
                  italiani.* Edited by Luciano Bellosi and Aldo Rossi.
                  Turin: Einaudi, 1986.

Vergerio 1934   Pier Paolo Vergerio. *Epistolario.* Edited by Leonardo
                  Smith. Rome: Tipografia del Senato, 1934.

Vida   *The "De arte poetica" of Marco Girolamo Vida.* Edited and
                  translated by Ralph G. Williams. New York:
                  Columbia University Press, 1976.

Villani   Filippo Villani. *Le Vite d'uomini illustri fiorentini.* Vol. 6
                  of *Cronica di Matteo e Filippo Villani.* Edited by
                  Giammaria Mazzuchelli. 1826. Reprinted Rome:
                  Multigrafica, 1980.

Weinberg   *Trattati di poetica e retorica del cinquecento.* Edited by
                  Bernard Weinberg. 4 vols. Bari: Laterza, 1970–74.

I. POLIZIANO TO CORTESI

1. "Features" (*lineamenta*) may refer to characteristics both of style (Cicero, *Brutus* 87.298) and of a face (Cicero, *De divinatione* 1.13.23). It literally refers to a line drawn with a pencil, hence an outline or sketch.

2. For the ape image, see Seneca the Elder, *Controversiae* 9.3.12–13; Pliny the Younger, *Epistles* 1.5.2; Horace, *Satires* 1.10.18–19; and especially Petrarch, *Familiares* 23.19. The ape image will appear in Cortesi's response as well as both of Pico's letters to Bembo and will be used frequently by Erasmus in the *Ciceronianus*; see the introduction to the translation by Betty I. Knott in Erasmus 1986, 330. The bull and lion images are found together in the *De oratore* 2.16.69 of Cicero, but in a different context.

3. Lucius Annaeus Seneca, known as Seneca the Younger (c. 4 BC–c. AD 65), the philosopher and tragedian, was usually confused in the Renaissance with his father, the rhetorician known as Seneca the Elder (c. 55 BC–c. AD 40). Some Renaissance authors thought that Seneca the philosopher could not be the same person as Seneca the tragedian. Both Seneca the Younger's *Epistulae morales* 84 and the Elder's *Controversiae* 1, Proem 6, speak of the necessity of multiple-model imitation, though neither directly says what Poliziano attributes to Seneca here. For Seneca's reflections on different styles, see *Epistulae morales* 100.6–7; for other pertinent classical sources, see Cicero, *De oratore* 3.7.26 and Tacitus, *Dialogus de oratoribus* 18. For a comparable contemporary argument, see Poliziano's letter to Bartolomeo Scala in Poliziano 1970, 1: 58–59.

4. Quintilian 10.2.18; see also Tacitus, *Dialogue on Oratory* 23. The expression *esse videatur*, "it would seem to be," becomes the tag phrase of the Renaissance Ciceronians. It will be ridiculed later by Pico, Calcagnini and Erasmus (Erasmus 1986, 370).

5. Horace, *Epistles* 1.19.16–20.

6. Identical parrot and magpie imagery will be used by Marc-Antoine Muret (Muretus) in his inaugural oration in Rome in 1572. See *Oratio* 1.21 in Muret. For the nature of parrots and magpies, see Pliny the Elder, *Natural History* 10.42.

7. Compare Horace, *Ars poetica* 359.

8. Poliziano may be the first to have used this verb as a reflexive. The notion of self-expression will be repeated by Erasmus in the *Ciceronianus* (Erasmus 1986, 441). See McLaughlin, *Literary Imitation*, 203.

9. The mendicant image was used by Petrarch (*Familiares* 1.8). It will reappear in the letters of Bembo and Cinzio. The term *frustillatim* ("piece by piece, piecemeal") derives from Plautus, *Curculio* 576. Quintilian expresses a similar idea in 10.2.6, where he alludes to those who have nothing but what is received "as charity from others."

10. The technique of excerpting phrases and placing them in one's personal notebook will be recommended by Erasmus in the *De copia* (Erasmus 1978); it will be discussed in detail by Possevino, Text 11. For barbarisms, see Quintilian 1.5.5.

11. The motif of disease and illness as characteristics of the extreme Ciceronian will be reprised in Erasmus' *Ciceronianus* in his caricature of Nosoponus, whose name stems from a Greek root meaning "suffering from illness."

12. This passage and the following draw on Quintilian 10.2.24–28. See also Petrarch, *Familiares* 22.2.

13. For the digestive image, see Quintilian 10.1.19, Seneca *Epistulae morales* 84.6–7, and Petrarch *Familiares* 22.2. It will be used later by Cortesi (Text 2, §2), Calcagnini, Erasmus in the *Ciceronianus* (Erasmus 1986, 402), in Cinzio's *Dei romanzi* (Cinzio 1864, 64 = Cinzio 1968, 32), and in Joachim Du Bellay's *Deffence et illustration de la langue françoyse* (Du Bellay, 1.7).

14. Cicero makes this point about the importance of acquiring knowledge of many matters in the *De oratore* 1.5.17 and 2.2.5–6.

15. For the image of swimming without a life preserver, see Horace's *Satires* 1.4, 120. This proverb will be noted by Erasmus in his *Adages* 1.8.42; it later appears in the treatises of Calcagnini and in Erasmus' *Ciceronianus* (Erasmus 1986, 446) and *On the Method of Study* (Erasmus 1978, 681).

16. For the idea of relying on one's own powers, see Quintilian 10.12.19.

17. Plautus, *Trinummus* 38. The situation in that text parallels that of Poliziano's letter to Cortesi, in that the older, wiser man (or *senex*) finds

himself in the reluctant position of needing to reprimand a friend. See on this point Shafer, "The Eclectic Style," 31–32.

18. For the image of imitation as following the tracks or footsteps of others, see Lucretius, *De rerum natura* 3.3–6; Seneca *Epistulae morales* 33.11; Horace, *Epistulae* 1.19.20–21 and *Ars poetica* 286; Cicero, *Brutus* 90.307; Quintilian 10.2.10 and 12.11.28; Petrarch, *Familiares* 22.2; and Pier Paolo Vergerio, *Epistolario* (Vergerio 1934, 29). It will reappear in both of Pico's letters to Bembo as well as in the *Adagia* (4.10.32) and *Ciceronianus* (Erasmus 1986, 444–446) of Erasmus.

19. Compare to Seneca, *Epistulae morales* 33.7.

2. CORTESI TO POLIZIANO

1. Compare Cicero, *De oratore* 3.7.26 and 3.8.29–31.

2. Cortesi's pessimism about the parlous state of Latin eloquence is a humanist trope, going back to Petrarch at least, and is also reminiscent of passages in Tacitus' *Dialogue on Oratory* 1, Cicero's *Tusculan Disputations* 2.2.5, and *Brutus* 6.22. Cortesi's sentiments will be echoed by Bembo as well as Calcagnini.

3. For the coupling of elegance and variety, see Cicero, *De oratore* 1.12.50. *Varietas* is a favored literary virtue of the Eclectics.

4. Contrast with Cicero's *De oratore* 2.23.98, where Antonius declares that "there are many who copy no man, but gain their objects by natural aptitude."

5. The image of a leader or guide (*dux*) comes from Petrarch, *Familiares* 22.2. Quintilian (7.Pr.3) uses the image of the lost traveler to describe oratory that lacks order. The term *dux* traditionally connotes a military commander as well as a guide, and Cortesi prolongs this metaphor in the next sentence through the image of a battle line (*acies*).

6. This language is repeated by Cortesi in his *De hominibus doctis* (Cortesi 1979, 146).

7. For a similar analogy between putting only good food in one's stomach and reading only good authors, see Bruni, *On the Study of Literature* (Kallendorf 2003, 97). But compare Quintilian 10.1.58, where he suggests

that one should first eat the best fare at a banquet, then the rest, "which in spite of its comparative inferiority is still attractive owing to its variety." The banquet image is reprised by Erasmus in the *Ciceronianus* (Erasmus 1986, 440); a similar analogy between variety of styles and variety of foods which are all appealing at different times can be found in Petrarch, *Familiares* 1.1.

8. The incongruous image of writers being nurtured on the milk of Cicero had been used in a well-known letter of Guarino Veronese (Guarino, 1: 367). For a similar analogy of nursing and early exposure to eloquence, see *Brutus* 58.211.

9. For the ape image, see Poliziano (1.1); for the likeness of son to father, see Seneca, *Epistulae morales* 84.8, Petrarch, *Familiares* 23.19, and Gasparino Barzizza (Quondam, 111–113). The image of apes and sons is reprised by Erasmus in the *Ciceronianus* (Erasmus 1986, 374).

10. For a warning against imitating defects, see Quintilian 1.3.1–2.

11. The phrase *aliquid suum* is reminiscent of Petrarch's admonishment that imitators should add something uniquely their own (*quiddam suum ac proprium* and *unum suum ac proprium*) to the imitation. See *Familiares* 22.2 and 23.19, respectively. See also Salutati's letter to Bruni in Salutati, 4: 148, Quintilian 10.2.28, and Poliziano (1.3).

12. The notion of *copia* or richness and abundance of expression is essential to Cicero, *De oratore* 1.6.21, Quintilian 10.1.5, and throughout the *De copia* of Erasmus. For more on its importance in Renaissance letters, see Cinzio's letter (6.6 and note).

13. See Cicero, *Orator* 23.76, where the true Attic style is deemed deceptively plain and easy to imitate. Cortesi repeats his judgment about the deceptive ease of imitating Cicero in *De hominibus doctis* (Cortesi 1979, 135–136).

14. Cortesi's reference to the *insignia* and *lumina* that decorate writing is an echo of Cicero, *De oratore* 3.25.96.

15. For the notion of decorum in speech, see Cicero, *De oratore* 3.14.53 and 3.55.210 as well as *Orator* 21.70–22.74.

16. A similar idea is expressed in Horace, *Art of Poetry* 1–13.

17. The last few lines of this paragraph are echoed in Cortesi, *De homini-bus doctis* (Cortesi 1979, 152).

18. These images are reprised by Cortesi in the *De hominibus doctis* (Cortesi 1979, 172), where also Poliziano's position is alluded to. The conflation of the pupil and ape imagery may owe something to two let-ters in which Coluccio Salutati was referred to—in a complimentary fashion—as a *simia Ciceronis* (Salutati 4: 491–492) and as an *alumnus splendidissimi Ciceronis* (ibid. 4: 465). See also Villani, 19, for the expres-sion *scimmia di Cicerone* used to compliment Salutati, and ibid. 49, for the expression *scimmia della natura*, used to describe a follower of Giotto who achieved an uncanny realism in his art. See Poliziano's letter to Cortesi (Text 1, n. 2) and Pico's second letter to Bembo (5.19) for more on ape imagery. For the image of the 'hanger-on' (*assecla*) see the comment of Sylvius: "The imitator is a servant [*assecula*] from the fact that he follows in attendance [*assequi*]. Livy has criticized this type of man."

19. For the idea of imitating no one, see Cicero, *De oratore* 2.23.98; the is-sue will be revisited by Bembo.

20. On the necessity of imitation, see Aristotle, *Poetics* 1447a. For man's instinct for and natural pleasure in imitation, see *Poetics* 1448b.

21. For the notion of the mind as a *tabula rasa* see Aristotle, *De anima* 3.4. The formula "nihil est in intellectu quod prius non fuerit in sensu" ("nothing is in the mind that was not first in the intellect") was an oft-re-peated maxim that is basic to Aristotle's psychology. This idea will be re-peated by Bembo (4.5) and appears in Pico's treatise *On the Imagination* (Pico 1930).

22. For a discussion of art as imitation of nature, see Seneca, *Epistles* 65.3.

23. On the idea of a single form of eloquence, see Cicero, *De oratore* 3.6.22. Much of this section of Cortesi's letter is reminiscent of the *De oratore* 3.6–26 and following, where different varieties of excellence in the arts are examined.

24. As McLaughlin notes (*Literary Imitation*, 205), Cortesi's list of au-thors who borrowed individual traits from Cicero appears to be especially

chosen to appeal to Poliziano's eclectic tastes. Indeed, the passage is reminiscent of Poliziano's letter to Scala (Poliziano 1970, 1: 58–59).

25. See Quintilian 10.1.32, who speaks of the "milky fullness of Livy."

26. Caecilius Firmianus Lactantius (c. 250–c. 317 AD), often called "the Christian Cicero," had been recommended as a model by Bruni (Kallendorf 2003, 97) and is praised by Gianfrancesco Pico in De studio divinae et humanae philosophiae, 1.7 (Pico 1969, 2: 21). He is discussed extensively by Erasmus in the Ciceronianus (Erasmus 1986, 412).

27. For the image of Cicero as a source or spring of natural talents and the embodiment of all stylistic virtues, see Quintilian 10.1.105–112.

28. The image of how early learning takes deep roots in the mind is a common one, found for example in Vergerio's popular educational treatise De ingenuis moribus (Kallendorf 2003, 59). See also Petrarch, Familiares 22.2.

29. See Cortesi, De hominibus doctis (Cortesi 1979, 126–127), for a similar use of the seed image. See also Cinzio (6.4). For Cicero's use of the image of sowing, see Orator 14.48.

30. Note the negative use of the varietas topos and the digestive metaphor, both favored by Poliziano. Compare Barzizza (Quondam, III), Vergerio (Kallendorf 2003, 61) and Macrobius, Saturnalia 7. The image is derived from Seneca, Epistulae morales 2.4 and 84.6–7.

31. For the image of mixing sounds from several sources, see Barzizza (Quondam, 113).

32. The commentary of Sylvius states: "In nearly every city of Italy live Jews who loan large sums of money for that purpose. From some they collect interest; from others, garments that people pledge so the lenders may find a buyer more easily."

33. See also Horace, Epistles 1.1.95 and following, Petrarch, Familiares 22.2, and Barzizza (Quondam, III) for another use of the cloak image. Cortesi will later accuse Poliziano of changing his style as one changes cloaks according to the weather. See Cortesi 1510, 95.

34. Quintilian (10.1.2) had compared writing without models to a ship drifting aimlessly.

35. Demosthenes (c. 384–322 BC), generally considered to be the greatest of Athenian orators and an important model for Cicero; Hyperides (c. 389 -322 BC), Attic orator and a pupil of Isocrates; Lycurgus (c. 396–342 BC), another Attic orator and pupil of Isocrates; Aeschines (c. 390–314 BC), an Athenian orator and rival of Demosthenes; Dinarchus or Deinarchus (born c. 360 BC), an Attic orator who gave a speech against Demosthenes. Quintilian reviews these and other "remarkable orators" in the *Institutio oratoria* 10.1.76–80 and goes on to review famous philosophers in 10.1.81–84.

36. Quintilian (10.1.112) likewise suggests that, merely by admiring Cicero's style, the novice writer demonstrates some measure of progress.

3. PICO, *ON IMITATION*

1. See *Republic* 10.597.

2. See *Epistles* 1.19.19–20.

3. Compare Quintilian 10.2.4 and 10.2.9 for the suggestion that imitation is not enough, and 10.2.10–11 for the shadow/substance imagery.

4. Perhaps an inference from the close relationship between *Orphic Hymns* 40 and *Homeric Hymns* 2 and 13.

5. Macrobius, in his *Saturnalia*, gives a detailed catalogue of Virgil's extensive borrowings from Homer. See also Aulus Gellius, *Attic Nights* 9.9 and 13.27 and Suetonius, *Life of Virgil* 44–46. Criticism of Virgil for excessive imitation was a Renaissance commonplace.

6. On the importance of good rhythm in prose and verse see Cicero, *De oratore* 3.44.173, *Orator* 20.67, 50.169, 52.175, and 53.179, as well as Quintilian 9.4.45–57.

7. For the distinction between imitation and emulation, see Quintilian 10.2. 7–11, where Quintilian also gives a three-fold distinction between *imitari, aequare* and *sequi*.

8. For the metaphor of stealing, widely used in Renaissance imitation debates, see Cicero, *De finibus* 5.25.74. Among Renaissance authors see Berni 1997, 196–197. For a positive use of the metaphor, see Longinus

13.4, Macrobius, *Saturnalia* 6.1.3, and Vida, *De arte poetica* (Vida, 243–263).

9. The classic comparisons of Demosthenes and Cicero are Quintilian 10.1.105 and Plutarch's parallel lives of Demosthenes and Cicero.

10. The Roman historian Sallust, known for his terse style (see Quintilian 10.1.32), was frequently compared to his predecessor Livy. See for example Quintilian 2.5.18–19. Much of this section is reminiscent of Poliziano's letter to Bartolomeo Scala, referred to in Texts 1 and 2.

11. Cicero makes a similar point about Sulpicius and Cotta, who chose as their models Crassus and Antonius, respectively; the result was that each was different from the other yet both were supreme among their contemporaries. See *Brutus* 55.204.

12. The allusion is to Thucydides, who was a general as well as the historian of the Peloponnesian war. A comparison of Herodotus and Thucydides can also be found in Cicero's *Orator* 12.39. A similar argument regarding the variety of equally pleasing styles (but with different examples) is made in Cicero's *De oratore* 3.7.26–31.

13. For praises of the literary style of Aristotle and Plato, see Cicero's *Brutus* 31.121 and *Orator* 19.62 as well as Quintilian 10.1.81–83. The praise of Aristotle for his supposed eloquence was a humanist theme from the time of Petrarch and Leonardo Bruni (see Bruni 1987, 290).

14. I.e., Xenophon, the Greek historian and disciple of Socrates. The epithet is probably inspired by the *Orator* 19.62; see also Quintilian 10.1.33.

15. The primary sense behind the play on *koina* (common) and *kala* (beautiful) is that Xenophon used a simple style, Plato an ornate one. For a detailed description of the natural beauty of Plato's language, see Dionysius of Halicarnassus, *On Literary Composition* (Dionysius 1969, 114).

16. I.e., Plato, with whom Aristotle studied for 20 years according to his ancient biographers.

17. For the image of blazing one's own trail, see Horace, *Epistles* 1.19.21–22, as well as Petrarch, *Familiares* 22.2.

18. Marcus Terentius Varro (116 BC–c. 28 BC) was a contemporary of Cicero who wrote many encyclopedic treatises in a more familiar or popular style than Cicero. For a comparison of the styles of Cicero and Varro, see Augustine, *City of God* 6.2.

19. Cicero calls Varro "of all men . . . the most learned." The phrase is quoted by Augustine (ibid.) from a now lost passage of Cicero's *Academica*.

20. These terms refer to the parts of a sentence in the classical theory of speech. The period generally expresses a complete thought and normally consists of at least two members or subordinate clauses; clauses consist of words. By varying the length of the members in a precise fashion, the writer could achieve different effects. The issue of prose rhythm is discussed extensively by Cicero in Book III of the *De oratore*.

21. Compare Quintilian 2.6.7. The image of the fledgling bird will be reprised by a "converted" Cinzio in his *Dei Romanzi* (Cinzio 1968, 132) where he likewise suggests that maturing writers should eventually try their own wings.

22. The image of culling or plucking a flower derives from Seneca, *Epistulae Morales* 84.3.

23. Aulus Cornelius Celsus (fl. first century AD) was an encyclopedist who wrote on both medicine and rhetoric. Columella was a Roman agricultural writer (fl. first century AD).

24. The word here is *genius* rather than the more common *ingenium*. As Jean Lecointe points out (*L'Idéal et la différence*, 221), the juxtaposition of the more familiar phrase *propensioque naturae* and the unusual term *genius* is revelatory: no doubt the notion of natural inclination is meant to be taken as a gloss on the word *genius*, which is used here for the first time in this manner. Chomarat (*Grammaire et rhétorique*, 2: 833–834) notes that Erasmus will uses this term, which carries connotations of divine power, seven times in the *Ciceronianus*.

25. See pseudo-Aristotle, *Problems* 30.6.

26. See Aristotle, *Poetics* 1448b 4–8.

27. See Cicero, *Orator* 2.8–3.10 as well as Plato, *Symposium* 211a for a discussion of the idea, form or pattern of ideal beauty. The term is also used by Hermogenes in his treatise on ideas, forms, or types of style, which Pico could have known in several Latin translations or via George of Trebizond's rhetorical handbook.

28. The notion that the perfect idea of correct speech cannot be fully instantiated in human language is Platonic in inspiration.

29. Zeuxis (fl. 435–390 BC), a famous ancient artist who chose five maidens from Croton in Southern Italy as models for his painting of Helen. See Pliny, *Natural History* 35.61–66 and Cicero, *De inventione* 2.1.1–3. The story of Zeuxis became a commonplace among proponents of eclecticism. See for example, Erasmus 1986, 357.

30. Cicero, who tells of choosing a wide variety of oratorical models for his treatise *De inventione* (2.1.4–5), in imitation of Zeuxis' use of multiple models.

31. Instead of *idea*, Pico here uses the terms *forma* and *species absoluta*, all synonyms for idea in Latin Platonic sources.

32. Compare Cicero, *Orator* 3.9: "so with our mind (*animus*) we conceive the ideal of perfect eloquence."

33. See Cicero, *Orator* 29.104: "Although [Demosthenes] stands pre-eminent among all in every style of oratory, still he does not always satisfy my ears. . . . ." See also *Orator* 66.221.

34. Because Livy was from Padua (*Patavium* in Latin), his tone appeared provincial to Roman critics. For more on the notion of Livy's *patavinitas* see Quintilian 1.5.56 and 8.1.3. Gaius Asinius Pollio (76 BC–5 AD) was an Augustan orator and rhetorician.

35. Tacitus, *Dialogue on Oratory* 18.

36. See Quintilian 12.10.12, who reports the view of some of Cicero's contemporaries that his style was "Asiatic, bombastic, redundant and effeminate." The Asiatic style was richly ornate and often contrasted with the direct and simple Attic style embraced by Brutus.

37. Quintilian 10.2.24.

38. For comparable imagery, see Cicero, *De oratore* 2.39.162, *Tusculan Disputations* 3.1.2, Quintilian 1.1.21, Bembo, *Prose* 1.3 (Bembo 1966, 80), and Erasmus, *Adagia* 1.7.54. Caecilius is probably Caecilius of Calacte (fl. late first century BC), the author of the lost treatise *On the Character of the Ten Orators*, who, in his comparison of Demosthenes and Cicero, preferred Demosthenes; he is referred to in Quintilian 9.3.47.

39. Compare Quintilian 2.2.8, which speaks of "how much more readily we imitate those whom we like."

40. Ibid. 10.1.81.

41. This passage is probably inspired by Quintilian 2.8.1, which also deals with the variety of natural inclinations, and 2.8.2–3 which treats of the natural human similarities that facilitate the imitation of one model more than another.

42. See Plutarch, *Moralia* (*Quomodo adulator*, 9); Horace, *Sermones* 1.3.39–40. The theme of imitating moles and scars becomes a Renaissance commonplace and is a favorite of Pico's, who uses it several times in his two letters. See also Erasmus, *Ciceronianus* (Erasmus 1986, 365–366).

43. Compare Leonardo Bruni's similar claim that if Plato were brought back from the dead, he would deny that the medieval translations of his work were genuine; see Bruni 1741, 1: Ep. I.1.

44. A reference to the five parts of rhetoric: invention (*inventio*), arrangement (*dispositio*), elocution (*elocutio*), memory (*memoria*), and delivery or action (*actio*). See Quintilian, *Institutio oratoria* 3.3.1 and the pseudo-Ciceronian *Rhetorica ad Herennium* 1.2.3, as well as Cicero's *De inventione* 1.7.9 and *De oratore* 1.31.142–143.

45. Invention (from the verb *invenire*, to come upon or find) refers to the finding of a topic or argument or subject matter.

46. Terence, *The Eunuch*, Prologue 23–24.

47. A paraphrase of Pliny the Younger, *Epistolae* 3.13.3.

48. Gaius Lucilius (180–102 BC), a writer of satires; the reference is to his *Satires* 26.623, where the meaning is "from conception." The elder Pico had quoted this expression in his *Oration on the Dignity of Man*

(Cassirer et al., 225), while Lilio Giraldi will refer to it in his *Dialogues on Poets of Our Time*. See Giraldi 1999, 110–111.

49. The denial of nature's weariness is a motif that recurs in the writings of the earlier humanists, including the elder Pico (see *On the Dignity of Man*, Cassirer et al., 244) and Alberti (*De commodis* in Alberti 1971, 39 and *De pictura* in Alberti 1972, 33). This optimism on the part of Alberti and both Picos contradicts the opinions of Lucretius that nature is indeed growing old (*De rerum natura* 5.1150 ff.). See also Quintilian 10.5.5, which suggests that nature and eloquence are not so poor that there is only one way to achieve proper expression. Pico uses this topos in the prefatory letter of his collection of epistles and once more in a letter lauding Poliziano, the elder Pico, and Barbaro. See Pico 1969, 2: 1268 and 1335.

50. See Cicero, *Orator* 9.31, where the allusion is to the legend that mankind subsisted on nuts alone until the sowing of grain was brought about with the blessings of Demeter.

51. Compare Quintilian 12.11.22.

52. Pico is referring elliptically to the common argument of Quattrocento humanists that they deserved more praise than the ancients for their literary achievements since it was harder to learn Latin well in modern times; this is found, for example, in the prefaces to Lorenzo Valla's *De elegantiis linguae latinae*.

53. Compare Poliziano (1.3).

54. The shoe image appears in the elder Pico's letter to Barbaro (Garin, 810; Pico-Barbaro, 18). See also Pico's second letter, 5.22.

55. For the topos that everything ancient is good and modern bad, see Horace, *Epistles* 1.1.1 and 2.1.76; Tacitus, *Dialogue on Oratory* 15; and Quintilian 1.6.41.

56. See, for example, Vasari 1896, 4: 51–52, which describes the reception of a now-lost statue known as the Sleeping Cupid that was presented as ancient before being revealed as the work of Michelangelo.

57. Aristarchus of Samothrace, head of the Alexandrian Library (c. 180 to 145 BC), was a famously sharp literary critic. See Horace, *Art of Poetry* 445–450.

58. The two Catos are Cato the Elder (234–149 BC), known as the Censor, and his great-grandson, Marcus Porcius Cato of Utica the Younger (95–46 BC), a statesman and contemporary of Cicero. Timon of Phlius (fl. c. 250 BC) was a Skeptic philosopher. Momus was the ancient god of fault-finding and criticism: see Alberti 2003 and Erasmus, *Adages* 1.5.74.

59. A similar story of a false and true Ciceronian text is presented in the *Ciceronianus* (Erasmus 1986, 364). In *The Courtier* of Baldassare Castiglione (2.35), a similar story is told regarding the writing of verses under the name of the acclaimed poet Jacopo Sannazaro; when the name of the real author was revealed, the same verses were declared "less than mediocre."

60. *Virgulae, asteriskoi,* and *obeloi* were used by ancient editors to indicate interpolations or defective passages in a text. *Notae censoriae* ("critical marks") were marks attached by a Roman censor to the name of a person on the citizen list who had been guilty of immoral or unpatriotic conduct (see Cicero, *Pro Cluentio* 46.129) and by extension came to indicate defective passages in literary works.

61. Aesop was traditionally known as the Greek writer of animal fables, which were later translated into Latin by Phaedrus. The story of the jackdaw dressed in the peacock's borrowed plumes can be found in *Fables* 1.3. A similar image can be found in Horace, *Epistles* 1.3.15–20, Petrarch, *Familiares* 22.2, and Erasmus' *Ciceronianus* (Erasmus 1986, 411).

62. See Cicero's *Orator* 60. 232–233. The idea of a sentence whose words and word-order cannot be changed without weakening its clarity or effectiveness came to be a principal measure of stylistic excellence.

63. For the topos "ocean of eloquence" see Quintilian 10.1.46 and 10.1.61, who uses the image to describe Homer and Pindar. For the river of eloquence, another common image, see for example Cicero, *Academica* 2.119, where it is applied to Aristotle.

64. Presumably a reference either to the pseudo-Ciceronian *Rhetorica ad Herrenium* or to Cicero's youthful *De inventione*.

65. *De universitate* was the title of Cicero's partial translation of Plato's *Timaeus*.

66. In the *Brutus* 2.8, Cicero refers to the time "when my oratory had attained a certain ripeness and maturity of age." See also Quintilian 11.1.31.

67. For the idea that style should vary in accordance with the genre in which one is writing, see Erasmus 1986, 407.

68. The general point is also made by Alberti, where it is said that "eloquence is so varied that even Cicero is sometimes very un-Ciceronian." See Garin, 180 and Alberti 1987, 127. For another reference to Cicero's stylistic inconsistency in his various writings, see Poliziano in Garin, 877.

69. Pico's adverb *Ciceroniane* will be transformed into *Tulliane* and used in a similar fashion by Erasmus in the *Ciceronianus* (Erasmus 1986, 348).

70. The image of the wall made of Ciceronian stones is adopted in Du Bellay, 1.11. For a classical precedent in which building imagery is used to express the importance of proper arrangement, see Quintilian 7.1.1. For the related image of a mosaic, see Cicero, *De oratore* 3.43.171–172, *Brutus* 79.274, and *Orator* 44.149, each of which refer to Lucilius (84–85, ed. Marx) as the originator of the image; see also Alberti 1960–73, 2: 160–162, and Erasmus 1986, 438 and 601, n. 838.

71. Erasmus uses this image in the section of the *Ciceronianus* (Erasmus 1986, 425) where, in the guise of Nosoponus, he criticizes his own hasty literary production, calling them "abortions."

72. The epithets used here (the power of Demosthenes, the richness of Plato, the charm or delightfulness of Isocrates) are commonplaces of Renaissance rhetoric, derived from Quintilian, *Institutio oratoria* 10.1.108; see also Cicero, *De oratore* 3.7.28. Pico had used these epithets in his early tract, the *De studio divinae et humanae philosophiae* 1.7 (Pico 1969, 2: 21).

73. *Chriae* according to the *Oxford Latin Dictionary* are "topic(s) of general application set for study and exercise in a school of grammar or rhetoric." See Seneca, *Epistulae morales* 33.7 and Quintilian 1.9.3–4 and 2.4.26.

74. See Cicero, *Orator* 16.52.

75. A reference to the three kinds of oratorical styles outlined in the *Orator* 5.20 and 21.69 (the *genus vehemens* or grandiloquent, the *genus humile* or

plain, and the *genus medium* or tempered or middle style). See also *De oratore* 3.45.177, where the three styles are described as *gravis*, *subtilis*, and *medium*.

76. See *Brutus* 12.49–13.51. The Laconic or Spartan style was known for its terseness. On the Attic style, see Cicero's *Orator* 23.76; for the opposition of the Asiatic and Attic styles, see Cicero, *De optimo genere oratorum* 3.8–9, as well as Quintilian, *Institutio oratoria* 10.2.17 and 12.10.12–16. For the expression "golden mean," see Horace, *Odes* 2.10.5. The Rhodian style, so called because of its leader, Apollonius Molon of Rhodes, Cicero's teacher, aimed to be more eclectic, moderate and appreciative of a variety of styles.

77. Compare Aristotle's *Rhetoric* 3.8.4 and Cicero's *Orator* 57.192 and *De oratore* 3.47.183. The technical term here is *clausulae*, referring to the final cadence of a period. Aristotle's interest in prose meter is mentioned by Bruni in Bruni 1987, 291. For Quintilian's criticism of excessive attention to *clausulae*, see *Institutio oratoria* 8.5.13.

78. For the idea of style fitting like a garment, see Cicero's *Brutus* 79.274, Quintilian 11.1.31–32, Petrarch, *Familiares* 22.2 and Erasmus 1978, 306.

79. For the image of weaving as a metaphor for literary creation, see Quintilian 9.4.19 and David Quint, *Origin and Originality*, 35.

80. Carmenta was a minor Roman deity who had the gift of prophecy. She was credited with transforming the Greek alphabet into Roman letters. See Boccaccio, *Famous Women*, ed. and tr. V. Brown (Cambridge, MA: Harvard University Press, 2001), 107.

81. I.e. Romulus and Remus.

82. A paraphrase of Horace, *Art of Poetry* 56–58.

83. A reference to the Apuleian style, named for Lucius Apuleius, most famously the author of *The Golden Ass*, a work seen as characterized by an extremely eclectic style full of archaisms and other verbal rarities. Renaissance stylists who were considered "Apuleians" include Filippo Beroaldo and Giovanni Battista Pio, as well as the mature Cortesi. See D'Amico, "The Progress of Renaissance Latin Prose."

84. A reference to Pico's recent poem, the *De Venere et Cupidine expellendis carmen*, or the *Expulsion of Venus and Cupid*, which he must have shared with Bembo in manuscript form before its publication in 1513. The work is critical of the abundance of classical pagan statuary found in Christian Rome.

4. BEMBO TO PICO

1. A classical oath popular among humanists though considered unacceptably pagan by some. Even Erasmus, who wrote several letters mocking the use by Christians of pagan language and severely criticizes it in the *Ciceronianus* (Erasmus 1986, 384, 388, and 565, n. 356), uses the Greek equivalent of this oath at Erasmus 1986, 366. Possevino will chastise Bembo for this and other pagan oaths found in this text and his other writings; see below, 10.3.

2. On these ancient Greek painters and sculptors, see Pliny, *Natural History* 35.79–97, though the immediate source here is Cicero's *Brutus* 18.70.

3. Alexander the Great was said to have permitted no artists but Lysippus and Apelles to portray him. See Horace, *Epistles* 2.1.237–241.

4. Bembo may be reminding Pico of what the latter had earlier written concerning the mind as a clean slate or *tabula rasa* in his *On the Imagination* (Pico 1930, 40–43), an Aristotelian view which contrasts with the Platonic psychology he invokes in Text 3. See also on this point Cortesi, 2.4.

5. Lucius Licinius Crassus and Marcus Antonius were famous Roman orators in the generation before Cicero and interlocutors in Cicero's *De oratore*; Julius Caesar was known as an orator as well as a general and statesman; see Cicero's praise of him in the *Brutus* 71.251–253.

6. I.e., consciously apply the idea of good style to their writing.

7. See Cicero, *Orator* 2.7.

8. See *Republic* 9.592b.

9. A similar point is made in Quintilian 1. Pr. 26–27.

10. *Aeneid* 5.716–717.

11. *Aeneid* 5.754.

12. Compare to Pico's first letter, 3.24. For a variation on Bembo's building image, see *Ciceronianus* (Erasmus 1986, 403), where Erasmus suggests that an architect who "sets out to create a splendid mansion [does not] derive all the details from one single building."

13. See Poliziano's letter to Cortesi (1.2) for the mendicant image.

14. "in a disorderly way" (*structura inconcinna*): the notion of *concinnitas*, the putting together of parts in a harmonious, symmetrical fashion, was a common classical stylistic virtue, praised by Cicero and especially cultivated by Bembo.

15. This "Ciceronian" definition of imitation actually derives from the pseudo-Ciceronian *Rhetorica ad Herrenium* 1.2.3. It is surprising that Bembo should have thought this work to be authentically Ciceronian, given that doubts about its authenticity were raised two generations before by Lorenzo Valla.

16. Compare Cortesi 2.5.

17. For an analogous discussion of the futility of an artist's following one model after another, see Cennini 1932, §27 (= Cennini 1933, 15).

18. See Quintilian 10.1.114.

19. I.e., moderation and disregard for eloquence.

20. This passage, while recalling Quintilian 10.2.25, directly contradicts it; Quintilian had maintained that one should attempt to imitate the best features of different authors.

21. The image of the woman who is more beautiful without cosmetics was used by the elder Pico in his letter to Barbaro (see Garin, 816; Pico-Barbaro, 21). Cortesi reverses the image in the proem of his *Liber Sententiarum* (Cortesi 1972, 22–24; Cortesi 1973, 32–33). For a classical antecedent, see Cicero, *Orator* 23.78.

22. That is, he never showed more than one form at a time. In Homer's *Odyssey* 4.410–420, Proteus has the power to take on different forms. Erasmus will also use Proteus as a figure for copious variety in *De copia* 1.8 (Erasmus 1978).

23. In establishing different primary models for different genres, Bembo here anticipates the advice he will give concerning vernacular models in his *Prose*, wherein Petrarch is cited as the model for Italian verse and Boccaccio for prose.

24. For the metaphor of a guide (*dux*) see Cortesi (2.2).

25. The metaphor of the pot being tainted by the scent of its first contents is a classical topos; see Quintilian 1.1.5 and Horace, *Epistles* 1.2.54 and 67–70 for examples of its use. Alberti uses the metaphor in *Della famiglia* (Alberti 1960–73, 1: 71), Erasmus in *Adagia* 2.4.20, *De conscribendis epistolis* of 1522 (CWE 25: 34), and *De pueris instituendis* of 1529 (CWE 26: 343).

26. This apprenticeship model is similar to that outlined by Poliziano in his *Oration on Quintilian and Statius* (Garin, 870); see also Quintilian, 1.2.26.

27. A reminiscence of Virgil, *Georgics* 1.145. Erasmus alludes to the same passage in the *Ciceronianus* (Erasmus 1986, 397).

28. A reference to Bembo's *Asolani* (1505) and his vernacular love poetry written in the Petrarchist style (collected in the *Rime* to be published in 1530). Bembo was also in the midst of composing his *Prose della volgar lingua* (published in 1525) at the time of his debate with Pico.

29. Pessimism about the state of eloquence was a humanist commonplace, at least as commonplace as humanist boasts of having revived eloquence; for an extended example see Calcagnini, 8.4–7.

30. See Quintilian 10.1.85–86 and Erasmus 1986, 397.

31. See Tacitus, *Dialogue on Oratory* 18 and 22. An example of Cicero's relentless self-praise may be found in the *Brutus*, where Cicero first quotes Caesar praising him (72.253), repeats it with a commentary by Brutus (72.254), and then comments on it himself (72.255). For examples of the criticism levied against Cicero's all-too-frequent self-praise, see Plutarch's *Life of Cicero* 24.1; Quintilian 11.1.17–25 and 12.10.12 ff. as well as Erasmus 1986, 360 and 366.

32. For the common image of Cicero as the father of eloquence, see Pliny, *Natural History* 7.30 and Petrarch, *Familiares* 24.4.

33. See Seneca, *De brevitate vitae* 5.1–2.

34. Pico will make a similar distinction between Cicero's moral character and his stylistic excellence. See also Petrarch, *Familiares* 24.4; Erasmus 1986, 366, and Quintilian 12.1.14. The need for the good orator to be a good man as well, a *vir bonus dicendi peritus*, was a classical and Renaissance commonplace. See Quintilian 1 Preface 9; 1.2.3, 12.1.1–12.1.4; Seneca the Elder, *Controversiae* 1, Preface 10; and Erasmus 1986, 366.

35. See Pico's first letter to Bembo (3.12).

36. See note 2, above. Phidias was a Greek sculptor of the fifth century BC, famous for the Parthenon sculptures. Polyclitus was the second most celebrated Greek sculptor of the fifth century after Phidias. Agelades (fl. c. 520–c. 450 BC) was a Greek sculptor and teacher of Polyclitus and Phidias. The name Eladus is apparently a corrupt form of Agelades, though Bembo clearly thought the two were different personages. Pamphilius (fl. early fourth century BC) was a Greek painter and the teacher of Apelles.

37. Compare Quintilian 1.2.29.

38. Compare Quintilian 10.2.10. In the *De' Romanzi*, Cinzio will similarly state that "it is easy for a runner, after reaching the point set before him, to pass it and leave it behind" (Cinzio 1864, 142 = Cinzio 1968, 133).

39. This opinion is a commonplace of late Quattrocento criticism, according to McLaughlin, *Literary Imitation*, 264.

40. Probably a reference to Ovid, whom Bembo imitated in several of his Latin poems. See Bembo 2005 for Bembo's debts to the Latin lyric poets.

41. For a comparable distinction between correctly imitating the style of one author alone and appropriately borrowing from several authors, see Barbaro's letter to Giovanni Antonio Panteo in Barbaro, 1: 44–45.

42. See Horace, *Ars Poetica* 58–59.

43. Marcus Atilius (fl. 200 BC) was a Roman playwright who translated the *Electra* of Sophocles from the Greek. This translation was criticized by Cicero in *De finibus* 1.2.5, though he admits it is worth reading.

44. Virgil's *Georgics* are compared to the *Works and Days* of Hesiod in Aulus Gellius, *Noctes Atticae* 9.9.3. Poliziano wrote a commentary on Gellius' comparison.

45. See 4.13.

46. Compare Salutati 4: 148.

47. A reference to Pico's *De amore divino*. Bembo is perhaps also reminding Pico and the reader that he has already published a book about love, namely the *Asolani*.

48. Pico's writings critical of secular philosophy include his *De studio divinae et humanae philosophiae* (1497), which formed the foundation for his later treatise against Aristotelian philosophy, namely the *Examen vanitatis doctrinae gentium et veritatis Christianae disciplinae distinctum in libros sex*. Though the latter work was not published until 1520, it may have been begun by 1502, and thus might have been known to Bembo.

49. Bembo's response is thus dated 100 days after Pico's letter. The interval may be indicative of the length of time Bembo spent composing his response, which may be contrasted with the few hours that Pico says he has spent in writing his first letter. Bembo's slow work pace was seen as typical of the Ciceronian who belabored the choice of every word. See on this point Quondam, 154.

5. PICO TO BEMBO

1. For the proverbial use of this expression, see Erasmus, *Adages* 1.1.60 and Plautus, *Amphitruo* 707.

2. I.e. honey from Arpinum, the birthplace of Cicero.

3. Paeonian herbs, so called after Paëon, the physician of the gods (*Iliad* 5.401, 899), were known for their medicinal value.

4. The wordplay on "points" (*puncta*) again evokes the image of the stinging hornets.

5. *Scrupulosos* ("punctilious") also means "sharp, pointed," and may be intended to recall the earlier image of the hornet's stingers.

6. *Simpliciter* and *absolute* are scholastic terms meaning "without remainder," "without possibility of further distinctions."

7. See 3.2.

8. See 3.4

9. See 3.8.

10. See 3.12.

11. For an analysis of Poliziano's eclectic imitation, see Shafer, "The Eclectic Style," as well as Greene, *Light in Troy*, 156–158.

12. See Cicero, *De inventione* 2.2.4.

13. See 3.10.

14. *Orator* 1.2. Later, in the *Orator* 11.36, Cicero will declare, "I held that in all things there is a certain 'best,' even if it is not apparent, and that this can be recognized by one who is expert in that subject." See also *De optimo genere oratorum* 1.4, which declares that "there is one best, and the next best is that which resembles it most."

15. *Orator* 2.7.

16. *Orator* 2.8.

17. The passage in question is *Orator* 2.8–3.10. On Phidias see 4.28.

18. *Orator* 2.9–10.

19. The verb here is *colere*, which can mean "to cultivate" but also "to worship" when used in the context of deities; Pico perhaps wished to exploit this ambiguity so as to hint at the inherent paganism of extreme Ciceronianism.

20. Democritus, fragment D 6.

21. See *Orator* 4.18.

22. See Plato's *Phaedrus* 275a 1–5.

23. See Ficino, 2001–2006, 1: 241–247.

24. See *Orator* 2.8.

25. *De officiis* 1.31.110.

26. *De officiis* 1.31.113.

27. Compare Bembo's language in 4.13.

28. The sculptor Lysippus of Sicyon was said not to have been anyone's pupil. In this he was like the painter Eupompus, who, "when asked which of his predecessors he took for a model . . . pointed to a crowd of people and said that it was Nature herself, not an artist, whom we ought to imitate." The story of Lysippus and Eupompus is told in Pliny, *Natural History* 34.19.61; Pico seems to be conflating the painter and the sculptor in this passage.

29. Zeuxis. See Pico's first letter, 3.10.

30. Poliziano, *Miscellaneorum centuria secunda*, ed. Vittore Branca and Manlio Pastore Stocchi (Florence: Olschki, 1978), 97.

31. Another allusion to the practice of keeping a commonplace book or lexicon from which to draw appropriate expressions. Alberti uses similar language to deride those who "grow old" collecting ornaments. See Alberti 1964, 127 and Alberti 1987, 34. See also Seneca, *Epistulae Morales* 33.7.

32. See 4.13.

33. For a similar warning against a facile imitation that might lead to the reproduction of faults, see Cicero, *De oratore* 2.23.90–91, Horace, *Satires* 1.19.17, and Seneca, *Epistulae Morales* 114.17. A similar passage, remarking on the elder Pico's ability to follow a variety of styles exemplified by great classical writers without falling into the vices so often attributed to them can be found in his nephew's *Life of Pico* (Pico 1963, 314–315).

34. The reference to the Spartan woman is unclear; it may be a reference to the model for the Diana of Apelles, as related in Pliny, *Natural History* 35.96, or it may refer to Helen, Queen of Sparta. The Thespian is Phryne, the courtesan who was the lover of Praxiteles and the model for his statue of Venus. Lampetia is the daughter of Helios, the Sun; see Ovid, *Metamorphoses* 2.349. The story of the Cyclops' love for Galatea is told by the Greek lyric poet Philoxenus and retold in Ovid's *Metamorphoses* 13.738.

35. The word *centos* used here refers to the "patchwork" poems composed by Neo-Latin writers who took whole lines from classical sources, such

as Virgil, and wove them into new poems, often on Christian topics; the ancient model was the fourth-century Christian poetess Proba. Erasmus criticizes such a practice in his *Ciceronianus* (Erasmus 1986, 368).

36. Hymettus, a mountain overlooking Athens, and Hybla, in Sicily, were renowned for the quality of the honey they produced. For this transformative apian metaphor, see Seneca, *Epistulae Morales* 84.3–5, Quintilian 1.10.7, and Petrarch, *Familiares* 23.19.

37. Pico here employs the technical term *epicheiremata*, found in Quintilian 5.10.1- 2 and 5.14.14. See also *Rhetorica ad Herennium* 2.2.

38. Not the more famous playwright, but the critic Aristophanes of Byzantium (257–180 BC), head of the Library of Alexandria. He edited and commented on Homer, Hesiod, Plato, the Greek dramatists, and lyric poets.

39. See 3.13.

40. Manilius, *Astronomicon* 2.58. He does not precisely say that he follows "no one person" but that he owes his enterprise to *nulli vatum*, none of the poets.

41. See 3.13–15.

42. According to Pliny, the affection of dolphins for their offspring was legendary. See *Natural History* 9.7. Erasmus will use the image in the *De copia* (Erasmus 1978, 638). For the affection the writer naturally exhibits towards his writing, as if for children, see Quintilian 10.3.7 and 10.4.2.

43. For the story of the student of Apelles, who, "unable to make Helen beautiful, made her rich," see Clement of Alexandria, *The Pedagogue* 2.12.125.

44. Augustine, *Confessions* (3.4): "Cicero, whose tongue almost all men admire but not his heart."

45. The use of the term *ferruminari* is reminiscent of the Apuleian style affected by Beroaldo in a letter to Poliziano (Poliziano 1970, 1:17). The word is also central to the polemic between Poliziano and Scala, who uses the agent noun *ferruminator* (a "cementer," that is, someone who cuts and pastes various stylistic units) in reference to Poliziano and Ermolao

Barbaro. For the Scala-Poliziano correspondence, see ibid. 1:58–62. On this point see also McLaughlin, *Literary Imitation*, 201–207.

46. Virgil, *Georgics* 2.108.

47. For Cicero's exhortation to trust the senses, see *Orator* 51.173.

48. The primitive Roman law code.

49. See Poliziano's letter, 1.1.

50. See *De oratore* 3.46.182 ff.

51. See 3.19.

52. I.e., extremely elegant boots. See the *De oratore* 1.54.231 and the elder Pico's letter to Barbaro (Garin, 810 = Pico-Barbaro, 18) for other instances of this image.

53. A misquotation, presumably from a mispunctuated text of Aulus Gellius (*Noctes Atticae* 18.7.3): "Vos philosophi mera estis ut M. Cato ait, mortuaria; glosaria namque conligitis et lexidia" ("You philosophers are, as Cato says, nothing more than mortuaries; you merely collect glossaries and lexicons.") A similar misquotation is found in the elder Pico's letter to Barbaro (Garin, 820 = Pico-Barbaro, 23). See on this point McLaughlin, *Literary Imitation*, 260.

54. See 4.19.

55. See Horace, *Epistles* 1.1.14.

56. The term *apices* refers to the long mark over a vowel; the *puncta* are punctuation marks.

57. See Aristotle, *Rhetoric* 3.8. Pico uses the Greek phrase here.

58. See 3.9, 27.

59. Ermolao Barbaro (c. 1453–1493), an Italian humanist and opponent of the elder Pico, was well-respected by both sides of the imitation debates. Like Bembo, Barbaro was from Venice, hence the appellation "your compatriot." Theodore Gaza of Salonika (1398–1475) was a Greek scholar and translator who taught in Ferrara and later worked in the papal curia in Rome.

60. Pico praises the style of Poliziano, Barbaro, and the elder Pico in much the same terms in another letter in his epistolary; see Pico 1969, 2: 1334–1335.

61. Theodore had translated Aristotle's zoological and Theophrastus' botanical works.

62. Picenum (the southern part of the Marche) and Benacus (near Verona) were two regions famous for paper-making in Renaissance Italy.

63. See 4.20.

64. Pindar, *Olympian Odes* 1.33–34.

65. The sentence ends in a self-consciously ironic use of the Ciceronian tag-phrase *esse videatur*.

66. For this Pauline *imitatio Christi* see, for example, 1 Thessalonians 1: 6–7. See also Erasmus, *Ciceronianus* (Erasmus 1986, 388), where Bulephorus prefers the imitation of Christ over that of Cicero.

67. A contaminated quotation from Horace's *Art of Poetry* 322 ("nugaeque canorae") and Cicero's *Tusculan Disputations* 5.25.72 ("inanes sonos"). Given the preceding reference to Pauline imitation in this context, however, it is also reminiscent, in substance if not in words, of the first letter of St. Paul to the Corinthians 13: 1 "If I speak with human tongues and angelic as well, but do not have love, I am a noisy gong, a clanging cymbal" ("factus sum velut aes sonans, aut cymbalum tinniens").

68. This juxtaposition of *verba* and *res* or words and matter is reminiscent of the Pico-Barbaro debate, in which the elder Pico championed substance over style. For more on the *verba/res* dichotomy, see Cicero, *De oratore* 3.5.19.

69. Pico uses here the word *norma*, which literally refers to a carpenter's square and which is used metaphorically to indicate a standard or rule.

70. This is a malarial fever characterized by paroxysms occurring every fourth day. For praising the quartan fever, see the elder Pico's letter to Barbaro (Garin, 822 = Pico-Barbaro, 24). Favorinus, a second century AD sophist, was said to have praised fever in one of his works, none of which has survived. For the story, see Aulus Gellius 17.12. It is also men-

tioned by Erasmus in his dedicatory letter to Thomas More in *The Praise of Folly*, itself no doubt the best example of the Renaissance rhetorical practice of praising unworthy subjects. For a similar critique of ridiculous themes, see Lilio Giraldi's *Progymnasma adversus literas et literatos* in his *Opera* (1580), 2: 422–443, especially p. 441. This text, written in 1527 but not published until 1551, addresses the younger Pico and was dedicated to Calcagnini (who himself wrote an encomium of the flea).

71. In the *Iliad*, Thersites was the embodiment of ugliness and evil; Homer provides a long description of his deformities in the *Iliad* 2.211–219. See also Erasmus, *Adagia* 4.3.80.

72. Vida will write a poem on silkworms (*De Bombyce*) in 1527. Isocrates warns against an excessive search for originality which he saw could result in the composition of encomia of such ridiculous topics simply because they had not been dealt with before. See on this point his *Encomium on Helen* 12–13 and *Panegyricus* 7–8. See also Alberti 1971, 44.

73. A reference to Pico's problems concerning the inheritance of Mirandola, for which see the Introduction, xi.

74. A reference to Pico's well-known scepticism about ancient and modern philosophers and his fideistic position with respect to belief in Christianity.

6. CINZIO TO CALCAGNINI

1. The general sense (though not the exact wording) can be found in the *De oratore* 2.21.89–90.

2. See Lucretius, *De rerum natura* 3: 10–12; Horace, *Odes* 4.2. 27–32; Erasmus, *De copia* (Erasmus 1978, 639). For a different use of the bee image, see Pico's second letter to Bembo, 5.16.

3. One classical precedent for describing style in physiological terms is Tacitus, *Dialogue on Oratory* 18 and 21. Cinzio will reprise this anatomical imagery in the *Dei Romanzi* (Cinzio 1864, 54 = Cinzio 1968, 16).

4. Compare Cortesi's image of multiple seeds, 2.5.

5. See Poliziano, 1.2, for the mendicant image.

6. For the concept of *energia*, a Greek term, see Quintilian 8.3.89, where the word is glossed as *vigor*. Giraldi Cinzio returns to this concept in the *Dei Romanzi* (Cinzio 1864, 80 = Cinzio 1968, 55).

7. The derogatory comments regarding Erasmus were expunged from the 1540 edition of Cinzio's works.

8. Italian and Latin. Note that Giraldi is aware of Pico's second letter to Bembo, presumably from the printed edition of c. 1515 or 1518. Though some critics have suggested that the letter was "probably never sent" (e.g., McLaughlin, *Literary Imitation*, 259) and was not widely circulated, the present passage shows that Pico's second letter, although not acknowledged by Bembo, was known to at least some humanists.

9. See Cicero, *Orator* 10.36 and *De optimo genere oratorum* 1.4.

10. The 1540 edition interestingly replaces "certainly" with "perhaps."

11. See Bembo, 4.7.

12. See Cicero, *Orator* 1.4 and Quintilian 12.11.26.

13. The expression that Cinzio uses here, *maximam rerum copiam*, suggests the presence in the background of Erasmus' *De copia*, first published in 1512 and reprinted in expanded versions in 1514, 1526, and 1534. Although *copia verborum*, i.e. a rich and ready vocabulary, was considered a virtue by all Renaissance stylists, Cinzio will use the word *copia* three times in his letter, demonstrating a concern with this rhetorical virtue which had thus far been of little interest to the correspondents in the imitation quarrel. The same term will be used in Calcagnini's response, which also seems to reflect the influence of the *De copia*. See Quintilian 10.1.5 and Cicero, *Brutus* 72.253 for the use of the word *copia* as a synonym for eloquence in general.

14. A reference to the three-fold task of the orator, described by Cicero (*Orator* 21.69) as *flectere, probare, delectare*, that is, to persuade, to examine and to please. Cicero here establishes a parallel between these three functions and the three styles of oratory (for which see Pico's first letter, 3.26); Quintilian does the same at 12.10.58. See also Cicero's *Brutus* 49.185 and 79.276 as well as his *De optimo genere oratorum* 1.3 and 5.16, where the

three tasks are described as *docere, delectare, movere* (or to teach, to please, and to influence) as well as Quintilian 3.3.11; 8.Pr.7 and 12.2.11. The style of this passage is reminiscent of the *Brutus* 16.65, where Cato's style is described. See also Quintilian 10.1.110 for similar stylistic devices.

15. Cinzio removes this adjective, which might be seen as sacrilegious, in the 1540 edition.

16. For similar battle imagery and the portrayal of weapons of eloquence, see Quintilian 10.1.2 and 10.1.29–30. The thunderbolt image can be found, in reference to Demosthenes, in Cicero's *Orator* 60.334.

17. For the opinion that Cicero "is supreme in all the different qualities which are praised in each individual orator," see Quintilian 12.10.11–12.

18. See Pico's first letter, 3.17.

19. Compare Cicero, *De oratore* 2.27.117 as well as Cortesi, 2.4.

20. Compare Quintilian 12.10.15.

21. In his *Dei Romanzi* (Cinzio 1864, 64 = Cinzio 1968, 31), Cinzio makes it even clearer that "though good things which heaven can give us mortals are dispersed among men, they are never found in one single man." This becomes the basis for his advice to imitate eclectically, a position which differs drastically from the one espoused in this early letter to Calcagnini.

22. See Quintilian 2.5.23–24. The distinction between the youthful and mature imitator will take on greater importance in the imitative advice proffered by Lilio Giraldi and Possevino. Note that the program suggested here, which allows for eclectic imitation in the mature writer, is the opposite of that suggested by Poliziano in his *Oration on Quintilian and Statius* (Garin, 870–885) and the method Bembo says he tried in 4.22–23.

23. I.e., Cicero, who was born at Arpinum. For the image of contending with swans, see Lucretius, *De rerum natura* 3: 6–8. Calcagnini will quote Cinzio's own use of this image in a subsequent (but undated) letter to Cinzio himself (Calcagnini, 188), in which he remarks that Cinzio used to "contend with the Arpinian swan" but now "roars with the Apuleian ass." For this last image, see Pico's first letter to Bembo, 3.26 and note.

7. CALCAGNINI TO CINZIO

1. Calcagnini frequently complains of stomach ailments in his letters.

2. I.e. "in complete accord with." The expression comes from the language of builders in ancient Rome, who applied chalk to plumb lines in order to mark stones accurately.

8. CALCAGNINI, *ON IMITATION*

1. Evidently with reference to Giraldi's status as a physician. In the 1537 edition, Giraldi is styled *physicus* in the dedication; a medical doctor would have studied Aristotelian and Galenic science at university. What we would call "science" is in this period often called "natural philosophy" or simply "philosophy," as below. Calcagnini was himself an accomplished scientist and around 1525 wrote a work arguing for the diurnal motion of the earth.

2. This reference to a previous generation of scholars who debated whether eloquence and scientific or philosophic matter were compatible may be an allusion to the Pico-Barbaro correspondence; see Pico-Barbaro. Or it may refer simply to the long-standing rivalry in the ancient tradition between philosophy and rhetoric, which goes back at least to Plato and Isocrates.

3. Proverbial expressions condemning superfluous acts; for the pig who teaches Minerva, the goddess of wisdom, see Cicero *De oratore* 2.57.233, and Erasmus, *Adages* 1.1.40; for bringing wood to the forest see Horace, *Sermones* 1.10.34–35, and Erasmus, *Adages* 1.7.57, as well as Giraldi Cinzio, *Dei Romanzi* (Cinzio 1864, 46 = Cinzio 1968, 5).

4. I.e., of the three functions of the orator (see Cinzio's letter, 6.7), he will be able only to narrate or describe, but not perform the more difficult tasks of persuading and pleasing.

5. These disparaging comments against vernacular theorists are possibly aimed at Bembo and his recent *Prose della volgar lingua*. The opposition of Latin and the vernacular Italian is part of the larger debate known as the *Questione della lingua*, for which see Mazzocco, *Linguistic Theories*. For an-

other criticism of writers who dare to elevate the vernacular, claiming that it equals or surpasses Latin, see Giraldi 1551, 212–215.

6. The same wording is used by Cinzio in his letter to Calcagnini, 6.7, and similar wording is found in Pico's first letter, 3.17.

7. See Pico's first letter, 3.11.

8. On solecisms and barbarisms, see Quintilian 1.5.5 ff.

9. The term *tabulae* is commonly used for account-books, public records, state papers, lists, wills, and testaments; *formulae* are formula regulating judicial proceedings of lawsuits, contracts, covenants, and agreements. So Calcagnini is probably referring here to bureaucrats, lawyers and notaries. Compare Erasmus, *Ciceronianus* (Erasmus 1986, 405) for a similar argument.

10. Calcagnini is referring elliptically to an argument made by Giovanni Pico della Mirandola in his famous letter to Ermolao Barbaro (Garin, 818 = Pico-Barbaro, 22). Pico imagines Ermolao Barbaro objecting to the scholastic use of *causari* to mean "to cause"; in classical Latin *causari* means to plead a cause or to object.

11. Calcagnini is here mocking non-classical usages of scholastic natural philosophers and lawyers respectively.

12. For this image, see Pico's first letter, 3.21.

13. An allusion to the three traditional parts of philosophy: moral philosophy, natural philosophy, and logic or epistemology.

14. See Plutarch's *Moralia* (*Quomodo Adulator*) 53, and Athenaeus, *Deipnosophistae* 6.249f–250a for similar stories.

15. Compare Cicero's *De oratore* 2.39.162–165 and *Topics* 2.8.

16. Publius Clodius was a political enemy of Cicero; he appears in the letters of Cicero and is attacked in one of Cicero's most celebrated speeches, the *Pro Milone*.

17. See Cicero, *De oratore* 2.41.178, for the three functions of an exordium.

18. I.e., the power of *dispositio*, the second traditional part of rhetoric after invention (or discovery of subject matter) and before style, memory

and delivery. See Cicero's *De oratore* 2.76.307 ff. The organization of Calcagnini's treatise follows this order but also complicates it with a second order, that of the parts of the speech itself: Exordium, narration, argumentation, refutation, peroration and amplification.

19. See Plato's *Phaedrus* 276e-277a and 277b-c.

20. See Cicero, *De oratore* 2.86.356.

21. See Quintilian 10.1.87.

22. For proper words, see Cicero, *De optimo genere oratorum* 1.4–2.5, *De oratore* 3.37.149, and *Orator* 26.92 as well as Quintilian 1.5.71 and 8.3.24. Giraldi Cinzio will discuss proper words and "transferred words" or metaphors in the *Dei Romanzi* (Cinzio 1864,144 = Cinzio 1968, 135).

23. In the *De lingua latina* 6.37.

24. See Plato's *Cratylus* 390d-e. The great dialectician is presumably Socrates, not Plato.

25. Compare Cicero, *De oratore* 3.37.149, *Orator* 26.93 and Quintilian 1.5.71 and 8.6.4–5, for a similar definition of metaphor or *translatio*. Erasmus likewise discusses metaphors in this way in *De copia* (Erasmus 1978, 333); Cinzio revisits the subject in the *Dei Romanzi*. See also Cicero's *Orator* 39.134 on ornaments and embellishments.

26. For "transferred words" or metaphors as stars see *Orator* 26.92.

27. Marcus Antonius, the Roman orator and older contemporary of Cicero who is an interlocutor in Cicero's *De oratore*, says something like this at 1.21.94. See also the *Orator* 5.18 and 29.100.

28. *Rhetoric* 1409a2–23. The four paeans are: (1) – ᵕ ᵕ ᵕ (2) ᵕ – ᵕ ᵕ (3) ᵕ ᵕ – ᵕ and (4) ᵕ ᵕ ᵕ –. Aristotle prefers the fourth to close a period, the first to begin one. For the forms of the paean, see *Orator* 215.

29. This disagreement between Aristotle and Cicero was mentioned in Pico's first letter; see 3.26. Cicero discusses rhythm at length in the *De oratore* 3.46.182.

30. See Cicero's *Pro Sexto Roscio Amerino* 26.72. It is cited in the *Orator* 30.107 as a passage much lauded by others, though Cicero there points out its faults. See also Quintilian 12.6.4.

31. This would include the famous Ciceronian closing, *és-sĕ vĭ-dĕ-á-tŭr*.

32. The *Defense of Cornelius* has been lost, but this passage is quoted in Cicero's *Orator* 70.232 as well as Quintilian 9.4.14.

33. The Ciceronian tag phrase "esse videatur." See Poliziano, 1.1.

34. See 1.3 for the digestive metaphor.

35. From this point on, Calcagnini's treatise bears a striking resemblance to the *De copia* of Erasmus, using a similar manner of presentation to show how to achieve fullness of expression.

36. See Cicero, *Stoic Paradoxes* 3.26.

37. See Cicero's *Orator* 3.13.

38. In the *De corona* (*On the Crown*) 52. Calcagnini is evidently citing this Greek text from memory as the quotation is inexact. In the speech Demosthenes deliberately mispronounces Aeschines' name as "aeschunes," the genitive of the word for "shame," and asks the people whether Aeschines is a guest-friend or a hireling of the Macedonian kings. They shout out "a hireling!" The passage showed Renaissance critics that Attic Greek was not a mandarin discourse that could not be understood by ordinary people. A similar question had arisen among humanists a century before about the intelligibility of classical Latin to ordinary Romans; see Mazzocco, *Linguistic Theories*.

39. Cicero recounts the story of how an old grocer woman recognized from his accent that Theophrastus was a foreigner, even though he had lived in Athens for many years and was acknowledged as "the most perfect speaker of his time." See *Brutus* 46.172. Quintilian later adds that the woman thought his speech was "too Attic" (8.1.2).

40. For the deterioration of diction due to the influx of foreigners, see *Brutus* 74.258.

41. Calcagnini's understanding of inspiration offers a striking parallel to that of Longinus. See *On the Sublime* 13.2.

42. The word here is *compta*, meaning adorned or ornamented, and was often used to describe braided hair. This image also implies ornamentation that is well put together. The same term is used by Quintilian (10.1.79) to describe Isocrates's style.

43. Compare the similar language in Quintilian 10.1.79 and Cicero's *Orator* 13.42. The palestra or gymnasium was literally a wrestling school; by extension, it was the place for practicing rhetorical exercises. See also n. 82 below.

44. From the *Pro Milone* 37.102.

45. This image is used in Quintilian 10.1.2.

46. For the story of Greece's impoverishment due to Cicero's eloquence, see Plutarch's *Life of Cicero* 4.4. Apollonius Molon was a rhetorician and one of Cicero's teachers. Cicero describes his tutelage under him in the *Brutus* 89.307, 90.312, and 91.316. See also Quintilian 12.6.7.

47. See Quintilian 10.1.114.

48. Cicero, *De inventione* 1.8.

49. See Paul the Deacon, *Roman History* 2.9. When the Romans defeated the Samnites in 290 BC, they destroyed Samnium to the point where it was said that "today you'd have to look for Samnium in Samnium, and it wouldn't be easy to find."

50. Virgil, *Aeneid* 7.622 (the citation is inexact).

51. Ibid. 6: 846. In the *De senectute* 3.10, Cicero credits a similar phrase to Ennius, the ostensible source for Virgil.

52. For Virgil's borrowings, see Pico's first letter, 3.4. For a nearly contemporary example of the criticism that Virgil liberally imitated Ennius among others, see Berni, *Dialogo contro i poeti* (Berni 1997, 196–197), first published anonymously in 1526, which claims that of "seven things that Virgil says, six don't belong to him, but come from Homer, or Lucretius, or Ennius, or Catullus." Giraldi Cinzio also discusses Virgil's imitation of Homer (Cinzio 1864, 50).

53. The Virgilian and Ciceronian passages can be found in *Aeneid* 5: 320 and *Brutus* 66, 173.

54. From Cicero, *Tusculan Disputations* 4.8.19, citing Ennius.

55. Cicero, *Pro Cn. Plancio* 40.95; the expression, which means roughly "to make a mountain out of a molehill," was proverbial.

56. Livius Andronicus (c. 284–204 BC) was an early Roman playwright whose work survives only in fragments. The passage is cited from the *Eunuch* of Terence (3.1.426).

57. Lucian, *Iupiter Tragoedus* 14. Lucian's works were translated by both Thomas More and Erasmus and published in the early sixteenth century.

58. This is the first usage of the term "plagiarism" (*plagium*) in these debates. Literally, the word was used to refer to kidnapping and only by extension (and rarely) to literary theft. The more common rendering of this idea both in antiquity and the Renaissance was *furtum*.

59. The "little crow" probably refers to Fable 162 of the Chambry version of Aesop (see also Phaedrus, *Fables* 1.3), though that story specifies the bird as a jackdaw.

60. See Pico's second letter, 5.18.

61. This sort of rephrasing of a single idea takes up a considerable part of the *De copia*. Erasmus demonstrated two hundred variations upon the sentence "More's memory will never perish within me, unless I perish myself." See the *De copia* (Erasmus 1978, 355–364).

62. *De oratore* 1.34.154.

63. Note that for Quintilian, the exercise of paraphrase (done with a text in the same language) carries with it the connotation of contending with a prior text. Quintilian uses the term "emulation" to express this rivalry.

64. Compare Erasmus, *De copia* (Erasmus 1978, 297–298): "Cicero used to vie with his friend, the actor Roscius, to see whether Roscius could express the same material more often using different gestures." The same image appears in the *De conscribendis epistolis* of Erasmus (*CWE* 25: 43). See also Macrobius, *Saturnalia* 3.14.12 and *De oratore* 1.59.251 for classical antecedents.

65. The sense here is that, since we obviously can "contend with ourselves" by varying expression, we can also perform the same exercise with the speech of others and thus can contend with them as well.

66. Quintilian 10.5.5–8. Erasmus also recommends this exercise in the *De copia* (Erasmus 1978, 303).

67. An inaccurate quotation of Caesar, *Bellum Gallicum* 5.24.3, possibly quoted from memory.

68. Pliny the Younger (Gaius Plinius Caecilius Secundus), *Panegyricus* 38.3: "Egregie, Caesar, quod lacrimas parentum vectigales esse non poteris" ("It was nobly done, Caesar, to refuse to tax a father's tears.") He is called "Plinius Caecilius" in the Latin text to distinguish him from his uncle, Pliny the Elder (Gaius Plinius Secundus).

69. Cicero, *De natura deorum* 3.3.7.

70. Source not identified.

71. Seneca the Elder, *Controversiae* 9.15.17. For more judgments of Ovid, see *Controversiae* 2.2.12; Seneca the Younger (*Epistulae morales* 10.1.130) and Quintilian (10.1.98). Erasmus cites this same Senecan criticism of Ovid in *De copia* (Erasmus 1978, 299).

72. The italicized passage is found in the 1535 edition but was dropped from later ones.

73. *De amicitia* 16.58.

74. The Doryphorus was the most famous statue of Polyclitus, depicting a youth carrying a spear, which became known as the Canon or standard. See Cicero, *Brutus* 87.297 and *Orator* 1.5, Pliny, *Natural History* 34.55, and Quintilian 5.12.21. The confusion regarding the identity of this statue that came to be known as the Canon stems from the passage in Pliny, which first discusses the Doryphorus and then indicates that Polyclitus "also made what artists call a 'Canon' or 'Model Statue,' as they draw their artistic outlines from it as a sort of standard."

75. Pliny, *Natural History* 34.55. The editor of the Loeb edition of Pliny explains that Polyclitus "in a single work embodied the principles of his art. Polyclitus wrote a treatise on art, called it Κανών ["Canon"], then made his Doryphorus on his own principles, and called the sculptured work also Κανών."

76. The word here is *mango*, which literally means a "salesman," especially a slave-dealer. The verb formed on this word, *mangonicare*, means to smarten up an article for sale; this is presumably the "furbisher's skill."

77. Quintus Lutatius Catulus (fl. 100 BC) was a distinguished orator known for his pure diction and is an interlocutor in the *De oratore*. Quintilian notes Cicero's praise for Catulus (11.3.35), found in the *Brutus* 74.259.

78. Demosthenes studied delivery under the actor Andronicus. See Quintilian (11.3.7) for a discussion of nature and art in delivery which informs Calcagnini's text. See also Horace, *Ars poetica* 408–411, for the necessity of both art and nature in achieving excellence.

79. The word here is *phonascus*, a teacher of singing or elocution. See Suetonius, *Augustus* 84.2.

80. Roscius (d. 62 BC), was a Roman comic actor and a friend of Cicero; he influenced Cicero's oratorical delivery. See above, n. 64.

81. Aesopus (fl. late first century BC), the tragic actor, not the author of the fables. The rapid style of Roscius and the weighty style of Aesopus are contrasted in Quintilian 11.3.111. See also *Orator* 31.109.

82. Calcagnini uses the Greek ἀπάλαιστον for "foreign to the palaestra." Here, Calcagnini is quoting Quintilian's use of the term (9.4.56), where it is explained that Cicero promoted moderation in the use of prose rhythm, like a man not unacquainted with the palaestra. See also the *Orator* 13.42, where Cicero describes the copious style as "fit for the palaestra," and Erasmus' *Adagia*, 5.2.40. For another use of this word, see 8.16 and note 43.

83. See Poliziano, 1.3.

84. The reference to knee-splints is in the *De lingua latina* 9. 10–11. These were bandages used to straighten the crooked legs of children.

85. See Quintilian 2.4.5 and 2.6.7 and Cicero's *De oratore* 2.39.162. This image of pre-chewed food, along with that of swimming without the preserver, are found together in the *De ratione studii* (1511–1512) of Erasmus (Erasmus 1978, 681) as well as in his *De pueris instituendis* (CWE 26: 43).

86. In the *Art of Poetry* 38–40, Horace uses similar imagery, inciting writers to take on subjects that their shoulders can bear. See also Quintilian 10.2.19, Petrarch, *Familiares* 1.8, Giraldi Cinzio, *Dei Romanzi* (Cinzio 1864, 161 = Cinzio 1968, 156), and Du Bellay 1.3.

87. Alexander of Aphrodisias (fl. c. 200 AD) was an early commentator of Aristotle. The fable of Eros and Anteros is, in fact, not found among his extant works. Calcagnini is following the version of Themistius, *Orationes*, ed. Dindorf (Leipzig: Cnobloch, 1832), 367 (Oration xxiv), though the detail that Anteros' father was Mars comes from Cicero, *Tusculan Disputations* 3.28.59–60. But he seems not to have known the source directly, since in his *Anteros sive de mutuo amore*, published in 1544, the myth is ascribed to Porphyry. This explains the discrepancy between the attributions in the 1535 edition and subsequent versions (see the apparatus to the Latin text, note 83). Themistius' orations had been published by Aldus in 1534 under the title *Omnia Themistii opera . . . Alexandri Aphrodisiensis libri duo de anima, et de fato unus*; the combination of the two authors in the same volume may be the origin of the confusion, as is suggested by Merrill (below). The story was first popularized in the Renaissance in Mario Equicola's *Libro di natura d'amore* (1525). For the tradition of this myth in the French and Italian Renaissance, see Robert Merrill, "Eros and Anteros," *Speculum* 19 (1944): 265–284; Calcagnini is discussed on 274–76.

88. Calcagnini's conception of emulation as a kind of strife is again reminiscent of Longinus. For more on the eristic images in Calcagnini and Longinus, see Pigman, "Versions of Imitation," 16–18.

9. GIRALDI TO CINZIO

1. Fabio Antimaco was the son of Marcantonio Antimaco (1473–1552), a professor of Greek at Ferrara under whose tutelage Giraldi Cinzio studied. Fabio was a doctor but was well respected for his own knowledge of Latin and Greek.

2. Giovanni Manardo (1462–1536), a celebrated Renaissance physician and scientist who treated Ariosto, Pico, and the Este family in Ferrara; Giraldi Cinzio also studied medicine under him.

3. That is, Gianfrancesco Pico della Mirandola, Bembo's correspondent.

4. See Cicero, *De oratore* 2.162; Horace, *Ars poetica*, 439–441; and Erasmus' *Adagia* 1.9.98 for the image.

5. See Calcagnini, 8.2.

6. The exact relationship between Lilio Giraldi and Giraldi Cinzio is unclear.

7. An allusion to the Sack of Rome (1527) when Rome was invaded and pillaged by the troops of the Emperor Charles V. Lilio Giraldi suffered considerable personal losses in the Sack.

8. I.e., his note-taking pen; Lilio's fear is that his style will have become corrrupted by the variety of his reading.

9. For the common expression *invita Minerva*, see Cicero, *De officiis* 1.31.10 and Horace, *Art of Poetry* 385; see also Erasmus, *Adages* 1.1.42.

10. Lilio is here using the term *genius*, rather than *ingenium*, and is thus following Pico's usage. See on this point Pico's first letter, 3.8.

11. Isocrates' ointment box (*myrothecia*) is a proverbial expression referring to the flowery nature of Isocrates' style. Cicero says that a book of his "has exhausted all the scent box of Isocrates" ("Meus autem liber totum Isocratis myrothecium . . . consumpsit" in *Letters to Atticus* 2.1.13). The same expression is also used in Gianfrancesco Pico's *Life* of his uncle: "Even if he used up the whole ointment box of Isocrates (as they say), he kept his ornamentation within a fitting combination of neatness and majesty" (". . . etsi totum, ut aiunt, Isocratis myrotecion consumpserit, munditiae tamen et decorae maiestatis ornamenta servauit"). See Thomas More's translation of the *Life of Pico* (More, 314–315).

12. The expression means that Lilio feels he is capable only of low style. See Horace, *Art of Poetry* 28 for similar imagery of creeping along the ground.

13. For the image of flowers of eloquence, see Quintilian 10.5.23.

14. Lilio's expression *inepta imitatione*, his Latin gloss on the Greek term κακοζηλία, "unhappy imitation," "bad taste" or "affectation," appears to owe something to Quintilian, who uses this precise term to describe an "extravagant affectation" or excessiveness that must be avoided. See *Insti-*

tutio oratoria 2.3.9 and 8.3.56 (where it is glossed as "perverse affectation") and 8.6.73; in all three places the word is transliterated as *cacozelia*. The term is also found in Greek literary critics such as Demetrius Phalereus the Rhetor, *De elocutione* 186, 189, Longinus 3.4, and Hermogenes, *De inventione* 4.12. See also Possevino, 11.12.

15. For Lucian, see Calcagnini, 8.21. According to Lucian, *kakozelia*, or "bad taste," as it is translated in the Loeb edition, is committed by those who "exceed the due limit of mimicry and put forth greater effort than they should." See *The Dance* (*De saltatione*), 82.

10. POSSEVINO, *CICERO*

1. Juan Luis Vives (1492–1540) was a celebrated Spanish humanist. His ideas on imitation are developed in the *De tradendis disciplinis*.

2. Christophe de Longueil (1488–1522), also known as Longolio, the Italian version of his name, was a Frenchman who lived in Italy and was given honorary Roman citizenship at the instigation of Bembo and Sadoleto, his mentors. He is the only writer accepted as a true Ciceronian by Nosoponus in the *Ciceronianus* of Erasmus.

3. Bartolomeo Ricci (1490–1569) was the author of the *De imitatione libri tres* (1545) and an acquaintance of Possevino as well as of Cinzio and Calcagnini in Ferrara.

4. Giulio Cesare Scaligero (1484–1558), also known as Jules-César Scaliger, was an Italian who had lived in France and who responded vehemently against the *Ciceronianus* of Erasmus in two orations.

5. Aldo Manuzio (1449–1515) was an Italian humanist and printer who established the Aldine press, which published primarily editions of Greek and Latin classics. At the time of Possevino's treatise, the Aldine press was run by Aldo's grandson, Aldo Manuzio the Younger (1547–1597), the last of the clan to carry on the press. In 1583 (just ten years before Possevino's treatise was printed) Aldus published a ten-volume set of the complete works of Cicero, which included commentaries written by a number of eminent humanists, including the elder Aldo, his son, Paolo, and the younger Aldo. It is this edition and its commentaries to which Possevino is referring here. In chapter 16 of the Paduan edition (chapter

15 of the other 1593 editions), entitled "Ciceronis editio emendatior et interpretes in eum aliquot," Possevino lists the works and commentaries included in Aldus' 10-volume set.

6. Note that Possevino too was aware of both of Pico's letters. See Cinzio's letter, 6.5.

7. See Bembo, Letter 4, for several examples of his use of such pagan expressions.

II. POSSEVINO, *BIBLIOTHECA SELECTA*

1. Justus Lipsius (1547–1606), a Flemish humanist and a former disciple of Erasmus, published a treatise entitled the *Epistolica institutio* in which he outlined a program of imitative practice remarkably similar to that devised by Lilio Giraldi, without naming him as a source. Possevino paraphrases and quotes large portions of his treatise in the *Bibliotheca selecta*. This paraphrase is based on Lipsius, chapter 11.

2. Lipsius reads: "In the first phase, the sect of the Italians satisfies me, and for some time Cicero should not only be chiefly read, but solely read." ("In illa prima, Italorum haeresis mihi placeat, et aliquamdiu Cicero non praecipuus solum legatur, sed solus." Lipsius 1996, 36–37). It is significant that the Italian Possevino omitted this pejorative expression from his paraphrase.

3. The sustained image here is one of weaving and woven cloth (*textum, filum*) and may reflect the language of clothing metaphors found in the two letters of Pico.

4. Gaius Licinius Calvus Macer (82–c. 47 BC) was an orator and poet who was a staunch anti-Ciceronian or Atticist. None of the oratory produced by any of those Lipsius names here has survived.

5. M. Caelius Rufus (c. 82–48 BC), another orator who used the Attic style, was discussed in Cicero's *Brutus* 79.273.

6. Lipsius adds, pp. 36–37: "Just as a painter, when he takes up a canvas, first sketches in the whole man, then seeks the right colors and adds them to each part, so my imitator first forms the body of his eloquence, then looks for varied colors. Unless he does so (take heed now, young

man, or you will take heed too late), he always brings forth an elliptical, disorganized, motley shape in a medley of styles. Daily I see this and I am not unaware of the cause of the fault." ("Ut pictor, cum tabulam accepit, primum hominem totum delineat, colores mox aptos quaerit, et addit cuique parti, sic meus Imitator corpus eloquentiae suae formet, pigmenta deinde varie conquirat. Nisi facit (crede iuventus aut sero credes) hiulca semper, incomposita et e variis varia quaedam stili forma gignetur, nec satis sibi constans. Cottidie video, et peccati caussam non ignoro.")

7. Paolo Manuzio or Paulus Manutius (c. 1511–1574) was an Italian humanist who also wrote on the subject of imitation in the vernacular. He was the son of Aldo Manuzio, the famed printer (see Possevino, 10.1, n. 5). Samples of letters from all of the humanists mentioned here were published together in two volumes edited by Henri Estienne. See Bunel et al.

8. Jacopo Sadoleto (1477–1547) was an Italian humanist and papal secretary to Leo X. A member of the Roman Academy, he was a Ciceronian and staunch ally of Bembo and, like him, was made a cardinal in 1536.

9. Pierre Bunel or Petrus Bunellus (1499–1549) was a French humanist known for his letters, which were published posthumously.

10. Though he considered himself to be French, Longueil was in a sense a countryman of Lipsius, having been born in the Low Countries. This explains the appellation "our own Longolio."

11. Artemon is identified as the editor of Aristotle's letters. His dates are unknown, though it is thought that he may have lived in the second century BC.

12. Demetrius, about whom nothing is known, is often identified as the author of the treatise On Style, possibly written in the first century AD, though both the authorship and date of this treatise are much debated. The passage referred to here, which deals with epistolary writing, is On Style, 223. Lipsius gives a Latin translation of Demetrius' Greek text in his Epistolica institutio.

13. That is, they sound like passages from Plautus or Terence rendered into prose. See Pliny the Younger, Epistles 1.16.6.

14. Or, "that Tuscan Angel," a pun on the name Angelo Poliziano. Erasmus similarly puns on the words Angelo/angelic in the *Ciceronianus* (Erasmus 1986, 416). He likewise cites Poliziano as a suitable example for the epistle in *De conscribendis epistolis* (CWE 25: 21, 44) and in the *Conficiendarum epistolarum formula* (CWE 25: 260).

15. A reference to the simple toga (or "toga pura") worn by young Romans after the purple "toga praetexta" of childhood. The image refers to the use of a plain style. For the image of the hand held within the cloak, see Erasmus 1986, 370, which itself refers to Quintilian, 12.10.21.

16. The garland image is used here in conjunction with the notion of a thesaurus or anthology of expressive phrases. The garland has indeed been associated with the anthology genre since at least the first century BC, when the Greek poet Meleager compiled a collection of epigrams written by diverse poets under the title *Stephanos* or *Garland*, the first in the series of texts known collectively as the Greek Anthology.

17. Similar pruning imagery can be found in Cicero's *De oratore* 2.21.88 and Quintilian 2.4.3–4, a passage paraphrased by Erasmus in the *De copia* (Erasmus 1978, 300). Quintilian also recommends that Seneca be read at a later stage because of his excessive terseness. See *Institutio oratoria* 10.1.28. This advice is repeated by Erasmus in the *De conscribendis epistolis* (CWE 25: 259–260).

18. This paraphrase is taken from Lipsius, chapter 12.

19. Lipsius adds Poliziano's name to Pliny's (44–45).

20. For Apuleius, see Pico's first letter, 3.26. Lipsius' hesitation probably has to do with the salacious character of parts of the *Golden Ass*.

21. This is a paraphrase of Lipsius, chapter 13.

22. For the image of rouge and color (used in a more negative context), see Cicero, *De oratore* 3.25.96 and 3. 25.100 as well as *Brutus* 9.36. The term *fucus*, translated here as "rouge," actually denotes a white pigment used in Roman cosmetics.

23. For this practice, see Quintilian, *Institutio oratoria* 1.1.27.

24. For similar imagery, see Pico, note 71.

25. Lipsius uses the same word found in Lilio's letter, the Greek term κακοζηλία; see Lilio's letter, 9.9. The printed marginal annotation points out that this advice is the same as that offered by Lilio to Giraldi ("Haec eadem Gregorius Giraldus ad Cinthium Giraldum"). Possevino's next chapter will make this more explicit

26. See Letter 9. Possevino had transcribed portions of Lilio's letter in chapter 15 of the Paduan edition of the 1593 Bibliotheca selecta, as the marginal annotation informs the reader.

27. See 9.7. The marginal note here suggests that Lipsius has offered the same advice. It reads: "Idem Lipsius."

28. Guillaume Budé (1468–1540), a celebrated French humanist, was especially renowned as a scholar of Greek. For his remarks on style that show him to be anti-Ciceronian, particularly with regard to the use of pagan language, see especially his De studio literarum recte et commode instituendo (1532), ff. xxi–xxii.

Bibliography

꿏ᶄᶈ

SOURCE TEXTS

Angelus Politianus. *Epistolarum Liber Octavus.* In Politian's *Omnia opera.* Venice: Aldus, 1498. Contains texts 1 (lii^v–liii^r) and 2 (liii^r–liii^v).

Ioannes Franciscus Picus Mirandulae. *Physici libri duo. De appetitu primae materiae. De elementis et rhetorici quoque duo. De imitatione ad Petrum Bembum cum uno ipsius Bembi ea de re liber.* Rome: Mazzocchi?, c. 1515. Contains texts 3 (aa^r–bb^v), 4 (bbii^r–ddiii^r) and 5 (ddiii^r–ffiii^r)

Cynthii Ioannis Baptistae Gyraldi. *De obitu divi Alfonsi Estensis . . . Eiusdem super imitatione epistola, Coelii Calcagnini ad eundem super imitatione commentatio perquam elegans. Lilii Gregorii Gyraldi epistola bonae frugis refertissima.* Ferrara: Franciscus Roscius, 1537. Contains texts 6 (Ni^r–Nv^r), 7 (Nv^v–Nvi^r), 8 (Nvii^r–Pi^v) and 9 (Pii^r–Piii^v).

Antonio Possevino. *Cicero collatus cum ethnicis et Sacris Scriptoribus. Ad Bibliothecam Selectam auctoris pertinens quo agitur de ratione conscribendi epistolas. De arte dicendi, etiam ecclesiastica.* Padua: Paulus Meietus, 1593. Contains texts 5, part of 9, and 10 (Chapter 13: 27^r–28^r, Chapter 14: 28^v–36^r, Chapter 15: 36^r–36^v).

Antonio Possevino. *Bibliotheca Selecta, liber decimusoctavus. De arte conscribendi epistolas.* Venice: Altobellus Salicatius, 1603. Contains text 11 (Chapters 15–19: 574–578).

OTHER EDITIONS CONSULTED

Ioannes Francisci Pici Mirandulae. *Physici libri duo: I. De appetitu primae materiae . . . II. De elementis . . . Et Rhetorici duo, de imitatione ad Petrum Bembum. Petri Bembi Veneti de imitatione liber unus.* Basel: Froben, 1518. Contains texts 3–5 (53–123).

Angelo Poliziano, *Illustrium virorum epistolae XII libris distinctae cum succulentis Francisci Sylvii commentariis . . . et cum Iodoci Badii addititia explanatione.* Paris: Nicolaus de Pratis, 1520. Contains texts 1 and 2, with François du Bois' commentary on the Poliziano-Cortesi correspondence and additional comments of Josse Bade.

Petri Bembi. *De imitatione libellus.* In Bembo's *Opera.* Venice: de Sabio, 1530. Contains texts 3 and 4 (aaii^r–ccvi^v).

De imitatione eruditorum quorundam libelli quam eruditissimi. Strasbourg: Joannes Albertus, 1535. Contains texts 1–2 (e8^r–f4^r), 3–4 (b6^r–e7^v), 8 (a2^r–b5^v).

Jacobus Omphalius, ed. *De elocutionis imitatione ac apparatu.* Paris: Simon Colinaeus, 1537. Second edition. Paris: Gulielmus Julianus, 1555, 1565, 1575, 1579, 1591; Cologne: Birckmannus and Baumius, 1567, 1580. Contains texs 1 (44–45), 2 (51–56), 3–4 (232–272).

Cynthius Ioannes Baptista Gyraldus. *Poematia.* Basel: Robert Winter, 1540. Contains texts 6 (199–207), 7 (207–208), 8 (209–232) and 9 (233–236).

Caelius Calcagninius. *Opera aliquot.* Basel: Froben and Episcopius, 1544. Contains texts 7 (188) and 8 (269–276).

Epistole di Gaio Plinio, di Messer Francesco Petrarca, del Signor Pico della Mirandola et d'altri eccellentissimi huomini. Edited and translated by Lodovico Dolce. Venice: Giolito, 1548. Contains texts 1 (161^r–162^r) and 3 (131^r–139^r) in Italian translation.

Lilius Gregorius Gyraldus Ferrariensis. *Operum quae extant omnium . . . tomi duo.* Basel: Thomas Guarinus, 1580. Contains text 9 (2: 633–634).

Justus Lipsius. *Epistolarum centuriae duae, quarum prior innovata, altera nova.* Frankfurt: Wechel and Fischer, 1591.

Antonio Possevino. *Cicero . . . Ad Bibliothecam Selectam auctoris pertinens quo agitur de ratione conscribendi epistolas. De arte dicendi, etiam ecclesiastica.* Rome: Typographia Apostolica Vaticana, 1593; Lyon: Joannem Pillehotte, 1593; Cologne: Birckmann, 1593. Contains texts 5 and 10.

Antonio Possevino. *Bibliothecae Selectae Tomus Secundus. Ad artem oratoriam conscribendi epistolas cum Appendice.* Cologne: Ioannes Gymnicus, 1607. Contains texts 10 and 11 (500–503).

Collectio praestantissimorum opusculorum de imitatione oratoria. Edited by Friedrich Andreas Hallbauer. Jena: Christianus Franciscus Buchius, 1726. Contains texts 1 (275–276), 2 (276–280), 3 (234–248) and 4 (248–274).

Pietro Bembo. *Opere del Cardinale Pietro Bembo*. Edited by Anton Federigo Seghezzi. Venice: Francesco Hertzhauser, 1729. Facsimile edition Ridgewood, NJ: Gregg Press, 1965. Contains texts 3 (4: 329–333) and 4 (4: 333–341).

Izora Scott. *Controversies over the Imitation of Cicero*. New York:, Columbia University Teachers College Press, 1910. Reprinted Davis, CA: Hermagoras Press, 1991. In two parts, separately paginated. Contains English paraphrases of texts 1 (1: 17–19), 2 (1: 19–22), 3 (2: 1–7), and 4 (2: 8–18), based on the 1553 Basel edition of Poliziano's *Opera omnia* and on the 1556 Basel edition of Bembo's *Opera*.

Prosatori latini del Quattrocento. Edited by Eugenio Garin. Milan: Ricciardi, 1952. Contains texts 1 and 2 (902–911) with a facing Italian translation.

Le Epistole "De Imitatione" di Giovanfrancesco Pico della Mirandola e di Pietro Bembo. Edited by Giorgio Santangelo. Florence: Olschki, 1954. Critical edition of texts 3 (24–38), 4 (39–61) and 5 (62–76), based on the Basel edition of 1518.

Bernard Weinberg. *Trattati di Poetica e Retorica del Cinquecento*. Vol. 1. Bari: Laterza, 1970. Contains texts 6–8 (199–220), based on the 1540 edition.

Introduzione al Rinascimento: Materiali didattici per il corso 1993–94. Edited by Amedeo Quondam. Rome: Bulzoni, 1994. Reprinted in revised form as *Rinascimento e Classicismo: Materiale per l'analisi del sistema cultura di Antico regime*. Edited by Amedeo Quondam. Rome: Bulzoni, 1999. Contains texts 1–4 with a facing Italian translation.

De l'imitation: Le modèle stylistique à la Renaissance. Translated by Luc Hersant. Introduction by Giorgio Santangelo. Paris: Aralia, 1996. Contains texts 1–5 with a French translation.

Giovan Battista Giraldi Cinzio. *Carteggio*. Edited by Susanna Villari. Messina: Sicania, 1996. Contains texts 6–9.

SECONDARY LITERATURE

Baxandall, Michael. *Giotto and the Orators. Humanist Observers of Painting in Italy and the Discovery of Pictorial Composition 1350–1450*. Oxford: Clarendon, 1971.

Besaucèle, Louis Berthé de. *Etude sur l'évolution des théories littéraires en Italie au XVIe siècle.* 1920. Geneva: Slatkine, 1960.

Brizzi, Gian Paolo. *La "Ratio Studiorum". Modelli culturali e pratiche educative dei Gesuiti in Italia tra Cinque e Seicento.* Rome: Bulzoni, 1981.

Camporeale, Salvatore. "Poggio Bracciolini contro Lorenzo Valla: Le *Orationes in L. Vallam.*" In *Poggio Bracciolini 1380–1980,* 137–161. Edited by Riccardo Fubini, et al. Florence: Sansoni, 1982.

Cave, Terence. *The Cornucopian Text: Problems of Writing in the French Renaissance.* Oxford: Clarendon Press, 1979.

Chomarat, Jacques. *Grammaire et rhétorique chez Erasme.* 2 vols. Paris: Les Belles Lettres, 1981.

Croll, Morris. *Style, Rhetoric, and Rhythm.* Edited by J. Max Patrick, Robert O. Evans, et al. Princeton: Princeton University Press, 1966.

D'Amico, John. "Paolo Cortesi's Rehabilitation of Giovanni Pico della Mirandola." *Bibliothèque d'Humanisme et Renaissance* 44 (1982): 37–51.

———. *Renaissance Humanism in Papal Rome: Humanists and Churchmen on the Eve of the Reformation.* Baltimore: The Johns Hopkins University Press, 1983.

———. "The Progress of Renaissance Latin Prose: The Case of Apuleianism." *Renaissance Quarterly* 3 (1984): 351–392

D'Ascia, Luca. *Erasmo e l'umanesimo romano.* Florence: Olschki, 1991.

Dunn, Catherine. "Lipsius and the Art of Letter Writing." *Studies in the Renaissance* 3 (1956): 145–156.

Fumaroli, Marc. *L'Age de l'éloquence: Rhétorique et "res literaria" de la Renaissance au seuil de l'époque classique.* Geneva: Droz, 1980.

———. "Rhétorique d'école et rhétorique adulte: remarques sur la réception européenne du traité *Du Sublime* au XVIe et au XVIIe siècle." *Revue d'histoire littéraire de la France* 86 (1986): 33–51.

Gmelin, Hermann. "Das Prinzip der *Imitatio* in den romanischen Literaturen der Renaissance." *Romanische Forschungen* 46 (1932): 83–360.

Godman, Peter. *From Poliziano to Machiavelli. Florentine Humanism in the High Renaissance.* Princeton: Princeton University Press, 1998.

Grayson, Cecil. *A Renaissance Controversy: Latin or Italian?* Oxford: Clarendon Press, 1960.

Greene, Thomas. *The Light in Troy: Imitation and Discovery in Renaissance Poetry*. New Haven: Yale University Press, 1982.

Greswell, William Parr. *Memoirs of Angelus Politianus, Actius Sincerus Sannazarius, Petrus Bembus, Hieronymus Fracastorius, Marcus Antonius Flaminius, and the Amalthei, translations from their poetical works, and notes and observations concerning the other literary characters of the fifteenth and sixteenth centuries*. London: Cadell and Davies, 1801.

Guerrieri-Crocetti, Camillo. *Giambattista Giraldi ed il pensiero critico del secolo XVI*. Milan: Abrighi, 1932.

Jones, Howard. *Master Tully: Cicero in Tudor England*. Nieuwkoop: De Graaf, 1998.

Lecointe, Jean. *L'Idéal et la différence: La perception de la personalité littéraire à la Renaissance*. Geneva: Droz, 1993.

Marsh, David. *The Quattrocento Dialogue: Classical Tradition and Humanist Innovation*. Cambridge, MA: Harvard University Press, 1980.

Mazzocco, Angelo. *Linguistic Theories in Dante and the Humanists. Studies of Language and Intellectual History in Late Medieval and Early Renaissance Italy*. Leiden: Brill, 1993.

McLaughlin, Martin L. *Literary Imitation in the Italian Renaissance: The Theory and Practice of Literary Imitation in Italy from Dante to Bembo*. Oxford: Clarendon Press, 1995.

Murphy, James J. *Renaissance Eloquence: Studies in the Theory and Practice of Renaissance Rhetoric*. Berkeley: University of California Press, 1983.

Pigman, George W. "Barzizza's Treatise on Imitation." *Bibliothèque d'Humanisme et Renaissance* 44 (1982): 341–52.

———. "Imitation and the Renaissance Sense of the Past: The Reception of Erasmus' *Ciceronianus*." *Journal of Medieval and Renaissance Studies* 9 (1979): 155–177.

———. "Versions of Imitation in the Renaissance." *Renaissance Quarterly* 33 (1980): 1–32.

Pomilio, Mario. "Una fonte italiana del *Ciceronianus* di Erasmo." *Giornale italiano di filologia* 8 (1955): 193–207.

Quint, David. *Origin and Originality in Renaissance Literature: Versions of the Source*. New Haven: Yale University Press, 1983.

Sabbadini, Remigio. *Storia del Ciceronianismo e di altre questioni letterarie nell'età della Rinascenza*. Turin: Loescher, 1885.

Santangelo, Giorgio. *Il Bembo critico e il principio d'imitazione*. Florence: Sansoni, 1950.

Scott, Izora. *Controversies over the Imitation of Cicero*. New York: Columbia University Teachers' College, 1910. Davis, CA: Hermagoras, 1991.

Shafer, Keith A. "The Eclectic Style in Theory and Practice in Angelo Poliziano's Ep. VIII.16." *In Laudem Caroli: Renaissance and Reformation Studies for Charles G. Naurert*. Edited by James V. Mehl. Sixteenth Century Essays and Studies, 49. Kirksville, MO: Thomas Jefferson University Press, 1998.

Spingarn, Joel Elias. *A History of Literary Criticism in the Renaissance*. Second edition. New York: Columbia University Press, 1930. New edition with an introduction by Bernard Weinberg. New York: Harcourt, Brace and World, 1963.

Spongarno, Raffaele. Review of *Le Epistole "De Imitatione"*, ed. Santangelo. *Giornale storico della letteratura italiana* 131 (1954): 427–437.

Vitale, Maurizio. *La questione della lingua*. Palermo: Palumbo, 1984.

Weinberg, Bernard. *A History of Literary Criticism in the Italian Renaissance*. 2 vols. Chicago: University of Chicago Press, 1961.

Witt, Ronald G. *"In the Footsteps of the Ancients": The Origins of Humanism from Lovato to Bruni*. Leiden: Brill, 2000.

Wittkower, Rudolf. "Imitation, Eclecticism, and Genius." *Aspects of the Eighteenth Century*, 143–161. Edited by Earl R. Wasserman. Baltimore: The Johns Hopkins University Press, 1965.

Index

❧❦❧

References are to item and paragraph numbers. References to Notes to the Translation are by page number and note number, indicated by *n*. Lowercase roman numerals refer to page numbers in the Introduction.

Aeschines, 2.6, 239n35
Aesop, 3.22, 8.21, 8.27, 266n59, 268n81; *Fables*, 245n61
Agelades, 4.28, 251n36
Alberti, Leon Battista, xvi, 246n68, 254n31; *De commodis*, 243n49; *Della famiglia*, 250n25; *De pictura*, 244n49
Aldine press, 271n5
Alexander of Aphrodisias, 8.29, 268n87
Alexander the Great, 248n3
altercation, 8.9
amplification, 8.9
ancient writers, and imitation, 3.1–8. *See also names of authors*
Andronicus, 8.27
Anteros. *See* Eros and Anteros, story of
Antimaco, Fabio, 9.1, 269n1
Antonius, Marcus, 4.6, 8.12, 248n5, 263n27
ape image, 1.1, 2.2, 3.12, 5.4, 5.19, 233n2
Apelles, 4.4, 4.28, 5.15, 5.20, 5.22, 248n3, 251n36, 254n34, 255n43
Apollonius Molon of Rhodes, 8.18, 247n76, 265n46

apprenticeship model, 4.22–24, 11.2–4, 11.10–12, 11.13
Apuleians, 247n83
Apuleius, Lucius, 11.8, 247n83
archaism, 11.11
architecture image, 3.4, 4.11, 249n12
Aristarchus of Samothrace, 3.20, 244n57
Aristophanes of Byzantium, 5.18, 5.22, 8.21, 255n38
Aristotle, 3.6, 3.26, 5.23, 5.24, 8.13, 8.19; *De anima*, 237n21; *Poetics*, xiii, 237n20, 241n26; *Problems*, 3.8; *Rhetoric*, 247n77, 256n57, 263n28. *See also* Ps.-Aristotle
arrangement, 3.14, 5.19, 5.21, 8.16, 8.26
art, 3.20, 4.4, 244n56; imitates nature, 2.4. *See also names of artists*
Artemon, 11.3, 273n11
Ascham, Roger, *Scholemaster*, xxxviii n13
Asinius, 3.10
Athenaeus, *Deipnosophistae*, 262n14
Atilius, Marcus, 4.31, 251n43
Augustine, 5.20, 241n19; *City of God*, 241n18; *Confessions*, 255n44

283

INDEX

Publication of this volume has been made possible by

The Myron and Sheila Gilmore Publication Fund at I Tatti
The Robert Lehman Endowment Fund
The Jean-François Malle Scholarly Programs and Publications Fund
The Andrew W. Mellon Scholarly Publications Fund
The Craig and Barbara Smyth Fund
for Scholarly Programs and Publications
The Lila Wallace–Reader's Digest Endowment Fund
The Malcolm Wiener Fund for Scholarly Programs and Publications